MONSTERS FROM THE ID

# MONSTERS FROM THE ID

*The Rise of Horror in Fiction and Film*

E. MICHAEL JONES

SPENCE PUBLISHING COMPANY · DALLAS
2000

Published in the United States by
Spence Publishing Company
111 Cole Street
Dallas, Texas 75207

*Library of Congress Cataloging-in-Publication Data*

Jones, E. Michael.
    Monsters from the Id : the rise of horror in fiction and film / E. Michael
    Jones
        p.  cm.
    Includes bibliographical references and index.
    ISBN 1-890626-06-6
    1. Horror tales—History and criticism.  2. Psychological fiction—
History and criticism.  3. Motion pictures—psychological aspects   4.
Horror films—History and criticism.     I. Title.
PN3435.J66  2000
809.3'8738—dc21                                             99-049602

Printed in the United States of America

# Contents

PART III

THE MONSTER TRAVELS FROM
GERMANY TO AMERICA

CONCLUSION

Everyone who is tempted is attracted and seduced by his own wrong desire. Then the desire conceives and gives birth to sin, and when sin is fully grown it too has a child, and the child is death.

James 1:14-5


The Krell forgot one thing, monsters from the Id.

*The Forbidden Planet*

# A Legacy of Horror

UNTIL RECENTLY, Mary Wollstonecraft Shelley, unlike her husband, Percy Bysshe Shelley, was not part of the pantheon of English literature. The cover of the Lion Books edition of *Frankenstein,* brought out in 1953, gives an accurate picture of the literary status of *Frankenstein* at the time. In the background stands the monster, looking like Marlon Brando on a bad day, staring at his blood-stained hands. In the foreground, an unconscious Blanche DuBois figure exposes a tantalizing bit of cleavage.

The cover of the Lion Books edition was just one artifact on display in the Carl H. Pforzheimer Collection exhibit, "Shelley and His Circle," at the New York Public Library over the summer of 1997. The exhibit was, in many ways, a definitive statement that Mary Shelley has finally joined her husband as a star of English literature after years of languishing in Hollywood and on the margins of pulp fiction. Moreover, the Shelleys' art has finally been understood in the context of the lives that inspired it. Yet even as it grasps the connection between art and life, our culture cannot seem to understand horror or *Frankenstein,* the book that created the genre. "The show's curators," AP writer Joan Brunskill wrote in her review of "Shelley and His Circle," felt the writings of Mary and her mother, Mary Wollstonecraft, "challenged the sexual oppression and possessive morality of their day."

Thus *Frankenstein* is lumped in with challenges to tradtional sexual morality, without any suspicion that the novel was written precisely as a protest against theories of sexual revolution by someone who had suffered badly because of them.

The fact that the creator of the horror genre is celebrated as a proponent of sexual liberation indicates that our culture still does not understand horror. If our culture could make up its mind about sexual liberation, it would not need horror. It would either embrace sexual license wholeheartedly, as Mary's husband did, or repudiate it wholeheartedly, as Christianity does. But horror is a sign that the culture cannot make up its mind. Sexual liberation is so frightening, I cannot talk about it, those like Mary Shelley seem to tell us. But then they turn around and say the opposite: It is so frightening, I cannot *not* talk about it. The monster speaks the unspeakable for them.

If ambivalence signifies the beginning of horror and the end of the Enlightenment, then the film *Mimic* is a sign that both may be coming to an end: the unconscious repudiation of the Enlightenment, the basis of horror, is perhaps becoming conscious. Other, weaker evidence shows that the horror genre may be aware of itself. Wes Craven's *Scream* tries to make sense of the clichés of the slasher film, though without much success. *Mimic*, on the other hand, is neither campy nor self-conscious. It is a classic horror film in the tradition of *Them!*, the famous science fiction-horror film of the 1950s.

*Mimic* begins with a plague carried by roaches in the subterranean tunnels of New York City. In order to stop the plague, which is killing the city's children, a female entomologist, who wants to have children herself but cannot, invents a new bug—referred to in the film as a "Frankenstein"—by recombining DNA from two different species. The bug is supposed to be sterile but, as in other such movies, is not. Soon it has mutated and multiplied throughout New York's subway system.

*Mimic* is deeply pessimistic about the promises of the Enlightenment, a fact underscored by its setting, the ruins of the advanced Industrial Age—rusted, dripping, dank, bug-filled, darkened tunnels. The first victims of the mutant bugs are the homeless who live in the subway tunnels. The existence of the homeless, the "mole people," is another sign that the Enlightenment has failed.

According to the Enlightenment view of scientific progress, we should by now have no more dirty poor and no more dirty dwellings. The Enlightenment fantasy of the "radiant city" consigned squalor to the past. Percy Shelley shared this fantasy, as Claire Clairmont, Mary Shelley's half-sister, recounts:

> Shelley said there would come a time when no where on the Earth, would there be a dirty cottage to be found—Mary asked what time would elapse before that time would come—he said perhaps in a thousand years—We said perhaps it would never come, as it was so difficult to persuade the poor to be clean. But he said it must infallibly arrive, for Society was progressive and was evidently moving forwards towards perfectibility—and then he described the career made by man—I wish I could remember the whole—but half has slipped out of my memory—only I recollect men were first savages—then nomadic tribes wandering from place to place with their flocks—then  they formed into villages—then to towns, and the improvement in mind , morals comforts etc. set in—and then next came Art—and then the Sciences and from this point, Society would go on to almost perfection.

As in *Them!*, in *Mimic* we are in tunnels fighting giant bugs whose origins lie in our violations of the natural order. But when Hollywood made *Them!* it had more of the patrimony of the West to draw on. The army is brought in, but is restrained in its use of force; soulless technology triumphs, but it is a technology in the service of humanitarian ideals such as the defense of innocent life.

Though *Mimic* is in the tradition of *Them!*, it is different in important ways. There is no army waiting to save the people from the giant bugs: they are left to deal with the horror alone. The entomologist who created the bugs is not like the entomologist in *Them!*, who formulates a scientific solution. She does not know how to stop the bugs. She created a monster, and trapped with it in the subway all she can do is shout impotently as the creature stalks its child victim.

As technological solutions fail, the only solution left is one that involves self-sacrifice. The heroine remembers that the child's father, before he was killed by the bugs, had dropped his rosary on the subway track and that she had picked it up. She takes the rosary's crucifix, stabs herself in the palm of her hand and, like Jesus Christ standing before the Apostle Thomas, holds up her bleeding palm to the bug. Distracted by the scent of blood, the bug turns and flies at the entomologist, only to be run over by an oncoming subway train.

We have in this scene a gesture that is a complete repudiation of the Enlightenment, and hence something that presages the end of horror. *Them!* retains the post–World War II optimism that the culture can make good use of technology. In *Mimic*, however, all such hope is gone. Out of the bowels of Hollywood, the seat of the secular humanist regime—in other words, from the quarter where we would least expect it—we have not just generic religion, but Catholicism in particular, invoked as the only hope of destroying the monsters created by Enlightenment science.

*Mimic* implies nothing less than a thinking through of the premises of the Enlightenment to their logical, contradictory conclusions. Reliance on "scientific" reason leads not to light and peace but to ruin and darkness. And the antidote to all this, Hollywood is now telling us, is faith and self-sacrifice. The entomologist who created the monster by the application of Enlightenment science redeems herself by shedding her blood in defense of an innocent child. At the end of the film, after being told that no one could have survived the explosion that killed the remaining bugs, the entomologist gazes into the subway and sees her husband emerge miraculously, like Lazarus from the dead. In the final scene, as husband and wife and newly adopted child embrace, the camera tracks over the rosary firmly attached to the wife's wrist and dangling, crucifix and all, over her husband's back. After two hundred years of Enlightenment-inspired horror resulting from utopian experiments gone bad, even the most obtuse moviegoer realizes that the Enlightenment has failed, which is what horror has been telling us cryptically since Mary Shelley wrote *Frankenstein.*

This book attempts to make what is cryptic in this tradition explicit. The Enlightenment tried to drive out religion and morality, but found that they returned in the form of a monster. That monsters have destroyed the fondest hopes of the Enlightenment should be obvious by now. The Enlightenment is dead. Its only lasting legacy will be the horror stories told by its survivors.

PART I

# The Monster Travels
# from France to England

I

## Why the French Revolution Failed

AT THE BEGINNING OF 1812, the year when the forces of revolution under Napoleon would meet decisive defeat in Russia at the hands of nature and the czar, William Godwin, England's most famous philosopher, now in eclipse because of his notorious defense of the French Revolution, received a letter, posted from Keswick in the Lake District, asking for an interview. The author of the letter was a nineteen-year-old aristocrat by the name of Percy Bysshe Shelley, lately expelled from Oxford for writing an anonymous pamphlet in defense of atheism, and even more lately married to a sixteen-year-old girl (a friend of one of his sisters) named Harriet Westbrook. Shelley informed the once-popular Godwin that he was writing an inquiry into why the French Revolution had failed to benefit mankind and wanted Godwin to advise him in the project. Shelley had read Godwin's magnum opus, the *Enquiry Concerning Political Justice*, and had been swept away by the breadth of its vision: "It is now a period of more than two years since first I saw your inestimable book on *Political Justice*; it opened to my mind fresh and more extensive views; it materially influenced my character, and I rose from its perusal a wiser and better man."[1]

Shelley was not alone in his adulation. The book's effect on the older romantic generation had been just as dramatic. "Throw aside

3

your books of chemistry," Wordsworth said to one of his contemporaries, "and read Godwin on necessity."[2] During the mid-1790s, when enthusiasm for the French Revolution was still high in progressive circles in England, Godwin, in the words of William Hazlitt, "blazed as a sun in the firmament."[3] Samuel Taylor Coleridge, who used to give dramatic readings of his poetry at the Godwin household (Mary Godwin Shelley later remembered hiding behind a sofa and listening to "Christabel"), wrote that Godwin

> Bade the bright form of justice meet my way
> And told me that her name was happiness.[4]

Unfortunately, the Godwin who had written *Political Justice* in 1792 was not the same man tending a bookshop in 1812. Much water had flowed over the revolutionary dam in the meantime. There was no getting away from the Terror, proof that the event seemingly predicated on universal love and virtue had culminated in one of the most dramatic bloodbaths Europe would ever see. Twentieth-century Nazis and Communists may have killed more people, but neither group engaged in public carnage with the relish of the French revolutionaries, who, more even than the Bolsheviks, according to Erik von Kuehnelt-Leddihn, "engaged in tortures and massacres with a truly popular élan, quite different from their Nazi imitators who perpetrated their crimes in a bureaucratic and almost always clandestine way. The tortures to which the officers of the Bastille were submitted were carried out by the 'dear people' in full daylight. The fiendish dissection of the Princess de Lamballe, the frenetic work of these sadists and sex maniacs, can be ascribed to 'ignoble savages,' to our deified friend, the Common Man."[5]

The revulsion at the excesses of the French Revolution was palpable among the once-enthusiastic English. Indeed, by the end of the eighteenth century reaction against the Enlightenment was strong enough to lead to sedition trials, although Godwin himself was spared and was never called to denounce his friends. By the time Shelley's letter found its way to Godwin's insolvent bookshop on Skinner Street, Godwin was more ignored than reviled.

Godwin's story—from luminary to forgotten bookman—is in many respects a classic study in the history of ideas. Born into the Glassites, a strict dissenting Calvinist sect that believed that God predestined men to Hell not according to the merits of their actions but according to His own sovereign pleasure, Godwin first studied to be a minister of the Gospel. But his colleague, the Reverend Joseph Fawcett, loaned Godwin his copy of *Le système de la Nature*, by the *philosophe* Baron d'Holbach, and as if by magic, the Calvinist system of Godwin's youth collapsed like a burning building and the French Enlightenment began to rise phoenix-like in its place.

Liberty was the bridge that allowed Godwin to move from Calvinist fideism to French rationalism without too much self-inflicted intellectual injury. The dissenting tradition in England was committed to religious and political liberty as well as liberty of thought, and along with that liberty went the right to overthrow any government that violated those rights. In a sense, revolutionary France was now doing what dissenters in England had merely discussed. Godwin was not alone in his hope for the Revolution. Charles Stanhope, the English scientist and politician, gave this analysis of the events in France: "France and the whole human race are to enter into possession of their liberties when the ideas of justice and truth, of intellectual independence and everlasting improvement, are no longer to remain buried in the dust and obscurity of the closet, or to be brought forth at distant intervals to be viewed with astonishment, indignation, and contempt, but universally received, familiar as the light of day, and general as the air we breathe."[6]

Lester Crocker states well the Enlightenment premise: "Accompanying these developments was the desire for a total integration of man in nature, with refusal of any transcendence, even though it was admitted that his more complex physical organization gave him certain special abilities and ways of living. The important thing, as La Mettrie, d'Holbach, and others made clear, is that he is submitted to the same laws; everything is response to need—mechanically, some added, like a tree or a machine. Man merely carries out natural forces —without any freedom whatsoever—in all he does, whether he loves or hates, helps or hurts, gives life or takes it."[7]

Man is a work of nature, Baron d'Holbach proclaimed, and is subject to the laws of nature. Instead of vainly looking outside the world for supernatural beings to bring him the happiness which he cannot find on earth, man should study nature, should learn her laws, and submit to her mandates. "God" is a meaningless term, d'Holbach stated. Religion arose from men's primitive fears, which priests then exploited in order to enslave their minds.

Godwin's other reading only confirmed his determination to see d'Holbach's project through. In addition to d'Holbach, Godwin read *De l'esprit* by Claude Helvétius, one of the Encylopaedists, a book that had been banned in 1758 in one of the generally ineffectual attempts by the *ancien régime* to combat the dissemination of revolutionary literature in France.

La Mettrie, another Enlightenment thinker in prerevolutionary France, stated clearly the ideology of mechanism, another significant element of the Enlightenment:

> Among animals, as I have sufficiently proved, everything depends upon the diversity of this organization: these admissions suffice for guessing the riddle of substances and of man. It [thus] appears that there is but one [type of organization] in the universe, and that man is the most perfect [example]. He is to the ape, and to the most intelligent animals, as the planetary pendulum of Huyghens is to a watch of Julien Leroy. More instruments, more wheels and more springs were necessary to mark the movements of the planets than to mark or strike the hours; and Vaucanson, who needed more skill for making his flute player than for making his duck, would have needed still more to make a talking man, a mechanism no longer to be regarded as impossible, especially in the hands of another Prometheus.[8]

Commenting on La Mettrie, Abbé Barruel, in his influential *History of Jacobinism*, stated: "As to La Mettrie the doctor, if he appeared to rave, it was only from the sincerity of his heart. His man-machine, or his man-plant, only caused the Sect to blush from the open manner in which he had said what many of them wished to insinuate."[9] The Enlightenment was in effect an attempt to transform man into a machine, with Newtonian physics as its guide. "With Voltaire," Abbé

Barruel wrote, "man is a pure machine; Frederick the Great maintains . . . 'I know that I am an animal organised, and that thinks; hence, I conclude that matter can think, as well as that it has the property of being electric.'"[10]

Common to all Enlightenment thinkers, moreover, was the desire to discover the human or social equivalent of the role gravity plays in Newton's physics. According to Crocker, "There existed in the eighteenth century a widespread desire to equate the moral with the physical world: to see in it an order comparable with the order of Nature. If self-interest was selected as the fundament for moral values, it was in part because pseudoscientific thinkers were seeking for the moral counterpart to gravitation."[11] The machine known as man had to be regulated somehow, and Godwin concurred with many other contemporary figures that self-interest was the way: "It is uniformly found in practice, that masses of intellectual individuals are guided by as regular a gravitation, and directed by as mechanical principles, as are the planets in their orbits. So long as the inequality of mankind shall subsist, so long as one shall be rich and another poor, as one shall have the power of conferring benefits and another the need for receiving them; just so long will men cohere and act together from sympathy, from gratitude, and from expectation."[12] But declaring self-interest the moral equivalent of gravity was the easy part; difficulties arose when Enlightenment thinkers like Godwin were pressed to explain how self-interest could be regulated by something other than force. Thus arose the term "enlightened" self-interest—but it was not clear how that term entailed anything other than a circular argument.

Godwin nevertheless saw how the Enlightenment at least solved the Reformation's epistemological problem. Religion had become a battlefield of warring sects whose only answer to questions of faith, if not morals, was superior force. The idea of a magisterium, a divinely-sanctioned teaching authority, had disappeared with the rise of Protestantism. *Sola fide, sola scriptura* and the other tenets of the reformed faith had proved inadequate in this regard. And this left a problem: the collapse of a universal magisterium as an intellectual court of final appeal led to the discrediting of all knowledge, and once that had happened, power alone could decide right and wrong.

It was precisely this moral vacuum and the fear it engendered that led to the rise of science as magisterium, or more precisely, science as ideology. Science, in an odd way, seemed like an answer to prayer: it had arrived on the scene just in time. By the end of the eighteenth century, science had become *the* arbiter of true and false. But the crucial question for the eighteenth century was whether science could function as an equally convincing arbiter of good and evil. For if nothing but self-interest operated in a Newtonian universe where individual judgment was supreme, how could one adjudicate competing self-interests and contradictory individual judgments? Given their materialist outlook, Enlightenment thinkers could have no answer to that question.

Thus the road seemed open to simple hedonism. A combination of La Mettrie's anthropology with d'Holbach's morals, yielded a society populated by machine-like, amoral men whose thoughts about higher things were chimerical but whose pleasures were very real. When the mind is befuddled or worn out with the fruitless effort of theorizing, pleasure always seems real and compelling—as Faust discovered. Mephistopheles tells Faust that all theories are gray, and as a result of that intellectual impasse, tempts him with life's pleasures as the only consolation available: "Grau, teurer Freund, ist alle Theorie/ Gruen aber des Lebens goldener Baum."[13]

All told, then, the Enlightenment was a classic instance of bad faith. It espoused nature instead of morality (or religion) and then expected its adherents to act like civilized human beings—even though it could find no rational basis for doing so. Essentially negative, the Enlightenment tore down institutions that had regulated human behavior, but could do nothing to prevent reason from disintegrating into and justifying pure desire, even destructive desire. In this regard, the Enlightenment could only stand helplessly by as the Marquis de Sade or, at a later date, Nietzsche proclaimed nihilism the logical outcome of Enlightenment rationalism. "Women," the Marquis de Sade wrote, "are nothing but machines designed for voluptuousness."[14]

Godwin came to understand the sadistic end of Enlightenment thinking, but it took the Terror to get him to see the logical import of his ideas. He did not, of course, experience the Terror himself; he learned of it the way most Englishmen did, through reports from those fleeing its horrors. Chief among these refugees of revolutionary France bearing bloody, terrible tales was, for Godwin, Mary Wollstonecraft, the famous English feminist.

Godwin first met Wollstonecraft in 1791, the same year he began writing *Political Justice*, and of the two occurrences, the former seemed the more auspicious. The first meeting between the two exponents of English radicalism did not go well. Godwin went to dinner at Joseph Johnson's, Wollstonecraft's patron-cum-employer, to hear Tom Paine, but found that Wollstonecraft, already famous, monopolized the conversation.

As one might expect in a gathering of English leftists in the 1790s, talk centered on the French Revolution and England's response. Richard Price, the Unitarian divine, had been the first well-known Englishman to endorse the Revolution, praising it as the logical sequel to England's Glorious Revolution of 1688. The French revolutionaries, Price had proclaimed, were the standard bearers for "the ideas of justice and truth, of intellectual independence and everlasting improvement, [which] are no longer to remain buried in the dust and obscurity of the closet, or to be brought forth at distant intervals to be viewed with astonishment, indignation, and contempt, but universally received, familiar as the light of day, and general as the air we breathe."[15]

Godwin, who heard the speech, had thrilled to Price's words. But in 1790 Edmund Burke wrote his *Reflections on the Revolution in France* in violent disagreement, prophesying not happiness and progress for France, but terror and ruin. One of the first responses to Burke, in turn, was Mary Wollstonecraft's *A Vindication of the Rights of Man*, which appeared in the same year. Wollstonecraft treated the revolution as an attempt to right injustice, specifically economic injustice, setting the tone for apologias for other revolutions that would follow.

One year later, Wollstonecraft followed her broadside against Burke with the more ambitious *Vindication of the Rights of Woman*, the first feminist tract. Although tame by twentieth-century standards (she objects, for example, to contraception), the tract prompted Horace

Walpole to call Wollstonecraft a "hyena in petticoats" and launched her career as England's most notorious bluestocking.

. . . . .

When the French Revolution broke out, Wollstonecraft was thirty and still a virgin. Hoping to rectify the situation, she planned to go to Paris with a group of friends. "At Paris, indeed," she wrote, "I might take a husband for the time being, and get divorced when my truant heart longed again to nestle with old friends."[16] Moreover, she had a personal reason for leaving England: unrequited infatuation with the Swiss painter Henry Fuseli. Awash in Jacobin thought, Wollstonecraft had proposed a *ménage à trois* to Fuseli's wife, Sophia, who had been appalled by the idea and had forbidden Wollstonecraft access to the house.

Even then, English leftists were drawn to countries that had experienced revolution. For Wollstonecraft and her ilk, utopia was definitely a somewhere. She seems to have decided that revolutionary Paris was the place where feminist theory would be transmuted into free-love praxis. When those who were to accompany her canceled their plans, Wollstonecraft decided to go alone. She arrived in Paris in December of 1792 just in time to see Citizen Capet (Louis XVI) being driven in a hackney coach to his trial for treason.

In France, the bliss at simply being alive had clearly passed by the time Wollstonecraft arrived in Paris. The euphoria of the crowds in the cafés and public squares had been replaced, beginning in September, with public massacres and, in Lady Palmerston's words, "an air of ferocity and self-created consequence."[17]

As with most revolutions, the initial phase of the French Revolution had involved a good deal of sexual license. Wordsworth begat an illegitimate daughter in France, whom he abandoned by the simple expedient of going back to England and turning his back on the Revolution for good. Male and female members of the new clergy—there being no women in the old, among other things—were encouraged to marry. The sexual liberation that flourished in Paris was in large measure the result of a Kulturkampf that had preceded the Revolution by decades. The anthropology of the variety taught by Margaret Mead was already rampant. Denis Diderot, for his part, had combined his attack on Christianity with his suggestion, in his *Supplement au voyage de Bougainville*, that men in the state of nature had no need of sexual prohibition. And then there was the popular pornography, whose origins lay in what Simon Schama calls the "rich and unsavory vein of court pornography" and which had "evolved into a particularly ripe phase during the last years of Louis xv, when 'histories' of his private brothel at Versailles, the *Parc aux Cerfs* (the Stag Park), were in vogue."[18]

The social and political consequences of an aristocracy that indulged freely in pornographic writings and art cannot be overestimated. The mores of an important sector of French society, Schama notes, actually favored hedonism and amoralism and made it difficult for its members to espouse, much less to practice, any moral precepts. Under the protection of the Duc d'Orleans, the denizens of the Palais Royale cast aristocrats and prelates as the main characters in the pornographic novels they produced and thus succeeded, in addition to titillating their friends, in destabilizing the ancien régime: "[T]he standard tales of buggery, adultery, incest and promiscuity thus became a kind of metaphor for a diseased constitution."[19] The revolutionaries simply put to their own use the libido that Versailles had unleashed. Sade, who more explicitly than any other in France described and reveled in the link between pornography and political revolution, was not an aberration of eighteenth-century French culture, but the culmination of the French predilection for pornography.

By 1792, when Mary Wollstonecraft arrived in Paris life was ready to imitate art. With illustrated copies of Sade's *Justine* already in circulation, and his *Aline et Valcour* soon to follow, the Parisian mob seemed bent on living a sadistic fantasy: "*Aline et Valcour, ou le Roman Philosophique*, a 'novel' in four volumes . . . was reprinted three times between 1793 and 1795. Totaling more than seventeen hundred pages, it had an enormous impact on the French Revolution which was, in so many ways, a sanguinary sex orgy. Hence its popular appeal."[20] The dismemberment of the Princess de Lamballe could have been taken from the latter chapters of Sade's *120 Days of Sodom*:

A door was opened off the interrogation room, where she saw men waiting with axes and pikes. Pushed into an alley she was hacked to death in minutes. Her clothes were stripped from her body to join the immense pile that would later be sold at public auction, and her head was struck off and stuck on a pike. Some accounts, including that of Mercier, insist on the obscene mutilation and display of her genitals, a story which Caron dismisses with the cloistered certainty of the archivist as intrinsically inconceivable. What is certain is that her head was carried in triumph through the streets of Paris to the Temple, where one of the crowd barged into the King's rooms to demand that the Queen show herself at the window to see her friend's head.[21]

Wollstonecraft, though unaware, found herself simultaneously in two separate trajectories of sex and horror. The English trajectory was just experiencing the first stirrings of sexual liberation; the French trajectory was ending in horror. What began as libertinage in France was now culminating in an unprecedented orgy of sadistic violence. To give some indication of how these two sexual trajectories were out of sync, Wollstonecraft wrote her *Vindication of the Rights of Woman* in England in the same year that the Marquis de Sade published *Justine* in France.

The waystations on the sex-horror trajectory are described differently by different thinkers, but the similarities outweigh the differences. "Everyone who is tempted," wrote St. James in his epistle, "is attracted and seduced by his own wrong desire. Then the desire conceives and gives birth to sin, and when sin is fully grown, it too has a child and the child is death." Sade gives his own version of the sex-horror trajectory in his pornographic Bastille reverie, *The 120 Days of Sodom*. Instead of St. James's tripartite trajectory of passion, sin, and death, Sade proposes a four-part division—simple passions, followed by complex passions, criminal passions, and murderous passions. Four women are chosen because of their debauched lives as narrators of the various fantasies:

Four women, I say, who having spent their lives in the most furious debauchery, had reached the state where they could provide an exact account of all these matters; and, as care had been taken to select four endowed with a certain eloquence and a fitting turn of mind, after much discussion, recording and arranging, all four were ready to insert each into the adventures of her life, all the most extraordinary vagaries of debauch, and to do so in such an order and at such a pace that the first, for example, would work in the tale of her life's activities the one hundred and fifty simple passions and the least esoteric or most ordinary deviations; the second, within the same framework, an equal number of more unusual passions involving one or more men with one or several women; the third was also to introduce into her narration one hundred and fifty of the most criminal whimsies and those which most outrage the laws of both Nature and religion; and as all these excesses *lead to murder* and as these murders committed through libertinage are infinitely various and are just as numerous as the occasions upon which the libertine's inflamed imagination adopts different tortures, the fourth was to adorn the events of her life with a meticulous report upon one and fifty assorted examples of them.[22]

After his description of the simple passions, Sade lapses into shorthand descriptions of torture and murder—mostly the murder of pregnant women and their unborn children. In this, the end of *The 120 Days of Sodom* was much like the end of the Terror. What St. James and the Marquis de Sade share is the realization that "all these excesses lead to murder." In this they differ from the early phases of the Enlightenment, which hold that releasing sexual passions from the confines of the moral order can be managed and its bad effects rendered harmless by legislation or technology. But what begins as sex emancipated from the moral order ends in murder and death.

On the evening of December 26, 1792, shortly after her arrival in Paris, Wollstonecraft, for the first time in her life, was too afraid to put out the candle by her bed. In a letter she wrote that cold evening in a city slipping into the grip of the Terror, she spoke of eyes glaring at her through the window and bloody hands threatening her from the street outside. The frightened tone of this letter was different from the breezy tone she had adopted earlier. Before arriving in France,

Wollstonecraft had written that the revolutionary mob should be compared to inexperienced children playing with sharp-edged tools: "[L]et me beg you not to mix with the shallow herd who throw an odium on immutable principles, because some of the mere instruments of the revolution were too sharp.—Children of any growth will do mischief when they meddle with edged tools. It is to be lamented that as yet the billows of public opinion are only to be moved forward by the strong wind, the squally gusts of passions."[23]

But "now she felt horror," Claire Tomalin observes, "and her nightmare fantasy—it cannot have been literal truth—of the bloody hands and glaring, peeping eyes, reads like a forecast of the Terror."[24] Yet no matter how moved she was in the moment, Wollstonecraft experienced no fundamental change of heart regarding morals and revolutionary freedom. Her fear was merely a preliminary to her own embarkation on the sex-horror trajectory.

It had all seemed so promising at the beginning, but clouds began to gather on the horizon. There was rioting in the street; freedom of the press disappeared as the mob destroyed the presses of journalists who had taken a wrong turn on the way to utopia. On April 12, 1793, all foreigners were forbidden to leave France. Rumors of bloody counterrevolutionary uprisings in the Vendée began to circulate through Paris. Madame Roland, the Girondist leader who eventually lost her head to the Revolution, described scenes of revolutionary terror in which "women were brutally violated before being torn to pieces by those tigers; intestines cut out and worn as turbans; bleeding human flesh devoured."[25] Wollstonecraft would witness similar scenes first hand. At one point, while crossing Paris on foot, she slipped, and looking down noticed that the square she was crossing was covered with blood. She became so distraught that the commotion she created could have led to her demise had not friends led her away. It hardly seemed a propitious time to unleash the dogs of passion, but that is precisely what Wollstonecraft did.

While dining with Joel and Ruth Barlow, two devotees of revolution from the United States, Wollstonecraft met another American by the name of Gilbert Imlay, the European agent of the Scioto Land Company of Ohio. Imlay was forty-one years old and had written a novel about an English woman living close to nature somewhere near Pittsburgh. He had also written about the charms of life in western Kentucky. Wollstonecraft had met Imlay once before and seems to have been repelled by his arrogance, but gradually, in spite of her fairly accurate assessment of his character, succumbed to his charms. He had told Wollstonecraft of his sexual involvements with other women and that he believed that marriage was a corrupt institution. But in this he was just mouthing the conventional left-wing wisdom of the times. Godwin said much the same thing in *Political Justice*; and Wollstonecraft herself had said similar things in *A Vindication of the Rights of Woman*. So Wollstonecraft could hardly be offended at Imlay's callousness, and she was not. She rushed headlong into an affair with him. Thus, as the revolution that was to bring about universal love and virtue descended into an orgy of sadistic violence and death, Wollstonecraft, in a colossal misreading of the times, decided to take her life into her hands by becoming involved with a sexual adventurer from the New World.

The affair took place at a little house with a garden in Neuilly-sur-Seine during the summer of 1793. It was an early version of the ultimate Boho idyll—sex with literary pretensions, playing at writing while playing at life. Wollstonecraft was convinced that she was hard at work writing "a great book," *An Historical and Moral View of the Origin and Progress of the French Revolution*. She shared her memories with Godwin during their marriage, and Godwin later tried to cast as positive a light as possible on the affair. "Her confidence," Godwin wrote, "was entire; her love was unbounded. Now, for the first time in her life, she gave loose to all the sensibilities of her nature."[26]

Imlay in due course registered Wollstonecraft as his wife at the American Embassy, but it was simply a diplomatic ruse to prevent Wollstonecraft from being arrested as an English citizen, since England was now at war with revolutionary France. Wollstonecraft, however, seems to have taken the gesture as something more, boasting in good revolutionary fashion to Ruth Barlow about the unconventional nature of her relationship with Imlay. Because it was contracted "freely," according to the Jacobin definition of that term— that is, without the sanction of state or Church—the sexual union paradoxically took on a "most sacred nature." In other words, whether the dissipated rake Imlay knew it or not, their sexual union was even more binding in Wollstonecraft's eyes than had they followed the conventional route and exchanged vows in front of the altar. She was offering herself up on the altar of revolutionary virtue. Wollstonecraft's sentiment evokes a feminism that came into being before the technological neutering of the female rendered it safe, or at least sterile (and therefore promotable as a mass movement). Back then, it was free love with live ammunition, and she paid the consequences by being looked upon by Imlay as just another of his many female conquests.

The Wollstonecraft-Imlay idyll ended, as such affairs usually do, when Wollstonecraft became pregnant in August of 1793. Suddenly, Imlay, who was perpetually involved in business ventures he seemed incapable of bringing to completion, was called to Le Havre, then to England, and did not return. Wollstonecraft, tasting the first bitter fruit of her journey along the sex-horror trajectory, returned to Paris in time to see the Revolution proceed to that trajectory's terminal phase, the inescapable phase of self-annihilation.

On May 30, 1793, just as the Imlay-Wollstonecraft idyll began, the moderate Girondins had found their position in the revolutionary Convention untenable and began to go into hiding to avoid arrest. During the summer, the Convention had moved the guillotine to the Place de la Revolution beside the Tuileries Gardens. Then, in the fall, just as Wollstonecraft returned pregnant from Neuilly, the killing began in earnest. In addition to the decapitations, hundreds of enemies of the revolution were drowned in the Loire. On October 9, all of the English who were foolish enough to have remained in Paris were arrested. Since Wollstonecraft's fictional marriage to Imlay conferred American citizenship on her, and since America was the French paradigm for revolution, Wollstonecraft was spared imprisonment and death, but her Girondin friends were not so lucky. On October 16, the queen was guillotined; two weeks later, Brissot and twenty other Girondins followed the queen to the scaffold.

Wollstonecraft had made contact with the Girondin faction shortly after her arrival in France, and because of her exalted status as the author of *A Vindication of the Rights of Woman* was invited by

Condorcet, who had the support of the Girondins, to submit a paper to the education committee, then hard at work trying to break the power of the patriarchal family and bring revolutionary freedom to wives and children. The death of the Girondins was a terrible blow to Wollstonecraft, who wept bitterly both for the people she knew and for the cause which she had espoused with such naïve fervor.

The loss of the moderate Girondins' hold on power had an uncanny parallel in the collapse of Wollstonecraft's affair with Imlay, as one of her biographers has noted. "Having accepted without question the Enlightenment presumption that passion can be controlled by reason," St. Clair writes, "she was surprised to find herself unable to keep her feelings under control."[27] With the passing of each day that Imlay failed to return, Wollstonecraft's irritation grew, at him in particular and at men in general. "Amongst the feathered race," she wrote, "whilst the hen keeps the young warm, her mate stays by to cheer her; but it is sufficient for man to condescend to get a child, in order to claim it.—A man is a tyrant!"[28] She lashed out against "the common run of men," who, after a drunken debauch, "suppose the wife, slave rather, whom they maintain, has no right to complain, and ought to receive the sultan whenever he deigns to return, with open arms."[29]

Gone were the plans of emigrating to America where they could live out the rustic idyll in the wilds of Pittsburgh or Kentucky described in Imlay's novel. All that was left was an absent father working for "whole knots of men turned into machines, to enable a keen speculator to become wealthy; and every noble principle of nature is eradicated by making a man pass his life in stretching wire, pointing a pin, heading a nail, or spreading a sheet of paper on a plain surface."[30] Wollstonecraft also had a hungry child, a sense of having been jilted, the wreck of the philosophy that had promised liberation both political and personal, and nightmare memories of the bloodiest days of the Terror. "I wish one moment," she wrote to Imlay, "that I had never heard of the cruelties that have been practised here, and the next envy the mothers who have been killed with their children."[31]

She also wrote Imlay letters mocking his sensual nature: "I have found out that I have more mind than you, in one respect; because I can, without any violent effort of reason, find food for love in the same object, much longer than you can.—The way to my senses is through my heart; but, forgive me, I think there is sometime a shorter cut to yours." She raged against her abandonment: "Am I always to be tossed about thus?" she wondered to Imlay. "Shall I never find an asylum to rest contented in? How can you love to fly about continually dropping down, as it were, in a new world—cold and strange!—every other day? Why do you not attach those tender emotions round the idea of home, which even now dim my eyes?—This alone is affection—every thing else is only humanity, electrified by sympathy." She lamented their different natures; hers, sensitive, his, animal: "I shall always consider it as one of the most serious misfortunes of my life, that I did not meet you before satiety had rendered your senses so fastidious, as almost to close up every tender avenue of sentiment and affection that leads to your sympathetic heart. You have a heart, my friend, yet, hurried away by the impetuosity of inferior feelings; you have sought in vulgar excesses, for that gratification which only the heart can bestow." She even employed Romantic psychology to win Imlay back: "The impulse of the senses, passions, if you will, and the conclusions of reason, draw men together; but the imagination is the true fire, stolen from heaven, to animate this cold creature of clay, producing all those fine sympathies that lead to rapture, rendering men social by expanding their hearts, instead of leaving them leisure to calculate how many comforts society affords."[32]

Wollstonecraft's protests ring hollow, given that the affair was as much her idea as his and her philosophy every bit as enabling as his. Indeed, she confessed at one point that she had not a leg to stand on when she condemned Imlay on moral grounds: "I have no criterion for morality, and have thought in vain, if the sensation which leads you to follow an ancle [sic] or step, be the sacred foundation of principle or affection. Mine has been of a very different nature, or it would not have stood the brunt of your sarcasm. The sentiment in me is still sacred. If there be any part of me that will survive the sense of my misfortunes, it is the purity of my affections. The impetuosity of your senses, may have led you to term mere animal desire, the source of principle."[33]

It had become painfully apparent to Wollstonecraft that liberated men and liberated women bring very different expectations to their approximation of the marriage bed. Men, she had discovered, tended toward promiscuity; absent an institution of indissoluble marriage, they remained in essence bohemians. But by entering the relationship on "philosophical" terms, Wollstonecraft had cut herself off from any authority which she could exert over her "husband." In other words, when she became pregnant, she came to realize that there was a certain asymmetry in sexual relations; that the female nature, which was bound up with nurturing, needed itself to be nurtured. She also intuited that the new life called into being was going to require care for a significant period of time.

Wollstonecraft, bluestocking feminist that she was, now perceived that matrimony was a natural state of affairs and not the tool of social oppression she railed against in her writings. In one letter to Imlay she wrote, "you perceive that I am acquiring the matrimonial phraseology without having clogged my soul by promising obedience."[34] What she really needed was to reinvent something she had spurned a few years earlier—namely, marriage. But, of course, the task exceeded her capacity as a thinker. Neither could she credibly condemn the misfortune visited upon her by Imlay because she was complicit in producing that unhappiness. All she could do was to express her revulsion at the libidinous philosophical underpinning of the doctrine of free love. In sum, Wollstonecraft was a perfect example of somebody hopelessly caught in the cage of her own thinking. Burke's phrase "unavailing sorrow" comes to mind as an apt description of her state of mind.

At one point in her largely unanswered stream of letters to Imlay, Wollstonecraft wrote:

> It seems to me, that my conduct has always been governed by the strictest principles of justice and truth.—Yet, how wretched have my social feelings, and delicacy of sentiment rendered me! I have loved with my whole soul, only to discover that I had no chance of return—and that existence is a burthen without it. . . . In truth I have been rudely handled. Do you judge coolly, and I

trust you will not continue to call those capricious feelings "the most refined,": which would undermine not only the most sacred principles, but the affections which unite mankind.—You would render mothers unnatural—and there would be no such thing as a father!—If your theory of morals is the most "exalted," it is certainly the most easy.—It does not require much magnanimity, to determine to please ourselves for the moment, let others suffer what they will!

But is it not possible that passion clouds your reason, as much as it does mine?—and ought you not to doubt, whether those principles are so "exalted," as you term them, which only lead to your own gratification? In other words, whether it be just to have no principle of action, but that of following your inclination, trampling on the affection you have fostered, and the expectations you have excited? [35]

Wollstonecraft thus reached the heart of the problem with the Enlightenment. Enlightenment morality was what its proponents said it was, namely, self-interest, which they tried to ameliorate by referring to it as "enlightened"—but which Wollstonecraft soon found out was synonymous with selfishness. Moreover, as she discovered in her dealings with Imlay, there was no higher court of appeal than the selfish self, unless one accepted the option of physical violence. Yet, despite her implicit condemnation of the Enlightenment as "mere animal desire" dressed up as "principle," no explicit condemnation followed. She was incapable of formulating it.

The Enlightenment myth had firmly stipulated that evil was imposed from without by the unholy alliance of church and state. Opposed to these "artificial" and deleterious restraints, the Enlightenment proposed "nature" and "nature's laws," which included desire and passion liberated from "unnatural"—that is, moral—restraint. Since there was no such thing as original sin, since man was "naturally" good, one need only remove external restraint, virtue would flourish, and the era of fraternal love would be inaugurated on earth. What happened in France—and what happened to Wollstonecraft—during the 1790s bespoke something different.

If the Enlightenment set out to prove that man could release passion from the bonds of religion, custom, and morals, and in the doing bring about a regime of universal brotherhood, then it is hard to imagine a more graphic refutation of that premise than the French Revolution. Even the most obtuse observer in France had to admit that the more the French people threw off restraint, the more suffering and death seemed to proliferate. Passion liberated from religious and moral restraint was simply passion, furious and uncontrollable. It followed no law but its own, which was the sex-horror trajectory described by both St. James and the Marquis de Sade. Crocker refers to the failure of the Enlightenment as a "tragedy," but this is just another way of saying that horror was the Enlightenment's logical outcome. The West, undeterred, would experiment with the sex-horror trajectory a number of times over the next two centuries, but the first instance was the most dramatic. By the mid-1790s the most ardent English supporters of the Revolution were having doubts in light of the ferocity and sadism exhibited by the Parisian mob. Burke had been prophetic in everything but the degree of ferocity he predicted. The Revolution was infinitely more terrible than he had warned it would be.

This pattern of the sex-horror trajectory contradicted, of course, the ideology of liberation, and as a result, people like Wollstonecraft found themselves at a loss when called upon to explain the train of events. Wollstonecraft remained essentially blind to the drama then reaching its bloody denouement, the most spectacular version of the political Enlightenment. She was blinded by the ideology of revolution she had come to Paris to justify, but also by the sexual passion that accompanied it. When it came to the murder of Louis XVI, Mary was of two minds. Her head seemed to be with the dissenting tradition and the English radicals who justified the regicide, one hundred years earlier, of Charles I, but her heart seemed to indicate that something else was at work, because she involuntarily wept when she saw the French king taken to his trial. It was another crisis of truth versus desire; and in the end, in spite of the evidence, Wollstonecraft justified ideology—the collective desire of her class, the English supporters of the Enlightenment—over the truth she had witnessed.

The book she eventually wrote on the Revolution was one of her worst, written mostly from outdated news accounts and never covering what she had actually seen. As a result, its optimism takes on the air of unreality common to ideologues. The excesses of the Revolution, she claimed, were the result of the repression which had preceded them. It was history based on plumbing psychology, in which the Revolution was cast in the role of safety valve. It was consequentialism of the sort Godwin espoused as well. Both Wollstonecraft and Godwin attempted to persuade their readers that once the excesses of repression imposed by the *ancien régime* had sweated themselves out of the body politic, the benefits in liberty would erase any lingering memory of the atrocities.

The naïveté of the English revolutionaries in this regard is traceable to the fact that the English were behind the French in the corruption of morals necessary to any revolution. The French had begun to emancipate the sexual impulse from the moral order some time before. Mary Wollstonecraft, as the representative of the morally more conservative English culture, had moved along the same trajectory by embarking on what seemed to be a harmless sexual idyll sanctioned by the Revolution's abrogation of traditional morals, but somehow also immune from its effects.

In the order of politics, the Revolution had destroyed any court of appeal higher than the guillotine. Political enlightenment, that is, had ended in terror; her own Enlightenment idyll had left her a penniless single mother abandoned in a foreign land. So she, as the representative feminist, was faced with unpleasant alternatives. The first was to repudiate the ideology of liberation and return to the tradition that articulated the moral order as part of the divine order of things. But this would have entailed a repudiation of her intellectual heritage and, in the absence of a religious conversion, was nearly impossible.

The second was the technological alternative, which subsequent feminists chose, namely, contraception. Neutering the female would eliminate offspring and the need to provide for them. This alternative was not historically untried, of course. Ancient Rome had had frequent recourse to "pharmakeia." The French, ever in the avant garde, had made unheard-of strides in developing poisons whose purpose was to allow unhappy wives to get rid of either unwanted husbands or unwanted pregnancies. But England, as ever, was in arrears when it came to progress (or degeneracy) in morals. In *A Vindication of the Rights of Woman*, the virginal Wollstonecraft was of the opinion that contraception was unnatural. "Surely," she writes, "nature never intended that women, by satisfying an appetite, should frustrate the very purpose for which it was implanted." In one of her last letters to Imlay, in November 1795, Wollstonecraft still seemed to feel that contraception was wrong, and that if she had stumbled in other areas, she still had not succumbed to the unnatural vice which required "vulgar precautions": "My child may have to blush for her mother's want of prudence—and may lament that the rectitude of my heart made me above vulgar precautions."[36]

Still, it did not take a genius to realize that free love practiced in a state of nature would lead to lots of children and the annoying responsibility of raising them. And the experience of Imlay and countless men like him showed that the men most likely to beget children outside of marriage were the least likely to support them. So a conflict arose along sexual lines among the enlightened, but it seemed a foregone conclusion that the conflict would eventually be resolved in favor of those who saw the technological solution of contraception as the *sine qua non* of free love and liberation, no matter how repugnant and unnatural the first generation of sexual revolutionaries considered these "vulgar precautions." Movements like this are technologically conditioned, if not technologically driven, as the discovery of the birth-control pill would show in the 1960s. But whether sexual liberation created the pill or the pill created sexual liberation is for our purposes a moot point. Wollstonecraft did not have at her disposal contraceptives, and having more children was out. Which is perhaps why she chose the third alternative, the one that became the family tradition, namely, horror.

Suicide loomed in the mind of Wollstonecraft. Imlay was not coming back, and as she wrote, "death and misery in every shape of terror haunts this devoted country." Shakespeare's Hamlet, the character of a devout age, wonders if suicide might not be a prelude to even greater suffering in Hell. But suicide held no such deterrent for

Wollstonecraft. By killing herself she could become Imlay's nemesis, his return to the moral order he had spurned. "Should your sensibility ever awake," Wollstonecraft wrote to him, "remorse will find its way to your heart; and in the midst of business and sensual pleasure, I shall appear to you, the victim of your deviation from rectitude."[37] Since enlightened reason failed to move Imlay to the correct moral position regarding his lover and child, Wollstonecraft would try terror instead. She would kill herself and thereby implant her ghost in Imlay's guilt-ridden conscience forever. It would be a perverse reinstatement of the marriage vows they had never taken. Like Banquo's ghost, she would stalk the banquet his life had become and plague the pleasures he was taking with actresses in London, but should have been sharing with her. While still in France, Wollstonecraft took an overdose of laudanum, half-heartedly hoping that the news would reach Imlay and soften his heart. It did not, and so Wollstonecraft returned to England to carry out her plans to restore moral equilibrium.

. . . . .

Returning to England did not improve Wollstonecraft's situation, however; in fact, it only worsened it. Now she was no longer the foreign bluestocking in the capital of revolution. She was a fallen woman returned to England, the land of her birth, where a rising tide of revulsion at things French and revolutionary prevailed, and where such unprogressive moral formulas as those limiting sexual activity to the married state were still current. Beyond that, Imlay was there too, living with an actress, a state of affairs that made Wollstonecraft's own situation even more transparent to society at large. She could no longer, as she had done in France, maintain the fiction that she was Mrs. Imlay.

And so she prepared to attempt suicide again, this time choosing death by water. In October, Wollstonecraft made provision for her daughter, Fanny; then, being a literary woman, she wrote a note that set forth what she intended to do and why. As she had already written Imlay from France, "Even at Paris, my image will haunt you.—

You will see my pale face—and sometimes the tears of anguish will drop on your heart, which you have forced from mine."[38]

Wollstonecraft walked up and down in the rain to weigh down her clothes and then threw herself off Putney Bridge into the Thames because the spot seemed remote and rescue unlikely. "I go to find comfort," she informed posterity in her suicide note, "and my only fear is, that my poor body will be insulted by an endeavour to recall my hated existence. But I shall plunge into the Thames where there is the least chance of my being snatched from the death I seek."[39] In this, she miscalculated once again: her clothing proved much more buoyant than she had imagined. Two men in a rowboat fished her out, and they took her to an inn of ill repute where she was revived and left to contemplate what to do for the rest of her life.

Wollstonecraft was later to say that the suicide attempt was so painful that the pains of an unhappy life seemed mild by comparison. Having failed twice to end her old life, Mary launched herself into a new life in the same intellectual environs. On January 8, 1796, she attended the tea party given by Mary Hays and met, for the second time, William Godwin. This most famous English philosopher, as mentioned, had fallen on hard times, primarily because the French Revolution, as Wollstonecraft had witnessed first hand, had taken such a marked turn toward savagery and horror. The man who was once the cynosure of the ladies' eyes had recently had two marriage proposals rejected, a sure sign that his intellectual stock was in decline. Not that his position was insignificant. In addition to the by-then widely execrated *Political Justice*, Godwin had written *Things as They Are: or, The Adventures of Caleb Williams*, a combination thriller and social tract that exposed social evils from the progressive point of view and was admired by people like Lord Byron. Nevertheless, Godwin was hardly the figure he had once been.

That his intellectual stock was available at remainder prices seems not to have deterred Mary Wollstonecraft; in fact, it seems to have encouraged her to cultivate his acquaintance. During the spring of 1796, she moved to a residence on Cumming Street to be close to the beleaguered remnant of Enlightenment bohemianism and to Godwin in particular, who was living nearby on Charlton Street, Somers Town. Godwin's presence seems to have helped her exorcise the ghost of Imlay. She wrote Imlay a last letter, not without acrimony and reproach, but at least ending with, "I part with you in peace."[40]

In many respects, the match promised success. To begin with, both Godwin and Wollstonecraft were intellectuals. Beyond that, they came from the dissenting tradition; both had repudiated it in favor of the Enlightenment, and yet both had retained (she in somewhat tarnished form) the morals that grew out of the Puritan tradition and antedated its transmogrification at the hands of French radicalism. In addition to those philosophical considerations, Godwin was still a virgin at the time Mary Wollstonecraft laid siege to his affections. It was as if her hope that she could have got to Imlay before he had become jaded by sexual excess was fulfilled in the virginal Godwin, who was feeling the pull of desire and the hearth, perhaps as a result of falling so abruptly from the firmament of literary fame.

The campaign had a directness to it that bespoke Wollstonecraft's years in revolutionary France. On the morning of April 14, 1796, in the manner of an emancipated lady, she arrived alone and unannounced at Godwin's house on Charlton Street. The affair may have begun as a meeting of the minds, but by August the two had become intimate. Godwin kept an account in his diary of the times they had sexual intercourse, along with his attempt to calculate the possibility of pregnancy and avert it, an early version of the rhythm method he referred to as the "chance medely system." Godwin, however, was not destined to become a pioneer in new methods of birth control. Toward the end of the year, Wollstonecraft discovered that she was pregnant.

To be back in counterrevolutionary England and now the mother of a second illegitimate child by a second father seems to have been a daunting prospect for Wollstonecraft, so on March 29, 1797, both Wollstonecraft and Godwin swallowed their revolutionary principles and got married at the Anglican Church of St. Pancras.

The decision was a tribute to the humanity of the liberated couple; unfortunately, it was not a ringing endorsement of their consistency as philosophers. In this they were typically liberated Enlightenment figures. They could only be human beings by reneging on their misguided philosophy; or conversely, they could be philosophers only by turning their backs on their humanity.

With the Wollstonecraft-Godwin marriage we contemplate the happier alternative, the subordination of ideology to common sense, no matter how expedient (or cowardly) it might have seemed to their radical contemporaries. Godwin's success as a husband and father may have come at the price of his failure as a philosopher, but there are worse tragedies in life. His description of the birth of their child in the Wollstonecraft memoir says as much in favor of matrimony as his philosophy said against it: "This, she seemed to say, is the joint result of our common affection. It partakes equally of both, and is the shrine in which our sympathies and our life have been poured together, by presents and tokens; we record and stamp our attachment in this precious creature, a creature of that species which is more admirable than anything else the world has to boast, a creature susceptible of pleasure and pain, of affection and love, of sentiment and fancy, of wisdom and virtue."[41]

The "this" in question was Mary Godwin, who would later write *Frankenstein*.

# 2

Passion and Electricity

S HELLEY INTRODUCED HIMSELF into the Godwin household in
1812. The adulatory tone of his letter to William Godwin makes
it clear that Shelley was looking for something more than a book
that ratified his belief in revolution. He was looking for an intellectual father, an older man who embodied the ideals Shelley wanted to
put into practice in a very specific way. "To you, as the regulator and
former of my mind," Shelley wrote, "I must ever look with real respect and veneration."[1] It was as if Shelley had stumbled across
Rousseau living in Yorkshire.

The revolutionary trajectory was evident in Shelley's life at an early
age. Born in 1792, the year Godwin published *Political Justice*, and heir
to a recent baronetcy, Shelley grew up as the little master at a country
estate, the idol of four adoring sisters. He was quite the spoiled child
and displayed that instrumental attitude toward human beings typical of the indulged youngster. Early fascinated by chemistry and electricity, young Shelley even experimented on his sisters, who uttered
no protest. As Shelley's sister Helen wrote, "when my brother com-
menced his studies in chemistry, and practiced electricity upon us, I
confess my pleasure in it was entirely negatived by terror at its effects.
Whenever he came to me with his piece of folded brown packing-
paper under him arm and a bit of wire and a bottle (if I remember

right), my heart would sink with fear at his approach; but shame kept me silent, and, with as many others as he could collect, we were placed hand-in-hand round the nursery table to be electrified."[2]  In another incident, a somewhat comical version of Victor Frankenstein's fictitious project, Shelley wired up a local tomcat to what his cousin called an "electrical kite" flying in a thunderstorm overhead.  Shelley also set off explosions in the meadow at Field Place, his country estate, started fires in the various stoves with the damper closed, and allowed various acids and caustics to burn holes in carpets and furniture.

But the idyll at Field Place was rudely disrupted when Shelley was sent to Eton, where he was treated in the brutal fashion customary among English public school boys when dealing with those deemed odd, like "mad Shelley." He discovered that he had a genuinely violent temper which he could at times barely control.  Shelley started to believe that he could overcome the world by sheer force of passion. That passion would later be transmuted through the romantic theory of poetry into a form of cultural warfare, but passion remained normative nonetheless.  Passion, of course, was simply desire writ large, and one of the shortcomings of Shelley's later politics, as well as his later poetics, was his inability to adjudicate desire.  "Whatever was, was right" is the closest he came to an explanation of how the parts fit together.  The result of this theory was a habit of rationalization.

Shelley's precocious learning only furthered his slide into rebellion.  The rigor of the public school training Shelley received meant he could read the classics in Latin and Greek by the time he reached Oxford; but it also meant that at an early age Shelley could delve into the literature of the revolution, congenial to his nascent sansculotte spirit, that had recently convulsed France.  Once deep in the treacherous waters of the Enlightenment, Shelly read its lessons back into the classics.  Prometheus, as a result, began to figure prominently in his own private revolutionary pantheon—Prometheus read through the gnostic lens of modern revolution.  That reading only added intellectual fire to a temperament that saw life as the realization of radical principle in action.  As Shelley was later to write in one of the interminable notes to his philosophical poem *Queen Mab*:

Prometheus stole fire from heaven, and was chained for this crime to Mount Caucasus, where a vulture continually devoured his liver, that grew to meet its hunger. . . . Prometheus (who represents the human race) effected some great change in the condition of his nature, and applied fire to culinary purposes; thus inventing an expedient for screening from his disgust the horrors of the shambles. From this moment his vitals were devoured by the vulture of disease. It consumed his being in every shape of its loathsome and infinite variety, inducing the soul-quelling slinkings of premature and violent death. All vice arose from the ruin of healthful innocence. Tyranny, superstition, commerce, and inequality, were then first known, when reason vainly attempted to guide the wanderings of exacerbated passion.[3]

*Queen Mab* had a long revolutionary reach: "Besides reaching American radicals, it is known that the poem was influential in liberal and revolutionary circles on the Continent, and the young Frederick Engels began a translation before the 1848 upheavals."[4]

Shelley continued his disordered intellectual life at Oxford. College chum Thomas Jefferson Hogg made explicit in his memoirs the connection between Shelley's interest in science and the occult:

He was passionately attached to the study of what used to be called the occult sciences, conjointly with that of the new wonders, which chemistry and nature philosophy have displayed to us. His pocket money was spent in the purchase of books relative to these darling pursuits—chemical apparatus and materials. The books consisted of treatises on magic and witchcraft, as well as those more modern ones detailing the miracles of electricity and galvanism. Sometimes he watched the livelong nights for ghosts. At his father's house, where his influence was, of course, great among the dependents, he even planned how he might get admission to the vault, or charnel-house, at Warnham Church, and might sit there all night, harrowed by fear, yet trembling with expectation, to see one of the spiritualized owners of the bones pile around him.[5]

By the middle of his first semester, Shelley was continuing the same sort of anarchic intellectual life he had pursued at Field Place, sleeping on the floor for a few hours a day, tinkering and reading through the night, burning the carpets and furniture with various acids and caustics, and paging though Paracelsus or a trashy novel from the Minerva Press. His room at Oxford was a metaphor for his chaotic state of mind. According to Jeff Hogg, in addition to Shelley's "solar microscope and several crates of chemical and electrical equipment, including a system of Voltaic batteries and hand-cranked generator," one could find

> Books, boots, papers, shoes, philosophical instruments, clothes, pistols, linen, crockery, ammunition, and phials innumerable, with money stockings, prints, crucibles, bags, and boxes, were scattered on the floor in every place. . . . The tables, and especially the carpet, were already stained with large spots of various hues, which frequently proclaimed the agency of fire. An electrical machine, an air-pump, the galvanic trough, a solar microscope, and large glass jars and receivers, were conspicuous amidst the mass of matter. Upon the table by his side were some books lying open, several letters, a bundle of new pens, and a bottle of japan ink, that served as an ink stand; a piece of deal, lately part of the lid of a box, with many chips, and a handsome razor that had been used as a knife.[6]

Shelley also continued his experiments with electricity. Hogg recorded an experiment Shelley performed on himself:

> He then proceeded, with much eagerness and enthusiasm, to show me the various instruments, especially the electrical apparatus; turning round the handle very rapidly, so that the fierce, crackling sparks flew forth; and presently standing upon the stool with glass feet, he begged me to work the machine until he was filled with the fluid, so that his long, wild locks bristled and stood on end. Afterwards he charged a powerful battery of several large jars; labouring with vast energy, and discoursing with increasing vehemence of the marvelous powers of electricity, of thunder and lightning; describing an electrical kite that he had made at home, and projecting another and an enormous one, or rather a combination of many kites, that would draw down from the sky an immense volume of electricity, the whole ammunition of a mighty

thunderstorm; and this directed to some point would there produce the most stupendous results.[7]

Shelley's experiments have a touching sort of naïveté to them, a
bit like a boy playing with his chemistry set on the way to inventing
the cure for some dread disease later in life. But there was a sinister
side to what he was doing as well. Science, from Shelley's point of
view, was a way of manipulating nature to get what he wanted from
it: science was successful magic. Moreover, as with Marx and Lenin
at a later date, the first step to successful revolution was a scientific
understanding of the universe. Shelley was a magus with a revolutionary agenda, not a boy interested in the workings of the world.
"Thou didst sport with life," the monster says to Victor Frankenstein,
and as Mary Shelley would learn, the charge applied to the young
Shelley.

It should come as no surprise that Shelley viewed Christianity as
the enemy. The more Shelley became convinced that he was in possession of the secrets of nature, the more violent became his hatred of
"unnatural" conventions like the family, the state, and religion. "Yet
here I swear," Shelley wrote in a letter, "and as I break my oath may
Infinite Eternity blast me, here I swear that never will I forgive Christianity! . . . Oh how I wish I were the Antichrist, that it were mine to
crush the Demon, to hurl him to his native Hell never to rise again."
"Oh! I burn with impatience for the moment of Xtianity's dissolution,"
he continued, "it has injured me; I swear on the altar of perjured love
to revenge myself on the hated cause of the effect which even now I
can scarcely help deploring. —Indeed I think it is to the benefit of
society to destroy the opinions which can annihilate the dearest of its
ties. . . . Let us hope that the wound which we inflict tho' the dagger
be concealed, will rankle in the heart of our adversary."[8]

He ended his letter with the battle cry of the Enlightenment,
"écrasez l'infâme; écrasez l'impie." The phrase comes from Voltaire,
who used to end his letters with it, in the manner of Cato the Elder
speaking of Carthage. But the reference to the concealed dagger in
Shelley's letter was straight from Barruel's account of the Illuminati—

that "the end sanctifies the means"—which along with electricity, became another of Shelley's obsessions.

Shelley's youth, and even more his Englishness, gave him an air of innocence and otherworldliness that have proved all but ineradicable in the minds of later generations. He had long brown hair when the style was to wear it short and features whose slight irregularities were quickly forgotten when he spoke. His boyish features made him look even younger than his twenty years, and if not exactly handsome, "yet was the effect of the whole extremely powerful," according to Jeff Hogg. Shelley's features "breathed an animation, a fire, an enthusiasm, a vivid and preternatural intelligence, that I never met with in any other countenance. Nor was the moral expression less beautiful than the intellectual for there was a softness, a delicacy, a gentleness, and especially. . . . [an] air of profound religious veneration."[9]

Shelley's intellectual development had a certain inexorable quality to it. Desires were repeatedly put forth as ideas that needed to be put into action, first by individuals filled by poetic afflatus, then by entire cultures in the name of revolutionary politics. Eventually, they were to coalesce into a philosophy of revolution, and Godwin's *Political Justice* was an important milestone in the progress of Shelley's desire. It was the summa of the English revolutionary. As Shelley wrote to Godwin, "I was haunted with a passion for the wildest and most extravagant romances: ancient books of Chemistry and Magic were perused with an enthusiasm of wonder almost amounting to belief.... It is now a period of more than two years since first I saw your inestimable book of *Political Justice*; it opened to my mind fresh and more extensive views; it materially influenced my character, and I rose from its perusal a wiser and a better man." Yet Godwin reacted with horror when Shelley linked chemistry and magic: "You talk of awakening them," Shelley wrote, "they will rise up like Cadmus' seed of dragon's teeth, and their first act will be to destroy each other."[10]

By the time young Shelley showed up at Godwin's door, Godwin still had much to say, but he no longer possessed the key to the secrets of the universe; he could no longer claim to be elucidating principles which would provide some underlying unity to the public and private spheres. Godwin had written *Political Justice* as a bachelor, but had answered Shelley's letter as a married man. William St. Clair writes that Shelley arrived on the scene in 1812 to pick up the philosophy that Godwin was in the process of discarding.

The year 1812 was to prove a watershed for Shelley. It was the year he married young Harriet Westbrook; he also made the first of several attempts to establish a commune in which property and women would be shared and from which the spirit of liberation would spread. Shelley spent much of the summer corresponding with a maiden schoolteacher, Elizabeth Hitchener, eventually persuading her to leave her job and join Shelley's ménage. The arrangement did not work out. Shelley, evidently repulsed by Hitchener's appearance, sent her packing after a short time, without a teaching position and encumbered by the general sense that she was a rich man's cast-off mistress. It was not the first life Shelley would wreck: he was just getting started.

In 1812 Shelley also embarked on another, related project—convincing his pregnant wife of a few months to have sex with Jeff Hogg. In this endeavor, Shelley proved less successful than he had in wrecking the life of Elizabeth Hitchener. Harriet Shelley seemed impervious to perverse sexual temptations. She was invariably seen as dull by Shelley's revolutionary friends. Shelley would eventually construe Harriet's refusal to go along with such schemes as a lack of spirit and finally use it as a pretext to leave her in favor of someone more "spiritual," that is, more in tune with the values of the Enlightenment.

In 1812, too, on October 4, ten months after his initial contact by letter, Percy Shelley finally got to meet his middle aged idol and living link with the French Revolution at the Godwins' residence-cum-bookstore on Skinner Street. Mrs. Shelley was there for dinner, as was the second Mrs. Godwin (Mary Wollstonecraft Godwin had died in 1798) and all of their children but one: Mary, Godwin's daughter by Mary Wollstonecraft, was living with a family in Scotland at the time, but would return in November and meet the Shelleys then. Everyone got along famously at the first meeting. The Godwins found the young couple enchanting; Godwin himself found Shelley's intellectual homage flattering and, more important, his financial prospects even more intriguing.

It was a case of codependency made in literary heaven. Godwin wanted money; Shelley wanted a revolution, and the Godwinian system seemed capable of accommodating them both: "Godwin borrowed on principle, for he believed his work had a right to financing and was valuable to the community, justifying his belief with the egalitarian arguments of *Political Justice*. Shelley, in his turn, forced his acts of generosity upon others.... Both men subscribed to the doctrine stated in Book III of *Political Justice* that 'morality as has been frequently observed, consists entirely in an estimate of consequences.'"[11]

As one meeting followed another, discomfort seems to have grown over the marriage-sex issue. Shelley was embarrassed by his abandonment of Godwinian principle in marrying Harriet Westbrook. Godwin, when a theoretician of social mores, had written that marriage was the "most odious of all monopolies":

> Another immoral and monopolistic institution is marriage, condemned both for its affront to truth and for its connections with the worst features of property.... The institution of marriage is a system of fraud; and men who carefully mislead their judgements in the daily affair of their life, must always have a crippled judgement in every other concern.... Add to this, that marriage is an affair of property, and the worst of all properties. So long as two human beings are forbidden by positive institutions to follow the dictates of their own mind, prejudice is alive and vigourous. So long as I seek to engross one woman to myself, and to prohibit my neighbour from proving his superior desert and reaping the fruits of it, I am guilty of the most odious of all monopolies.[12]

Godwin had, by the time he met Shelley, trimmed his theoretical sails to the exigencies of human nature, to the point that, by his own and Shelley's standards, Godwin was hardly a Godwinian by the time Shelley met him.

But Shelley was still a Godwinian, or desperately wanted to be. For in face of imperious sexual desire and a sixteen-year-old young lady who would not give in to those desires, Shelley had capitulated to social pressure and violated his Godwinian principles. But whereas

Godwin, with the wisdom that comes with age, had repudiated the Godwinian system, at least on this particular point, Shelley felt that the fault lay with his own failure of nerve. The longer Shelley lived with Harriet, the more his decision to marry, made in the heat of passion, rankled him as a fatal compromise; and the more he pondered Godwinian principle, the more dissatisfied he became with Harriet.

With the birth of the Shelleys's first child—compounded by the arrival of Harriet's elder sister Eliza as part of the household and Harriet's increasing opacity, if not resistance, to Shelley's revolutionary ideas—their estrangement solidified. When Shelley pleaded with Harriet to send Eliza home, Harriet refused, partly because she feared for her own safety: Shelley was prone to laudanum-induced hallucinations (during one he claimed to have seen a demon) and violent fits in which he often discharged his pistol, as he had done recently during a particularly harrowing evening at a remote retreat in Wales. By February 1814, the influence of the Godwinian system had nearly wrecked Shelley's marriage. Shelley and Harriet were living apart for weeks at a time.

.  .  .  .  .

On May 5, Shelley showed up at the Godwin household to negotiate a usurious post-obit loan, whereby Shelley would agree to outrageous terms for quick cash, largely for Godwin's benefit. In the course of his stay, Shelley, now estranged from his wife and content in Godwin's orbit, seemed drawn to Godwin's daughter Mary as well. And the attraction, it seemed, was mutual.

Under the guise of concerning himself with her education, Shelley began spending increasing amounts of time with Mary. In addition to being more intelligent and better educated than Harriet, Mary seems to have taken on a numinous quality precisely because of her parents. Mary Godwin embodied the revolutionary tradition in both the physical and metaphysical senses of the word. Shelley's dedication in "The Revolt of Islam" refers to Mary as "Of Glorious parents, thou aspiring child." For her part, Mary seems to have seen in Shelley the type of man she had been taught from birth to admire, a man who took ideas seriously—and put them into practice. The sexual threat was defused somewhat by Shelley's deliberately cultivated delicate appearance. He was convinced that he was going to die of consumption, the quintessentially romantic disease, at an early age, and as if to hasten its arrival, he refused to eat in any rational, wholesome manner, feeding himself instead on bread crusts he carried around in his pockets. When the pangs of hunger became too insistent to ignore, Shelley stilled them with doses of the ever-present laudanum. The myth of the angelic-looking Shelley grew out of these idiosyncrasies.

As part of his education of Mary, Shelley began plying her with his thoughts as expressed in his revolutionary poem, *Queen Mab*, a compendium of left-wing nostrums set to verse. At this point in his life, Shelley was unsure whether he was called to be a philosopher or a poet. After reading *Queen Mab*, Mary suggested poetry as his career, perhaps because his philosophy was derivative, chiefly from her father, as the poem's notes make clear. In an odd application of the man-as-machine metaphor which La Mettrie found so liberating, Shelley complains:

> Power, like a desolating pestilence,
> Pollutes whate'er it touches; and obedience,
> Bane of all genius, virtue, freedom, truth,
> Makes slaves of men, and, of the human frame,
> A mechanized automaton.[13]

Shelley explains the automaton image by referring in his notes to the "uncompromising first version" of *Political Justice*, specifically to Godwin's assertion that "one man can in no case be bound to yield obedience to any other man or set of men upon earth. . . . Man, when he surrenders his reason, and becomes the partisan of implicit faith and blind obedience, is the most mischievous of all animals. . . . He is, in the instant of submission, the blind instrument of every nefarious purpose of his principle; and, when left to himself, is open to the seduction of injustice, cruelty and profligacy."[14]

This is standard Enlightenment fare, assigning to reason the role of destroying "superstition." As *Queen Mab* proceeds, the poem makes clear that reason, no matter how helpful at the initial stages of revo-

lution, does not have the final word. Before long, we get to the heart
of the matter, which is the sexual agenda dear to all revolutionaries'
hearts. "Suicidal selfishness," the young poet tells us,

> Is destined to decay, whilst from the soil
> Shall spring all virtue, all delight, all love,
> And judgement cease to wage unnatural war
> With passion's unsubduable array.[15]

With the arrival of the leftist millennium, the lion of judgment
will lie down with the lamb of passion—or considering Shelley's belief that passion was "unsubduable," vice versa. In a letter to Jeff Hogg
announcing the completion of *Queen Mab* on February 7, 1813, Shelley
claimed that reason was in fact passion: "Reason is only an assemblage
of our better feelings, passion considered under a peculiar mode of its
operation. . . . A more elevated spirit has begun to diffuse itself which
. . . scarce suffers true Passion & true Reason to continue at war."[16]

What followed was a sort of sexual sorites, a series of linked syl-
logisms, that lays out Shelley's extrapolation of the sexual teachings
of the Godwinian system, which was in turn a sort of anglicization of
the French Enlightenment. Reason is man's distinguishing feature,
but reason, under the new dispensation announced by *Queen Mab*, is
really passion. So, therefore, in stifling passion we are really censor-
ing reason—that is, stifling what makes us truly human—which is a
vicious act. Therefore, to be truly virtuous, we must follow our sexual
passions wherever they lead. Referring to the reign of Queen Mab,
Shelley tells us:

> She left the moral world without a law,
> No longer fettering passion's fearless wing.
> Nor searing reason with the brand of God.
> Then steadily the happy ferment worked;
> Reason was free; and wild though passion went
> Through tangled glens and wood-embosomed meads.
> Gathering a garland of the strangest flowers,
> Yet like the bee returning to her queen,
> She bound the sweetest on her sister's brow,

Who meek and sober kissed the sportive child,
No longer trembling at the broken rod.[17]

The same paean continues a few lines later:

Then, that sweet bondage which is freedom's self,
And rivets with sensation softest tie
The kindred sympathies of human souls,
Needed no fetters of tyrannic law:
Those delicate and timid impulses
In nature's primal modesty arose,
And with undoubting confidence disclosed
The growing longing of its dawning love,
Unchecked by dull and selfish chastity,
That virtue of the cheaply virtuous,
Who pride themselves in senselessness and frost.[18]

Here Shelley draws on his other source of revolutionary thought, Mary Wollstonecraft, Mary Godwin's mother, who in *The Wrongs of Woman* wrote that "When novelists or moralists praise as a virtue, a woman's coldness of constitution, and want of passion . . . I am disgusted. . . . They want the fire of the imagination, which produces active sensibility, and positive virtue." Science is the gnosis that will make the millennium happen: "happiness/And Science dawn though late upon the earth" causing "Disease and pleasure," an oblique prognostication of penicillin as a cure for syphilis, to "cease to mingle here." This is another way of saying that "Reason and passion cease to combat there" and that a "happy Earth" is the "reality of Heaven!"

Even astronomy is part of the millennial conflation of reason and desire, specifically,

The [as yet undiscovered] plurality of worlds—, the indefinite immensity of the universe is a most awful subject of contemplation. He who rightly feels its mystery and grandeur, is in no danger of seduction from the falsehoods of religious systems, of deifying the principle of the universe. It is impossible to believe that the Spirit that pervades this infinite machine, begat a son upon the body of a Jewish woman; or is angered at the consequence of that necessity, which is a synonym of itself. All that miserable tale of the Devil, and Eve, and an Intercessor, with the childish mummeries of the God of the Jews, is irreconcilable with the knowledge of the stars.[19]

Shelley summarized the whole movement by saying, "The consistent Newtonian is necessarily an atheist."[20]

The bulk of Shelley's argument in favor of sexual liberation is carried on in prose in the notes of *Queen Mab*:

> Love withers under constraint: its very essence is liberty: it is compatible neither with obedience, jealousy, nor fear: it is there most pure, perfect, and unlimited, where its votaries live in confidence, equality, and unreserve. . . . How long then ought the sexual connection to last? What law ought to specify the extent of the grievance which should limit its duration? A husband and wife ought to continue so long united as they love each other: any law which should bind them to cohabitation for one moment after the decay of their affection, would be a most intolerable tyranny, and the most unworthy of toleration.[21]

Again and again, Shelley reiterates the Godwinian view of marriage: "Love is free: to promise for ever to love the same woman, is not less absurd than to promise to believe the same creed: such a vow, in both cases, excludes us from all enquiry. . . . Had they been suffered to part at the moment when indifference rendered their union irksome, they would have been spared many years of misery: they would have connected themselves more suitably, and would have found that happiness in the society of more congenial partners which is for ever denied them by the despotism of marriage."[22] Shelley wrote at another point: "Chastity is a monkish and evangelical superstition, a greater foe to natural temperance even than unintellectual sensuality; it strikes at the root of all domestic happiness, and consigns more than half of the human race to misery, that some few may monopolize according to law. A system could not well have been devised more studiously hostile to human happiness than marriage."[23]

Given Shelley's increasingly passionate attachment to Mary Godwin as both the embodiment of the revolution and the vehicle for its fulfillment, it is not surprising that *Queen Mab* should figure prominently in the surreptitious courtship. Of course, the fact that Shelley had dedicated *Queen Mab* to his wife of the time, Harriet Westbrook Shelley, would prove to be more than a little embarrassing. But it seems not to have dampened Mary Godwin's ardor, for she wrote, in response to the copy of *Queen Mab* which Shelley paid the shop porter to slip to her,

> I have pledged myself to thee & sacred is the gift
> But, ah, I feel in this was given
> A blessing never meant for me.
> Thou art too like a dream from heaven
> For earthly love to merit thee.[24]

What Mary Godwin overlooked, no doubt in the heat of passion, is that Shelley's passionate avowal of free love in *Queen Mab* was a double-edged sword. Mary could understand the statement "A husband and wife ought to continue so long united as they love each other: any law which should bind them to cohabitation for one moment after the decay of their affection, would be a most intolerable tyranny, and the most unworthy of toleration" as referring to Shelley's unhappy relationship with Harriet and as an easy rationalization of his fastening his affections to a new object, namely, Mary Godwin. But a little reflection would show that Mary Godwin was subject to the same rule herself, and she would in fact find herself in the same position. Mary Godwin was saved from Harriet Westbrook's fate only because Shelley died before he had a chance to act on his desires once again.

The dedication of *Queen Mab* notwithstanding, Shelley's marriage to Harriet Westbrook was proving hostile to his happiness, especially in the presence of such an alluring substitute lover, one who seemed more attuned to his radical ideas and willing to follow them to their logical sexual consequences. Given Shelley's notion of convention as tyranny, he was all but morally obligated by his misguided system to abandon his first wife and seduce Godwin's daughter.

On the evening of June 26, 1814, Shelley and Mary Godwin sat on her mother's tomb at St. Pancras cemetery and pledged the left-wing version of eternal love to each other. What followed is a matter of conjecture. William Godwin was of the opinion that Shelley had sexual intercourse with his daughter right then and there, and the date of her first pregnancy (which ended in miscarriage) seems to bear him out. The young couple, in obedience to Godwin's own writings, had decided to strike out against convention in true Promethean fashion. They would elope to the continent where they would live in Switzerland, home of Wilhelm Tell and other Protheans, in accord with Godwinian principles. But first, they would ask for Godwin's blessing. Godwin, to their stunned surprise, was appalled and refused to give his approval.

Godwin's philosophy was in many ways quintessentially Victorian. Its radical principles were modified by stern public opinion into an ethos that was really not much different from the Christian culture it aspired to replace. Many former Christians were relieved to find that the morality that Godwin's philosophy recommended differed little from superseded Christian ethics. The new philosophy—as the ideas that Godwin collected and codified quickly came to be called—was firmly in the tradition of religious dissent, appealing strongly to those of an inflexible, anxious, and puritanical disposition.

Unfortunately, in arguing with the perfervid Shelley, Godwin, despite his puritanical "new" philosophy, did not have a philosophical leg to stand on. He was hoist with his own revolutionary petard. What Godwin did not provide in his philosophy was a reason why his teenaged daughter should not run off with a married man, a prospect he viewed with horror. If anything, the Godwinian system provided a rationalization for that very act.

Complicating the situation was the fact that Shelley at that point had reached a crucial stage in negotiating a loan that was going to benefit Godwin. Godwin remained firm in his opposition to the elopement, but before long rumors began to circulate (probably at Harriet

Shelley's instigation) that Godwin had sold his daughters to Shelley for seven and eight hundred pounds respectively. Emily Sunstein detects a note of ambivalence in Godwin's refusal to give his daughter to Shelley. "If Godwin," she writes, "now had had the integrity to refuse Shelley's impending gift, he might have extracted the equivalent sacrifice of Mary from Shelley."[25]

But Godwin needed the money. The monetary needs of the middle-aged Godwin were the mirror image, in terms of desire, of the sexual needs of the adolescent Shelley. Godwin must have experienced a classic case of mixed emotions: wanting a wealthy aristocrat's money while loathing the price of that money, the bestowal on his creditor of the sexual favors of his favorite daughter. No wonder the rumor launched by Harriet Shelley had a ring of truth. That Shelley did not get Godwin's immediate approval seems not to have deterred him.

Shelley's behavior toward the Godwins by this point was starting to take on the characteristics of passion completely beyond the call of reason. Shelley's desire for Mary had become so imperious it was starting to be dangerous to oppose him. Shelley would show up at the Godwins' waving either a pistol or a bottle of laudanum, threatening to kill himself if he did not get his way. "Everyone who knows me must know that the partner of my life should be one who can feel poetry and understand philosophy," he exclaimed feverishly, waving a bottle of laudanum. "Harriet is a noble animal, but she can do neither." According to the second Mrs. Godwin, Shelley "looked extremely wild. He pushed me aside with extreme violence, and entering, walked straight to Mary. 'They wish to separate us, my beloved; but Death shall unite us,' and offered her a bottle of laudanum. 'By this you can escape from tyranny; and this,' Shelley said, taking a small pistol from his pocket, 'shall reunite me to you.'"[26]

Shelley's solution to his dilemma was to suggest that both Harriet and Mary live with him. Harriet declined. She found repugnant the proposed sexual sharing of her husband and thought it doubly offensive because the object of Shelley's affections was a member of the Godwin family, whose head, in Harriet's opinion, had corrupted Shelley's mind. Referring to her husband, she wrote:

Mr. Shelley has become profligate and sensual, owing entirely to Godwin's *Political Justice*. The very great evil that book has done is not to be told. The false doctrines there contained have poisoned many a young and virtuous mind. Mr. Shelley is living with Godwin's two daughters—one by Mary Wollstonecraft, the other the daughter of his present wife, called Clairmont. I told you some time back Mr S. was to give Godwin three thousand pounds. It was in effecting the accomplishment of this scheme that he was obligated to be at Godwin's house, and Mary was determined to seduce him. She is to blame . . . and here I am, my dear friend, waiting to bring another infant into this woeful world. Next month I shall be confined. He will not be near me. No, he cares not for me now. He never asks after me or sends me word how he is going on. In short, the man I once loved is dead. This is a vampire.[27]

Shelley begged Harriet to return to what he termed "philosophy and reason," in other words, Godwin's sexual theories as implemented according to Shelley's interpretation. But Harriet still refused. Harriet underestimated Shelley's connection to Mary and the sexual liberation Mary was willing to practice and rationalize as part of Shelley's grand scheme of revolution.

After Harriet's refusal to open her marriage bed, the Westbrooks, most especially Eliza, became, in Shelley's eyes, the incarnation of all that was evil. Harriet's refusal forced him to face his own guilt at abandoning her and their daughter, Ianthe, and in characteristic fashion he projected that guilt back on the person he had wronged and began to see her not only as the source of his own problems but the *radix malorum* in a malevolent universe.

Shelley, caught in the grip of "a sudden, violent, irresistible, uncontrollable passion,"[28] torn between loyalty to Harriet and love for Mary, tried to resolve the issue by attempting to kill himself with an overdose of laudanum, as had Mary Wollstonecraft almost twenty years earlier. But like Wollstonecraft he failed in his attempt. Someone from the inn where Shelley was staying warned the Godwins, and they rushed over to walk him up and down and, with the help of their friend Madame de Boinville, nursed him back to health.

For his pains, Godwin awoke on the morning of July 28 to find that Shelley had eloped to the continent with, not one, but two of his daughters. Shelley was, it seemed, determined to preside as the head of his own sexual commune, and so Mary's half-sister Claire Clairmont was persuaded to go along for the ride—and because her knowledge of French was superior to Mary's. What the three young revolutionaries encountered on the continent would not have inspired confidence in the French Revolution in the mind of a rational observer.

France had been torn by revolution, civil war, and finally foreign conquest over a period of twenty-five years. Now, even the most partisan supporter of revolution had to admit that the consequences had been disastrous. Shelley, Mary, and Claire traveled through villages recently pillaged by Cossacks, where they could hardly find food to eat and had to stay in mean, vermin-infested inns. The two young women were taking their lives in their hands simply by travelling on the roads. Our revolutionaries did not seem to notice, however. In Switzerland, Shelley removed his clothes to bathe in a roadside stream and tried unsuccessfully to persuade Mary to do the same. Mary, perhaps with stories of the rape and murders recently perpetrated by the invading Cossacks fresh in her mind, declined but still described the trip as something "like acting a novel, being an incarnate romance." Shelley described Mary in their joint journal of the trip as feeling "as if our love would alone suffice to resist the invasions of calamity." Apparently Shelley's angelic attitude to food began rubbing off on his companions. He noted in their journal that Mary "rested on my bosom & seemed even indifferent to take sufficient food," so happy was she—or so intent on making a virtue of necessity, since both money and food were scarce. Or perhaps Shelley was sharing his stock of laudanum. Whatever the reason, the trio made it to Switzerland only to turn around and come back, for their money had finally run out.[29]

Six weeks after they had started on their journey, they returned to England to find that their troubles had not gone on holiday with them. Harriet had contacted a lawyer to make sure she got her due as Shelley's wife and mother of the legitimate heir to the Shelley estate. Harriet and her lawyer were also spreading the rumor that Godwin had sold his daughters to Shelley to pay off his debts.

For our purpose—understanding *Frankenstein* and the genesis of horror out of the wreckage of the Enlightenment—the most significant thing about Mary's elopement and subsequent marriage to Shelley was the education she derived from it. True, Shelley may have used the idea of education as a pretext for seducing Mary, but that does not denigrate the seriousness of his efforts as an educator; for in the Shelleyan redaction of the Godwinian system, seduction and education were related.

· · · · ·

During the next two years, Mary would read over ninety books under Shelley's tutelage, and it was out of this intellectual stew that *Frankenstein* was confected. Most of the readings were predictable enough. They reread Godwin and Wollstonecraft, especially Wollstonecraft's letters to Imlay. Shelley also insisted that Mary read Barruel's *History of Jacobinism*, which St. Clair claims they "read not only as a history of why things had gone wrong but in order to learn the mind of the enemy."[30] In reading Barruel, Mary Godwin was confronted with the classical tradition of the West in both ethics and politics as it applied to the particulars of the revolution in France, whose consequences the young trio had just witnessed firsthand: "It is undeniable that virtue ought to be more particularly the principle of democracies than of any other form of government, they being the most turbulent and the most vicious of all, in which virtue is absolutely necessary to control the passions of men, to quell that spirit of cabal, anarchy, and faction inherent to the democratic form, and to chain down that ambition and rage of dominion over the people, which the weakness of the laws can scarcely withstand."[31]

According to the classical tradition, the soul is a microcosm of the state. The French Revolution was the logical consequence of liberating passion on a nationwide scale: "The French Revolution is in its nature similar to our passions and vices: it is generally known, that misfortunes are the natural consequences of indulging them; and one would willingly avoid such consequences: but a faint-hearted resistance is made; our passions and our vices soon triumph, and man is hurried away by them."[32]

Barruel's significance in Mary's education at Shelley's hands lay in the alternative his book provided to Enlightenment philosophy. Barruel's *History of Jacobinism* was not the only one that refuted the Enlightenment—the Shelleys reread Shakespeare, too—but Barruel's *History* was the one that did so most specifically in light of classical morals and politics. With Barruel, Mary Godwin encountered the Enlightenment in light of the tradition she and Shelley hoped to destroy. She read that unfettered passion, far from being compatible with reason, is its negation. The famous Enlightenment thinker Helvétius, according to Barruel,

> will at one time tell us, that the only rule by which virtuous actions are distinguished from vicious ones, is the laws of princes, and public utility. Elsewhere he will say, "that virtue, or honesty, with regard to individuals, is not more that the habit of actions be measured"; In fine, "that if the virtuous man is not happy in this world, we are justified in exclaiming, O Virtue! thou are but an idle dream."
>
> . . . . . . . . .
>
> The same sophister also says, that "sublime virtue and enlightened wisdom are only the fruits of those passions called folly; or, that stupidity is the necessary consequence of the cessation of passion. That to moderate the passions is to ruin the state. That conscience and remorse are nothing but the foresight of those physical penalties to which crimes expose us. That the man who is above the last can commit, without remorse, the dishonest act that may serve his purpose." That is, it little imports whether men are vicious, if they be but enlightened.

The fair sex too will be taught by this author, that "Modesty is only an invention of refined voluptuousness: that Morality has nothing to apprehend from love, for it is the passion that creates genius, and renders man virtuous." He will inform children, that "the commandment of loving their father and mother is more the work of education than of nature." He will tell the married

couple, that "the law which condemns them to live together becomes barbarous and cruel on the day they cease to love each
other."[33]

The last sentence, no doubt, made Mary Godwin sit up and take
notice. It was a fair description of what had become the Godwin family tradition of denigrating marriage—by the older generation in
theory, and by the younger in practice. This is the "scientific"
deconstruction of the moral tradition of the West proposed by the
Enlightenment, which Barruel condemns, retranslating it back into the
language of classical ethics and politics. According to that reading,
the carnage of the French Revolution was the result of passion, not
an aberration of a trajectory of sweetness and light leading to abun-
dant life. The Revolution in reality was a crucial stage in the trajectory of passion leading to death. Barruel sees the French Revolution
as a calculated effort to unleash passion as the vehicle of subversion,
but one that failed to reckon just how destructive these forces could
be once unleashed. The Terror, on this reading, is the logical outcome
of revolutionary principles.

It is important to point out that, in spite of their differences, both
the Enlightenment and Christian traditions agreed that passion was
the cause of the French Revolution. Where they differed was in their
assessment of passion as being, therefore, good or bad. The difference
had to do with the Aristotelian as opposed to the Newtonian system
of morals: stasis and tranquility were good according to the former,
but passion and motion were good according to the latter, which by
this time dominated in France.

The Jacobins had worked to suppress the Jesuits so that the
Jacobins could take over education in France: "In many colleges the
Jesuits being very ill replaced, the youth, neglected in their education,
left a prey to their passions." The same tactic was used to bring princes
under the conspirator's control. "They relish them," wrote Barruel,
explaining why princes protected the conspirators, "because they
flattered and unbridled their passions. This was the first step toward
the revolution." Subsequent steps follow the same trajectory: "The
French Revolution is in its nature similar to our passions and vices: it

is generally known, that misfortunes are the natural consequences of indulging them; and one would willingly avoid such consequences: but a faint-hearted resistance is made; our passions and our vices soon triumph, and man is hurried away by them."[34]

Barruel is well aware of the Newtonian dimensions of the revolutionary universe he criticizes, but he is careful to reanalyze the quasi-scientific transvaluation of values back into its classical components. Self-interest, according to the Enlightenment, was the human equivalent of gravity, the force that held everything in the universe together in dynamic motion. Just as the planets pursued their own way through the universe and thereby composed a dynamic harmonious whole, so those who pursued their own self-interest in this life would find their frequent selfish actions reconciled to harmony by some "invisible hand" or other convenient fiction. But twenty years after Adam Smith coined the term, France was giving some indication that individual passions might not work so benignly after all. If there was an invisible hand at work in France during the 1790s, its most significant characteristic was its invisibility. "It was only a constructive revolt which the philosophes had desired," Crocker writes, "but they were unable to halt the dynamics of revolution, even as the men of '89 could not prevent the coming of '93."[35]

Bernard Mandeville was, if anything, more naïve than Smith. He thought that prosperity would come from individuals pursuing a self-interest that was indistinguishable from vice. Morals were arbitrary restraints on "nature" and imposed by those who had the power to do so for their own benefit. Since man now has no transcendent goal or purpose, he is for all intents and purposes "a machine." He is "free" from moral constraints, but the price of his freedom is the determinism of nature as construed by the neo-Newtonians in France. According to La Mettrie, man gains his freedom from morals only by becoming totally subjugated to a sort of determinist quasi-physics. Man is now a clock in the hands of Nature, the clockmaker, in La Mettrie's words: "She has fashioned us as she wished, or rather as she could. In a word, we are no more criminal, when we follow the imprint of the primitive impulses which govern us, than the Nile is for its inundations and the sea for its ravages."[36]

Given a metaphysics that declares nearly every spiritual and intellectual trait man possesses illusory—and every vice a virtue—pleasure quickly becomes the only thing left that is undeniably real. "Physical passions," La Mettrie declares, "are the only real pleasures .... In regard to happiness, good and evil are indifferent, and he who gets greater satisfaction out of doing wrong will be happier than whoever gets less out of doing right."[37]

Remorse is quickly relegated to the realm of the chimerical as well because it impedes pleasure, but also because it testifies to the objective existence of a moral law. Since La Mettrie cannot seriously deny its existence, remorse becomes the result of cultural conditioning: "We should not, on the pretext of avoiding remorse, refuse to nature what she demands, nor above all, repent for pleasure. . . . We may, then, rightfully conclude, that if the joys derived from nature and reason are crimes, men's happiness lies in being criminals . . . he who has no remorse, because of so great a familiarity with crime that for him vices become virtues, will be happier than such another who, after a fine deed, is sorry he has done it, and so loses all its reward."[38] La Mettrie leads directly to Freud and psychoanalysis, the secular equivalent of sacramental confession that banishes remorse not through repentance, but by revealing its irrational roots in the cultural superego.

. . . . .

In intellectual trajectories of this sort, the conclusions of the first generation of revolutionaries become the premises of the second, and so if La Mettrie is the representative of Enlightenment optimism, the nihilism of the Marquis de Sade is Enlightenment's culmination. Once again, revolutionary passion—the desire for the abolition of sexual restraint—leads to terror. Sade, in many ways, wrote the scenario. Perhaps the best description of this trajectory can be found in Sade's rant in the pornographic *Philosophy in the Bedroom*: "Yet Another Effort, Frenchmen, If You Would Become Republicans." Sade begins with Enlightenment physics and proceeds to create out of it the politics of nihilism, classical politics turned on its head. Classical ethics proposes restraint as the means to freedom; Sade proposes vice. Indeed, Sade's political theory proposes freedom as a way of annihilating moral restraint, but ends by imposing another more severe restraint in its place, thus introducing the central paradox of the Enlightenment: freedom equals control. "As we gradually proceeded to our enlightenment," Sade writes, "we came more and more to feel that, motion being inherent in matter, the prime mover existed only as an illusion, and that all that exists essentially having to be in motion, the motor was useless; we sensed that this chimerical divinity, prudently invented by the earliest legislators, was in their hand, simply one more means to enthrall us."[39]

In classical physics, all objects were at rest unless moved by some agent; in Newtonian physics, all objects were in motion unless halted by some greater opposing force. The same could be said of Sade's politics, which he derived from Newton's physics. In an inversion of both Plato and Aristotle, Sade saw "insurrection" as the natural state of men, who are nothing more than machines made out of matter in which motion is inherent. Since the passions are the moral equivalent of gravity, the successful government is not one that stifles passion, but rather one that fosters it, and then directs the subsequent motions to its own ends. The state, in other words, should foster vice as an instrument of control:

> The Greek lawgivers perfectly appreciated the capital necessity of corrupting the member citizens in order that their moral dissolution coming into conflict with the establishment and its values, there would result the insurrection that is always indispensable to a political system of perfect happiness which, like republican government, must necessarily excite the hatred and envy of all its foreign neighbors. Insurrection, thought these sage legislators, is not at all a moral condition; however, it has got to be a republic's permanent condition. Hence it would be no less absurd than dangerous to require that those who are to insure the perpetual immoral subversion of the established order be moral beings: for the state of a moral man is one of tranquility and peace, the state of an immoral man is one of perpetual un-

rest that pushes him to, and identifies him with the necessary insurrection in which the republican must always keep the government of which he is a member.[40]

The key insight of both the Marquis de Sade and the Christian
West is that the moral man is in a state of peace; he is, in other words,
not in motion and therefore impossible to direct and control from the
outside. But—and this is a crucial point—the revolutionary's very
restlessness, his very rebellion against the moral order, holds within it
the seeds of his own subjugation because the state can control the
revolutionary's desires by controlling his passions. Sade is not slow
to draw this very conclusion: "Lycurges and Solon, fully convinced that
immodesty's results are to keep the citizen in the immoral state in-
dispensable to the mechanics of republican government, obliged girls
to exhibit themselves naked at the theater."[41]

Lust, in other words, is the force that keeps the citizenry of the
republic from succumbing to the inertia of tranquility, the fruit of
adherence to the moral order. At this point we enter into something
like a circular argument. Lust is good because it fosters the restlessness of republicanism, but republicanism is also good because it fosters lust. Either way, desire is an instrument simultaneously of
"liberation" and control; what was hitherto deemed pathological is now
to be seen as the social norm: "We are persuaded that lust, being a
product of those penchants, is not to be stifled or legislated against,
but that it is, rather, a matter of arranging for the means whereby
passion may be satisfied in peace. We must hence undertake to introduce order into this sphere of affairs, and to establish all the security
necessary so that, when need sends the citizen near the objects of lust,
he can give himself over to doing with them all that his passions demand, without ever being hampered by anything, for there is no moment in the life of man when liberty in its whole amplitude is so
important to him."[42]

"No passion has a greater need of the widest horizon of liberty
than sexual license," Sade writes:

[H]ere it is that man likes to command, to be obeyed, to sur-
round himself with slaves to satisfy him; well, whenever you with-

hold from man the secret means whereby he exhales the dose of despotism Nature instilled in the depths of his heart, he will seek other outlets for it, it will be vented upon nearby objects, it will trouble the government. If you would avoid that danger, permit a free flight and rein to those tyrannical desires which, despite himself, torment man ceaselessly: content with having been able to exercise his small dominion in the middle of the harem of sultanas and youths whose submission your good offices and his money procure for him, he will go away appeased and with nothing but fond feelings for a government which so obligingly affords him every means of satisfying his concupiscence.[43]

"Liberty," according to this line of thought, is the ability, not to act according to reason, but to gratify illicit passion, which means that in the very act of attaining his "liberty" man becomes the thrall of the passion he gratifies. Before long, it becomes clear that Sade's politics is in many ways just the physics he says it is. Man at the beck of passion is in many ways like a particle with no will of its own, since reason, especially moral reasoning, is the sole source of man's ability to govern himself. And once gratification of passion becomes the definition of "liberty," then "liberty" becomes synonymous with control. He who controls the passion controls the man. Liberty, as defined by Sade, must be seen as a prelude to a most insidious form of totalitarian control.

Sade was not alone in urging the repudiation of morals in revolutionary France. "Morals," Lester Crocker writes, citing Deschamps, "must be abolished, along with laws and the tyrannical society which imposes them on nature—in short, men must be freed from the very idea of right and wrong."[44] Sade's exhortation to Frenchmen is more consistent and more complete, for if sexual license is the most imperious of all the passions initially, it is not the ultimate, nor does its gratification stay within the bounds of sexuality. These passions always lead ultimately to murder, as Sade himself observed. Thus the Newtonian social order is threatened by the very strategies that purport to exercise control. Hints that things may turn out differently than planned appear here and there. To begin with, the gratification of sexual urges is first and foremost a male prerogative:

Has nature not proven that we have that right, by bestowing upon us the strength needed to bend women to our will? It is for the sake of the happiness of everyone that women have been given to us. All men therefore have an equal right of enjoyment of all women; therefore, there is no man who, in keeping with natural law, may lay claim to a unique and personal right over a woman. The law that will oblige them to prostitute them themselves, as often and in any manner we wish, in the houses of debauchery we referred to a moment ago and which will coerce them if they balk, punish them if they shirk or dawdle, is thus one of the most equitable of laws, against which there can be no sane or rightful complaint.[45]

What about people whose panoply of sexual desire includes the penchant for torturing young girls? Do the same rules apply here? "This consideration is utterly without value; once you concede me the proprietary right of enjoyment, that right is independent of the effects enjoyment produces; from this moment on, it becomes one, whether this enjoyment be beneficial or damaging to the object which must submit itself to me. Have I not already proven that it is legitimate to force the woman's will in this connection? . . . The issue of her well-being, I repeat, is irrelevant."[46]

Given Sade's view of male pleasure as the only absolute, it does not take too much imagination to foresee that someone will get hurt. And for those who lack imagination, there are always Sade's novels, where women sometimes are killed as part of the quest for pleasure. Sodomy, a form of sexual torture, is Sade's preferred form of sexual activity. If people get hurt, that is a small price to pay when gratification of sexual desire is the only reality: "As for the cruelty which leads to murder, let us dare to say boldly that it is one of the most natural feelings in man; it is one of his sweetest inclinations, one of the keenest he has received from nature." The greatest pleasure will come from corrupting, torturing, and finally killing small, helpless children. "What delight in corrupting innocence," cries the chevalier in *Philosophy in the Bedroom*, "to stifle in that young heart all the seeds of virtue and religion that her teachers planted in it."[47]

Murder is the ultimate form of pleasure. To kill the object of voluptuousness is the absolute of possession and mastery: "Death, the ultimate truth and act of life, can be experienced subjectively only once. But if one can die only once, he can kill several times and thus enjoy the 'ecstasy of death.' One can feel like God. Some of Sade's characters can reach the acme of sexual enjoyment only at the moment of murder. They describe their experience in detail, and modern criminology and psychology have confirmed Sade's findings."[48]

The difference between Sade and his forebears like La Mettrie and the rest of the Enlightenment optimists is that Sade does not avert his eyes from the logical consequence of making desire his god. "Is it not by dint of murders that France is free today?" Sade asks an audience with regicide fresh in its memory. "Savages," he says at another point, "the most independent of men, the nearest to Nature, daily indulge in murder which amongst them goes unpunished. In Sparta, in Lacedaemon, they hunted Helots, just as we in France go on partridge shoots. The freest of people are they who are most friendly to murder."[49]

We find, then, in Sade a perverse corroboration of the trajectory of horror adumbrated in the epistle of James and accepted implicitly by the orthodox Christian Barruel. Passion leads to sin, and sin, when it reaches its fullness, gives birth to death. Sade's only dispute with St. James is the value he places on the milestones of the same trajectory. Both admit that sexual passion released from the moral order leads to murder, terror, and death; Sade, nonetheless, remains firm in viewing these phenomena through the lens of sexual desire and fails to see them as evil. Vice, it turns out, and not self-interest is the gravitational force that both moves men and allows the revolutionaries to manipulate them to their own ends.

. . . . .

The genius of the Enlightenment was to make passion an instrument of political control. But the genius was not entirely Sade's. Adam Weishaupt, founder of the Illuminati and prototype—through Barruel's redaction of his writings—for Victor Frankenstein, played a significant role in rendering passion the facilitator of political manipulation. Mary

Shelley also learned Illuminism from Barruel, as had Shelley, at least in part.

Weishaupt, born in Bavaria around 1748—known later in revolutionary circles by the code name Spartacus—was associated, like the fictional Victor Frankenstein, with the University of Ingolstadt. Barruel saw Weishaupt as "an odious phenomenon in nature, an Atheist void of remorse, a profound hypocrite, destitute of those superior talents which lead to the vindication of truth; he is possessed of all that energy and ardour in vice which generates conspirators for impiety and anarchy. Shunning, like the ill-boding owl, the genial rays of the sun, he wraps around him the mantle of darkness; and history shall record of him, as of the evil spirit, only the black deeds which he planned or executed." Weishaupt, according to Barruel, made "the most absolute, the most ardent, the most frantic vow to overthrow, without exception, every religion, every government, and all property whatsoever. He pleased himself with the idea of a distant possibility that he might infuse the same wish throughout the world; he even assured himself of success."[50]

The means to this revolutionary end, according to Weishaupt, was first to find the adept among the powerful: "Seek out also those who are distinguished by their power, nobility, riches, or learning, nobles, potentes, divites, doctors, quaerite—Spare no pains, spare nothing in the acquisition of such adepts. If heaven refuse its aidance, conjure hell. *Flectere si nequeas superos, Acheronta moveto.*" Then after identifying the adept's dominant passion through study and the adept's confession, feed the passion. This should not be difficult: "Any fool may attract the people to the theatre, but the eloquence of a Chrysostom is necessary to tear them from it. With equal talents, he who pleads for license and impiety will carry more weight than the most eloquent orator who vindicates the rights of virtue and morality. Finally, Weishaupt taught, manipulate that passion as an instrument of control: "Study the peculiar habits of each; for men may be turned to any thing by him who knows how to take advantage of their ruling passions."[51]

Weishaupt admired Ignatius of Loyola, founder of the Jesuit order, and the Illuminati were in many ways an imitation of the Jesuits.

Their recruiting and control practices may be seen as a parody of the Jesuits' spiritual exercises. Whereas the traditional examination of conscience is used by the Jesuit superior to ferret out the faults in a novice in order to free him from his sins, the Illuminist examination of conscience is used by the Illuminist to discover the adept's sins as a means of controlling him by blackmail. "Now I hold him," Barruel writes of the newly initiated Illuminatus, "I defy him to hurt us; if he should wish to betray us, we have also his secrets. It would be in vain for the adept to attempt to dissimulate. He would soon find that the most secret circumstances of his life, those which he would most anxiously wish to hide, are known by the adepts."[52]

The method was powerful. Barruel maintained that the French Revolution came about after the French Masonic lodges became illuminized—that is, taken over by Weishaupt's revolutionary cells. Weishaupt, in turn, learned from the lodges the main "advantage to be reaped from SECRET SOCIETIES"—"the arts of knowing men and governing them without constraint."[53]

In sum, the goal of the Illuminati was threefold: "to teach the adepts the art of knowing men; to conduct mankind to happiness; and to govern them without their perceiving it."[54] In reality all three goals involved the same thing: the release of passion and the subsequent control of those who, because they had detached themselves from the moral order, had abdicated self-control. What emerges from the writings of Weishaupt is, therefore, a system of control similar to that proposed by the Marquis de Sade—a clear trajectory from liberation to bondage through passion first inflamed and then managed.

Shelley took Barruel's reading of Weishaupt as his model for the formation of his revolutionary cell and thus inserted himself, along with Mary whom he brought along for the ride, into that trajectory. Shelley had taken a great interest in the Irish struggle for independence and had decided that the Illuminist model of revolution from within would prove a successful one in that island:

Behind Sade's idea of the "quiet revolution," the revolution from within, rising silently through society like a yeast from an ever-extended chain of linked associations, lay the unmistakable form

of Illuminism. . . . Shelley secretly turned to the Masonic conception of revolutionary brotherhood as a viable form of reform
organization. He was attracted especially by its occultism, its
tight communal solidarity, and "seeding" of subversive political
ideas. He never wrote of Illuminism to Godwin, who would have
been appalled, but to Miss Hitchener in this same letter he recommended the authoritative book on the subject, by the Abbé
Barruel, *Memoirs Illustrating the History of Jacobinism*, a translation in four volumes, 1797–98. "To you who know how to distinguish truth, I recommend it." This letter marked the high
point of Shelley's political hopes in Ireland.[55]

There are other similarities between Weishaupt and Shelley.
Barruel's description of Weishaupt, including the latter's nocturnal
habits, corresponds uncannily to Hogg's description of Shelley at
Oxford. In addition, and most significant, Barruel tells us that "but a
single trait of his [Weishaupt's] private life has pierced the cloud in
which he had enveloped himself," namely, that he had incestuous relations with his sister-in-law, got her pregnant, and then tried to avoid
the ensuing scandal by attempting unsuccessfully to abort the baby:
"Incestuous Sophister! it was the widow of his brother whom he seduced.—Atrocious father! it was for the murder of his offspring that
he solicited poison and the dagger.—Execrable hypocrite! he implored,
he conjured both art and friendship to destroy the innocent victim,
the child whose birth must betray the morals of his father."[56]

"I am on the eve of losing that reputation which gave me so great
an authority over our people," Weishaupt wrote to his coconspirator
Hertel, "My sister-in-law is with child. . . . How shall I restore the
honour of a person who is the victim of a crime that is wholly mine?
We have already made several attempts to destroy the child; she was
determined to undergo all; but Euriphon is too timid."[57]

According to Barruel, since Weishaupt's goal was nothing less than
the overthrow of the moral order, it had to be violated in the most
telling, dramatic fashion, namely, through incest. Incest, as a result
of Weishaupt, took on numinous significance in the secret gnosis of
global revolution. "The preconditioning cause" of dominating nature,
Nietzsche wrote in *The Birth Tragedy*,

is the fact that beforehand a monstrous act against nature—something of the order of incest—must have taken place; then how is one to force nature to reveal her secrets other than by victoriously going against her, that is, through an act contrary to nature. I see this recognition sketched out in that hideous trinity of Oedipus' fate: the same man who solves the riddle of nature—that double-edged Sphinx—must also violate the most holy order of nature as both patricide and spouse of his mother. Indeed, the meaning of the myth seems inescapable, that wisdom, and especially Dionysian wisdom, is an unnatural horror, and that the man who through his knowledge plunges nature into the abyss of annihilation experiences in his own being the disintegration of nature.

"The point of wisdom turns against the wise," Nietzsche concludes. "Wisdom is a crime against nature."[58]

With this concatenation of incest and abortion, we come to the heart of the esoteric gnosis of Enlightenment Illuminism, and thus to the heart of horror that enveloped Shelley and the soon-to-be author of *Frankenstein*. Mary Shelley, at this point in our narrative, did not understand all this, but by the time she had finished writing *Frankenstein* she did not see things Shelley's way, either. She had by that time experienced the sadistic consequences of her sexual profligacy. *Frankenstein* was her attempt to make sense out of the conflict between the Enlightenment and the classical, Christian moral order.

The calamities described in horror fiction are really repressed moral truths. Horror is morality written backwards; it is the moral order viewed through the wrong end of the telescope. *Frankenstein* and Barruel's *History of Jacobinism* tell the same story, but in radically different ways. To say that "the French revolution is in its nature similar to our passions and vices" was, of course, the antithesis of the Godwin-Wollstonecraft family tradition; but then again so was *Frankenstein*, for both books describe how "misfortunes are the natural consequence of indulging" the passions. Barruel's history does this directly; *Frankenstein*, like the entire horror tradition, does it indirectly. Barruel's book is a warning; *Frankenstein*, an expression of regret—it is full, not of repentance, but remorse.

*Frankenstein* mirrors the mind of Mary Shelley, especially after the events of the fall of 1816 had left their indelible mark on her. Mary could never repudiate her family's radicalism, nor could she admit that her participation in that radicalism was wrong, nor could she deny that people had died because of her actions. Guilt bound her to Shelley, guilt over what she had done to Harriet Westbrook, but she had no way of dealing with the guilt because she could not bring herself to repent or avail herself of the vehicle of repentance, Christianity. Instead of repentance, she chose respectability as the antidote to the deadly radicalism of her family. In many ways, the Victorian Age was made for her.

.   .   .   .   .

Shelley had always been fascinated by the thought of kidnapping his sisters and spent a good deal of his time proposing them as sexual objects to friends like Hogg—hence Sir Percy's alarm and precautions regarding his son. Shelley's father, primarily because of his son's irrational and violent behavior at home, something often associated with alchemical experiments, seems to have decided—not inaccurately—that his son was either criminally insane or insanely criminal and acted accordingly by trying to prevent the lives of his daughters and the family estate and fortunes from falling into his son's hands.

Beyond that, Shelley had always been interested in terror, particularly when it came to dealing with his female companions—for instance, through hooking his sisters up to galvanic batteries to be electrified. Moreover, Shelley's poem about the French Revolution, the *Revolt of Islam*, originally had as its two main characters Laon and Cyntha, brother and sister, who engaged in incestuous sexual relations in order to produce good occult-revolutionary juju. Shelley's first wife, Harriet, had proved too opaque a medium when it came to sexual terror; her residual common sense rejected Godwin and his system. But Mary Shelley had been more receptive. During her first pregnancy, for example, Mary became sexually involved with Jeff Hogg.

Clearly, this step into perversion had delighted Shelley. But ever the disciple of Weishaupt, he wanted more than simple perversions like adultery: he wanted incest. Yet sex with Mary would be incestuous, and therefore of occult significance, only if it included sex with her half-sister Claire. So Shelley turned his attention to her during the fall of 1814 in order to expand the sexual commune, the *ignis fatuus* of all revolutionaries: the communality of wives, the communality of property, but more important, the means of making contact with the infernal powers.

During the winter of 1814–15, as Mary's pregnancy and her affair with Jeff Hogg proceeded apace, Shelley began to spend time with Claire; he took her, for example, to one of the city institutes to hear Garnerin, the French chemist who lectured on phantasmagoriana and gasses. More important, though, was what followed the lectures. Shelley would regale the young Claire with accounts of the sexual exploits of her half-sister and Jeff Hogg and then slowly bend the sexual excitement toward terror as a way of dominating Claire and using her as a medium for his theories.

Terror for Shelley was a way of heightening perception, a way of catapulting the mind out of its dull, sublunary sphere into contact with ethereal forces, which would suffuse the mind and bend it to a higher purpose. Shelley, according to Holmes, felt that an "'abnormal' state of sexual excitement" possessed "sensitizing and visionary properties" consonant with the "properties" students of the alchemical tradition sought to achieve. Shelley was "interested in the dream, and the sudden 'flash' of imagination during ordinary daylight affairs, as similar abnormal conditions of vision."[59]

On the night of October 7, 1814, Shelley remained up with Claire long after Mary, perhaps tired from the pregnancy and a walk that afternoon, had gone to bed. They talked about relations among the various members of Shelley's incipient commune as well as the possibility of a "subterranean community of women." During the course of the long night of conversation, Shelley most probably sketched out his views of a free love community and role it was to play in revolutionizing the world. At one in the morning, Shelley asked Claire "if it is not horrible to feel the silence of night tingling in our ears; in half an hour the question is repeated in different form; at 2 they retire awe-struck and hardly daring to breathe."[60] Shelley could not sleep and so decided to sit beside Mary and read until the morning. Claire, upon retiring, was in such a disturbed state that she could not sleep either and once she got to her room became convinced that poltergeist, were moving her pillow from the bed to a chair, which increased her agitation, until finally she could remain in the room no longer and came running down the stairs. Shelley wrote in his diary:

> Her countenance was distorted most unnaturally by horrible dismay—it beamed with a whiteness that seemed almost like light; her lips and cheeks were of one deadly hue; the skin of her face and forehead was drawn into innumerable wrinkles—the lineaments of terror that could not be contained; her hair came prominent and erect; her eyes were wide and staring, drawn almost from the sockets by the convulsion of the muscles; the eyelids were forced in, and the eyeballs, without any relief, seemed as if they had been newly inserted, in ghastly sport, in the sockets of a lifeless head. This frightful spectacle endured but for a few moments—it was displaced by terror and confusion, violent, indeed, and full of dismay, but human.[61]

If Shelley felt constrained to come to Claire's aid and attempt to calm her down, he seems to have been successful in resisting the impulse. Instead his actions and speech seemed more calculated to enhance the terror which Claire so abjectly displayed. Claire, moreover, seems to have discerned in Shelley's expression the source of her horror. Shelley continues:

> [Claire] remarked in me that unutterable expression which had affected her with so much horror before; she described it as expressing a mixture of deep sadness and *conscious power over her.* I covered my face with my hands, and spoke to her in the most studied gentleness. It was ineffectual; her horror and agony increased even to the most dreadful convulsions. She shrieked and writhed on the floor. I ran to Mary; I communicated in a few words the state of Claire. I brought her to Mary. The convulsions gradually ceased, and she slept. At daybreak we examined her apartment and found her pillow on the chair.[62]

Horrible as the sessions must have been from Claire's point of view, they continued on a regular basis. Eleven days later, Claire related another late-night seance during which Shelley and Claire stayed up to discuss things occult after Mary had gone to bed. Shelley recommended as part of Claire's education the same materials he had recommended to her sister, namely, the Zastrozzi, Barruel, and *Queen Mab*. When Claire finally did get to bed it was, as she wrote, "in a rather horrid mood . . . thinking of ghosts, cannot sleep all night."[63]

Soon after the return of the revolutionaries from their escapades on the continent, Shelley's grandfather died, freeing up some money immediately with the promise of a final arrangement of the estate in the spring of 1816, allowing Shelley to purchase a boat and sail up the Thames with his ménage of cultural terrorists. He wrote *Alastor* along the way. Also along the way, the group visited Oxford, prompting Charles Clairmont to write to Claire about Shelley's rooms there: "We visited the very room where the two noted infidels, Shelley and Hogg (now happily excluded from the society of the present residents), pored, with the incessant and unwearied application of the alchymist, over the certified and natural boundaries of human knowledge."[64]

In *Alastor*, we discern the beginning of Shelley's disenchantment with Mary—and in fact any particular woman. Once sexual desire is consummated, the object of the desire disappears, leaving the poet to substitute some fugitive ideal in its place. *Alastor* is in many ways the mirror image of *Frankenstein*. In the first instance, the poet pursues an ideal woman who is nothing more than his projected desires; in the second instance, the scientist pursues the monster he created so he can destroy it, while at the same time the monster stalks its creator to destroy him and his loved ones. Just as *Frankenstein* is about remorse, *Alastor* is about lust. Both involve pursuit, but are seen from different perspectives. The poet, in *Alastor*,

> dreamed a veiled maid
> Sate near him, talking in low solemn tones.
> Her voice was like the voice of his own soul
> Heard in the calm of thought.

The poet here is much like Shelley, the revolutionary pedagogue instructing sixteen-year-old girls like Claire and Mary, young ladies who echo his own deepest aspirations:

> Knowledge and truth and virtue were her theme,
> and lofty hopes of divine liberty,
> Thoughts most dear to him.

Soon the poet's thoughts descend to less ethereal realms. What is the purpose of liberty, after all, if not the satisfaction of the desires the young maid inspires in the young poet?

> His strong heart sunk and sickened with excess
> Of love. He reared his shuddering limbs and quelled
> His gasping breath, and spread his arms to meet
> Her panting bosom: . . . she drew back a while,
> Then, yielding to the irresistible joy,
> With frantic gesture and short breathless cry
> Folded his frame in her dissolving arms.
> Now blackness veiled his dizzy eyes, and night
> Involved and swallowed up the vision; sleep
> Like a dark flood suspended in its course,
> Rolled back its impulse on his vacant brain.

Shelley finds that as soon as desire disappears in satiation, the vision which inspired the desire disappears as well. Thus, fulfillment recedes forever in front of him, to use a metaphor that must have appeared familiar, like the horizon before a ship's bow. "Whither have fled," the poet wonders upon waking after his sexual encounter,

> The hues of heaven that canopied his bower
> Of yesternight? The sounds that soothed his sleep,
> The mystery and the majesty of Earth,
> The joy, the exultation?

Shelley wrote that the poem was about beauty and the frustrations involved in attaining it on earth. While it is certainly true that life is short and art is long, Mary Shelley in middle age came closer to the mark when she explicated the poem as being about "the sad and struggling pangs which human passion imparts"—another way of describing the insatiability of lust. No one woman can live up to the poet's expectations. The ideal woman becomes a chimera, a sort of personification of desire, and in proposing chimerical sexual liberation as his ideal, the poet instrumentalizes the very woman he idealizes and sees her as simply the vehicle for some cosmic breakthrough:

> The insatiate hope which it awakened, stung
> His brain even like despair.

In the end there is no vision, only, as Barruel had warned, passion, which comes at night

> Like the fierce fiend of a distempered dream,
> And shook him from his rest, and led him forth
> Into the darkness.

# 3

## *Frankenstein*

FROM THE INCEST AND TERROR SESSIONS with Claire arose the plot to seduce Byron, the most important poet in England at the time. Shelley, described as a vampire by both his wife and Byron's physician, Dr. John Polidori, seems to have hatched a plan with Claire to drain Byron's power, in Illuminist fashion, by controlling Byron's dominant passion.

Claire wrote to Byron, explaining in her letters, some of which Shelley composed himself, who Shelley was, that he had eloped with William Godwin's daughter, and that he had written a revolutionary poem entitled *Queen Mab*. Claire also forwarded to Byron a copy of *Alastor*, Shelley's latest opus, and announced that she was "interested in all he [Byron] does." She also informed Byron that she and her sister, Mary, practiced Godwin's free-love doctrines with Shelley, who had fathered a child by her, which they had aborted, and that Claire hoped to bear Byron's child, too. Claire also offered the lure of incest. If Byron would sleep with her, she would introduce Byron to Mary, who might prove susceptible to Byron's charms, thereby linking Byron and Shelley in a dual incest.

"You will, I daresay, fall in love with her," Claire wrote to Byron, describing Mary. "She is very handsome and very amiable, and you will no doubt be blest in your attachment; nothing would afford me more pleasure . . . . I will redouble my attentions to please her . . . do everything she tells me, whether it be good or bad."[1] In other words, it was not just another aspiring actress writing to Byron, but a contact from the nascent cultural terrorist underground willing to provide herself, and others, to him. He need only accept the offer.

Byron was already notorious for his incestuous affair with his half-sister, Augusta, but the possibility of sleeping with the same half-sisters Shelley had slept with offered numinous possibilities. Novelty, as Byron was to tell Augusta, when explaining why he has slept with Claire, is an essential ingredient to lust. And lust was Byron's dominant passion. Byron, later overcome with disgust, would refer to Claire as an "Atheist and Murderer," referring to both the Illuminist ideology she adopted under Shelley's tutelage and the abortion she claimed to have carried out on Shelley's child. But Byron at first fell hard for the Shelley-Godwin *ménage*. For her part, in a May 1836 letter to Edward Trelawney, Mary described her relationship with Claire: "We were never friends—Nor I would not go to Paradise, with her for a companion—she poisoned my life when young. . . . she still has the faculty of making me more uncomfortable than any human being."[2]

On April 18, Claire and Byron consummated their relationship. On the next day, Claire appeared at Byron's door with Mary, who although probably not part of the seduction plot, seems to have been pulled in the same direction by her own passions. "How mild he is! How gentle! How different from what I expected!" Mary told Claire, who promptly relayed the information to Byron.

Both Byron and Shelley were deeply entangled in personal troubles at the time and waiting for legal decisions that would free them to travel. Byron's separation papers from his wife came through on April 21, and Shelley's chancery decision, freeing up necessary funds, came down on April 23—the day Byron fled to the continent, there to survey the battlefield at Waterloo in his specially designed version of Napoleon's battle carriage.

Shelley's subsequent behavior indicates that he was involved in Claire's campaign to seduce Byron. In manner not unlike that advocated by Weishaupt, Shelley played a directorial role from behind the scenes. When Byron asked Claire for a description of her character, for example, Claire went directly to Shelley for the answer, and he wrote that she was "easily managed by the person you love as the reed is by the wind; it is your weak side." Shelley was the wind to Claire's aeolian harp; as Shelley would say to the west wind, so Claire would say to Shelley, "be thou me." When Byron, feeling the first onset of disgust at Claire and the seduction she had just perpetrated, refused to take her with him to the continent, Shelley abruptly changed his plans to go to Edinburgh and decided to follow Byron to Geneva, with Mary and Claire (and William, his and Mary's child) in tow, leaving Godwin high and dry (and starting the chain of events that would eventually cost Fanny Imlay, Mary Shelley's other half-sister, her life).

Furthermore, throughout the correspondence leading up to the meeting in Geneva, Claire invariably brought Shelley into the picture. While staying on the rue Richelieu in Paris, for instance, Claire wrote to Byron that she had persuaded "the whole tribe of Otaheite philosophers" to accompany her. The reference was to Tahiti, on the one hand, and Shelley and Mary Godwin on the other, the link being that both Tahitians and the Shelley ménage practiced free love and communal sex. In the same letter she said, rather curiously, that she would rather be Byron's male friend than his mistress, perhaps in an oblique reference to Byron's taste for young boys, something widely rumored in London at the time; she then sealed the letter with Shelley's signet, giving the unmistakable implication that the ménage held forth homosexual possibilities as well. Claire was, as Shelley indicated, an apt pupil, and her aptitude was evident in her letters, all of which were full of thinly disguised bits of Shelley's mind, aimed at impressing Byron with an erudition not her own. "Between her and Shelley," Holmes writes, referring to the sexual manipulation of Byron, "it seemed like a kind of conspiracy."[3]

At midnight on May 25, fresh from a trip down the Rhine and a visit to Waterloo, Byron rolled into town in his Napoleonic carriage with Dr. Polidori. On May 27, Claire, who was aware of Byron's arrival and anxiously awaiting a reunion, saw Byron and Polidori rowing on Lake Geneva and arranged to have Mary and Shelley walk along the beach in their vicinity, in order to bring about the long-anticipated meeting between the two poets. Polidori immediately perceived the sexual complexity of the Shelley ménage. From his point of view, a view shared by Byron, the most significant personage there was Godwin's daughter. "M Wollstonecraft Godwin," Polidori noted, was now referred to as "Mrs Shelley." Shelley, Polidori wrote, "the author of 'Queen Mab,' came; bashful, shy, consumptive; twenty-six; separated from his wife; keeps the two daughters of Godwin, who practice his theories." One of the two daughters, Polidori also mentioned, was Byron's mistress—a relationship that, in accordance with Shelley and Claire's plan—was renewed in Geneva.

The Shelleys left the expensive hotel where they had been staying and rented lodgings, the Maison Chapuis, for a longer stay. Lord Byron rented the grander Villa Diodati. Thereafter, intercourse between the houses was frequent, as were the excursions on the lake in Shelley's boat.

The locus of the Illuminist, incestuous coven was the Villa Diodati, a large house on the shore of Lake Geneva that had once been home to John Milton. During the summer of 1816, the villa fell under the notice of English tourists, who would spy on it with telescopes from the opposite bank, looking for evidence that the "League of Incest" was in session. Tablecloths hung out on the balcony to dry were taken for petticoats; one lady fainted when she thought she spied Byron in one of the bedrooms, and the Otaheite philosophers delighted in the scandal they were causing among the haute bourgeoisie.

The summer was late in coming in 1816—some might argue that it never came at all—largely because a volcanic eruption in Tambora, Indonesia, spewed tons of ash into the atmosphere, disrupting the climate. Storms abounded. When Shelley, Mary, and Claire had crossed the Alps on their way to Geneva in mid-May, they had needed a carriage drawn by four horses as well as ten men to accompany them and dig them out of the snow drifts. The storms would continue for the rest of the summer and the lightning that accompanied the rain would take on literary significance as the company of young Prometheans gathered around the fire and talked about things profound or spent their days sailing.

Polidori had begun a play that no one found inspiring or entertaining, and so the company began to amuse itself with conversation

about the theories in which they lived and moved and had their being. Mary, for instance, noted in her diary that "Shelley and I had a
conversation about principles—whether man was to be thought merely
an instrument."[4] Mary's diary entry noting their discussion indicates
a dawning awareness that her life was enmeshed in a conspiracy of
Shelley's and her half-sister's of which their meeting with Byron might
have been a part and that the conspiracy had to do with the sexual
manipulation of the parties. The context of the conversation was
Claire's pregnancy and the consequent flurry of speculation about who
the child's father was.

Byron seems to have concluded that, given the circumstances, he,
Byron, was the father. "Is the brat mine?" Byron wrote to his friend
Douglas Kinnaird. "I have reason to think so, for I know as much as
one can know such a thing—that she had not lived with S[helley]
during the time of our acquaintance—and that she had a good deal
of that same with me."

Shelley, it should be remembered, encouraged his wives to have
sex with his friends, but only after the women were safely pregnant
with his children, thereby forestalling important financial questions of
the sort that would continue to plague him with his children by Harriet
Westbrook. The converse of these considerations seems to have motivated him to orchestrate the affair between Claire and Byron. Byron,
as a result, was bound to Claire by their child, and while Shelley did
not deny that he had been intimate with Claire, he did deny that the
child she bore was his. Both statements were consistent with his Illuminist theories, specifically the idea of a revolutionary cell based on
sexual sharing and occult manipulation, enhanced by incest, into some
acheronian power that could be put to political use.

The conversation that evening turned quite naturally from the
instrumentality of men to electricity. Perhaps man was a mere instrument of natural forces? Was electricity the life force that could gal-
vanize mere matter into a living being? And was sexuality simply
another form of electricity? Could the man who controlled electricity control sexuality and thereby control man himself? Polidori, a
wunderkind who had qualified as a medical doctor at the age of nineteen, was conversant in the thought of the time, and so the company

passed the ideas back and forth like an electrical charge leaping from one pole to another, while the real electricity illuminated the night outside in a mockery of illumination and enlightenment.

Mary meanwhile sat in the background and mulled things over from the vantage point of someone who knew that things were taking an unforeseen and somehow sinister turn. Mary later wrote:

> Many and long were the conversations between Lord Byron and Shelley to which I was a devout but nearly silent listener. During one of these, various philosophical doctrines were discussed, and among others the nature of the principle of life, and whether there was any probability of it ever being discovered and communicated. They talked of the experiments of Dr. Darwin . . . who preserved a piece of vermicelli in a glass case till by some extraordinary means it began to move with voluntary motion. Not thus, after all, would life be given. Perhaps a corpse would be reanimated; galvanism had given token of such things: perhaps the component parts of a creature might be manufactured, brought together, and enbued with vital warmth.[5]

If we would understand the Enlightenment and its end in horror—particularly as that horror appeared, not in the pornography of Sade or in the sadism of the Terror, but in its first literary incarnation in *Frankenstein*—we should not forget that electricity, so commonplace today, suggested revolution in the moral and political spheres in the eighteenth and early nineteenth centuries.

Throughout the two hundred-year history of the revolutionary era, scientific discovery fueled the intellectual fires of those who felt that a truly scientific explanation of things human obviated both religion and morals. "With Voltaire," Barruel wrote, "man is a pure machine." Frederick the Great, Voltaire's protector and fellow *philosophe*, was of the same opinion, but according to Barruel, took the whole notion a step further to its logical conclusion: "I am well convinced that I am not twofold," Frederick wrote in a direct attack on the idea that man was a body informed by a soul, "hence, I consider myself as a single being. I know that I am an animal organised, and that thinks; hence, I conclude that matter can think, as well as that it has the property of being electric."[6]  Electricity was especially intriguing during the early phase of the revolutionary era because of Galvani's experiments with frog legs.  Because the current made even severed legs jump, electricity was seen as the *élan vital*, the scientific replacement for the soul, which, unlike the soul, could be infused mechanically and at will.  The revolutionary implications of this view of electricity should be immediately apparent.  For if man is nothing more than a complicated machine, then he who controls electricity, controls man.

Benjamin Franklin had been called the "Electrical Ambassador" by the French in the years preceding the Revolution, and not only on account of his famous experiments with kites in thunderstorms:

> Paris society at this time was hungry for scientific learning and there was no shortage of both amateur and professional scientists, from the most implausible frauds to the most rigorous empiricists, willing to popularize their findings.  Virtually every issue of the daily *Journal of Paris* was packed with reports of experiments from the provinces as well as the capital and advertisements for series of public lectures to be given by the best-known luminaries, like Fourcroy and Pilatre de Rozier.  So the image of Franklin, who could tap the heavens for the celestial fire of electricity, became woven into the celebration of his other "American" virtues, most especially that of liberty.  Turgot may have coined the famous epigram *Eripuit Coelo Fulmen, Sceptrumque* (He seized fire from the heavens and scepter from tyrants) as an innocuous play on words, but it very rapidly became a kind of byword for Franklin's role as the harbinger of liberty. . . . The link between the fall of tyrants and celestial fire had ominous implications in absolutist France.  For it inescapably suggested, in a Romantic vein, that liberty was a natural and hence ultimately irresistible force, and contributed further to a growing polarity between things natural on the one hand ("Humanity"; "Freedom"; "Patriotism") and things artificial on the other ("Privilege"; "Despotism"; the court).  Not surprisingly this equation of liberty and lightning was eagerly endorsed in the Revolution, so that in Jacques-Louis David's pictorial account of the Tennis Court Oath, for example, a bolt of electrically charged

freedom cracks over Versailles as a great gust of wind blows fresh air through the crowd-filled window spaces.

"It is universally believed in France," John Adams later wrote of Franklin, "that his electric wand has accomplished all this revolution."[7]

When the discussion of the life force and electricity at the Villa Diodati shaded over into a discussion of ghosts, the ambiance seemed to be gravitating in precisely the direction Shelley found congenial in his ritual horror sessions with Claire Clairmont. The sudden appearance of an extremely rare copy of German horror stories, the *Fantasmagoriana*, which had come into Byron's possession, helped deepen the terror in the nest of incestuous lovers. The company decided to write its own ghost stories, enhancing the gothic mood.

Everything seemed headed in the direction Shelley intended. Then something unexpected happened. Shelley lost control of his own seance, a failure, for our purposes, deeply symbolic of the sex-horror trajectory. With the ever-impressionable author of *Frankenstein* attentive, at midnight on June 18, as Polidori noted in his diary, the group "really began to talk ghostly."[8] Byron, taking his cue from the gothic literary tastes of his audience, began reciting Coleridge's poem *Christabel*, which describes a seduction at the hands of a beautiful lady who is in reality a serpent, which becomes apparent when she removes her clothes. The poem had long been part of the Godwin family lore, ever since Coleridge had recited it at Skinner Street with Mary listening from behind the sofa. When Byron reached the lines

> Behold! her bosom and half her side—
> Hideous, deformed, and pale of hue—

Shelley could take no more, but "suddenly shrieking and putting his hands to his head, ran out of the room with a candle."

Polidori eventually succeeded in calming Shelley down and, after throwing water in his face and administering a few whiffs of ether, began to elicit Shelley's confession in a way that would have inspired the admiration of Adam Weishaupt.

The immediate cause of Shelley's fit was a hallucination provoked by the poem. While looking at Mary, he told Polidori that "he suddenly thought of a woman he had heard of who had eyes instead of nipples, which taking hold of his mind, horrified him."[9] The image came from Mary herself, who had told Shelley that the breasts with eyes were Coleridge's original conception of *Christabel*. The image became fused in Shelley's mind with both Mary, its source, and Christabel, the seductress who was in reality a serpent. Eyes are the windows of the soul, and so it is hard not to see the image as indicative of Shelley's ambivalent relationship with Mary. She was the deeply desired object of his sexual affections, as well as his philosophical vision; but at the same time, the price of attaining her was the guilt he would carry for abandoning Harriet. The guilty, it seems, flee when none pursues.

Shelley's designs for the ultimate ritual horror session were overthrown at the last moment by nothing more, it seemed, than the pangs of his guilty conscience. "He married," Polidori noted in his diary, "and a friend of his liking his wife, he tried all he could to induce her to love him in turn. He is surrounded by friends who feed upon him and draw upon him as their banker."[10] Through his guilt, Shelley had been absorbed into the very terror he hoped to inflict on others.

Guilt had been the main reason the seance had failed, but Shelley had also misunderstood the personality of Lord Byron, who for all his rakishness still preserved a sense of decorum which Shelley found repugnant and a chill to his plans. Byron may have committed most of the sexual sins in the book, but was nonetheless scandalized when the waltz was introduced into England because the man held the woman in his arms in public. Byron may have practiced sodomy, but he did not preach it, and in this reticence to conform his theories to his life, he differed from Shelley and Shelley's adepts, and thereby disrupted the ritual horror sessions that Shelley had inaugurated with Claire, and which he wanted to take to a new level by including Byron.

Shelley's vision that night was of Mary as Lamia, the disguised serpent, who had seduced him from his first wife into a wilderness of repressed guilt. The eyes for nipples on her breasts meant that sexual pleasure would carry with it a terrible burden of guilty self-consciousness forever after. In his moment of delight, eyes would be watching him. But since she was Shelley's reason for leaving Harriet, who committed suicide at the end of 1816, Mary likewise owned part of the guilt that terrified Shelley. Out of this realization *Frankenstein* was born.

"I will be with you on your wedding night," the monster says to Frankenstein. Sexual enjoyment would be forevermore polluted with guilt. The monster would be there in their most intimate moments, to spoil them. The vision in all its clarity would come only later, however, after she had endured more suffering. But at the Villa Diodati, Mary came up with the initial vision, the inspiration for the tale. The vision involved someone who aspires to tamper with the forces of life and put them in the service of some unhallowed ideal.

On August 26, John Cam Hobhouse and Scrope Daves, Byron's friends from London, arrived at the Villa Diodati, and their arrival marked the end of one of the most famous literary moments in English literature. However, in the three months and more that the two groups had resided on Lake Geneva, a number of crucial changes had taken place. Claire's attempt to attach herself to Byron had failed, as had Shelley's manipulation of that hoped-for outcome for his own ends. Shelley had been overwhelmed at a crucial moment by the very forces he hoped to marshal, and he had been overwhelmed in front of everyone—but especially in front of Mary, who had undergone the most dramatic change of all.

Mary had embarked on the trip with an innocence that was matched only in intensity by the depth of disillusion that followed its sullying. Mary began the summer enraptured by her environment and her prospects. Summer on the threshold of the Alps was "divine" and the scenery a suitably sublime backdrop for the sublimation of her feelings. "I feel as happy as a new-fledged bird," she wrote to her other half-sister, Fanny Imlay, "and hardly care what twig I fly to, so that I may find my new-found wings."[11] Fanny, for her part, was feeling less than ethereal. She had been assigned the unwelcome task of financial intermediary between the impecunious Godwin and the increasingly irresponsible Shelley. She was also made increasingly aware that she was considered a financial burden on the Godwin household. That and the fact that Shelley's elopement with her two half-sisters had rendered her practically unmarriageable did not add to her happiness.

But by the end of the summer, and certainly by the end of the year, Mary was not feeling particularly happy, either. The vision of the student of the unhallowed arts was the sign that what she had been repressing about her relationship with Shelley was forcing its way to the surface. Before the end of the summer, she was aware that the trip to Geneva had involved a stratagem on the part of Claire and Shelley to ensnare Byron. Although that plot had failed, Mary had been victimized by her husband. She knew she had become, if she had ever been anything else, an instrument of Shelley's pleasure. Despite her complicity in the incestuous ménage and in the dabbling in the occult, Mary felt the sting of betrayal. She was also aware that her relationship with Shelley was tainted by guilt over Harriet that could not be banished by their radical theories. In addition, Shelley's breakdown and subsequent analysis at the hands of Dr. Polidori had shown that Shelley viewed Mary as a dangerous seductress, something that must have wounded her deeply.

There seemed little she could do, however, about her double problem (being simultaneously the victim and the perpetrator of a crime), other than "contrive" a tale "which would frighten my reader as I myself had been frightened that night." Apart from suicide, literary catharsis seemed the only way to deal with the pain. She could not go forward to an honest evaluation of her situation because she lacked the religious vehicle for repentance. At the same time, the events of the summer had severely weakened, if not obliterated, the radicalism she had inherited from her parents. Her mixed emotions over the conflict between her ideals and the reality she was living, while mirroring her father's, exceeded them in intensity.

To make matters worse, the contradictions in Shelley's personality were becoming as apparent to her as they would to the world at large later on. On one occasion, Benjamin Robert Haydon, an English painter, had dinner with Shelley, his wife, her sister, Leigh Hunt, and Keats. Haydon, attacked during dinner for his Christian faith, remembered how Shelley's self-righteous defense of the Romantic version of animal rights—he criticized Wordsworth's "inhumanity" in describing the death throes of a trout—contrasted ironically with the pain Shelley had caused in his own domestic circle. The one was a function of the other. Animal rights, Haydon rightly saw, was a compensation for the domestic terror he had inflicted on his teenaged wife: "He would lie with his sister & sophisticate himself into a conviction of its innocence, and then sell his coat for his Friend, if the produce would relieve his friend's necessities. He would kill his wife by infidelity, or himself by continence, whichever would make him most singular by appearing to suffer on principles not vulgarly acknowledged; Pride was the foundation of his heart, I suspect, though I certainly [saw] little of him."[12]

Thomas Peacock had similarly acute things to say about Shelley, named Scythrope in his novel *Nightmare Abbey*, who

> now became troubled with the passion for reforming the world. He built many castles in the air, and peopled them with secret tribunals, and band of illuminati, who were always the imaginary instruments of his projected regeneration of the human species. As he intended to institute a perfect republic, he invested himself with absolute sovereignty over these mystical dispensers of liberty. He slept with *Horrid Mysteries* under his pillow, and dreamed of venerable eleutherarchs and ghastly confederates holding midnight conventions in subterranean caves. . . . Scythrope proceeded to meditate on the practicability of reviving a confederation of regenerators.[13]

This disparity between idealistic intentions and brutal consequences found expression in the character of Victor Frankenstein. "Yet my heart overflowed with kindness and the love of virtue," Frankenstein tells us, adding "I had begun life with benevolent intentions, and thirsted for the moment when I should put them in practice, and make myself useful to my fellow beings. Now all was blasted: instead of that serenity of conscience, which allowed me to look back upon the past with satisfaction, and from thence together promise of new hopes, I was seized by remorse and the sense of guilt which hurried me away to a hell of intense tortures, such as no language can describe."[14]

How could someone who was so sincere cause so much pain? It

was a question that needed to be answered to explain the horror that was enveloping them, and Mary, the heir to the dissenting, radical tradition, did her best with the literary tools available to her.

. . . . .

Who opened Mary's eyes? In addition to the experience at the villa and the daily contact with her husband, it was most probably the Marquis de Sade who ripped off the scales. The role played by the Marquis de Sade, specifically his novel *Justine*, in influencing Mary Shelley's *Frankenstein*, has caused some comment. Mario Praz observes that one of the characters in *Frankenstein*, an "innocent woman, imprisoned, tried and executed, is called—by an odd coincidence— Justine, like de Sade's unhappy virtuous heroine." Both Justines suffer and eventually die as a result of their innocence. Indeed, Wolf notes, "though I cannot find evidence that Mary Shelley had read de Sade— it would not be surprising if she had suppressed the fact—there is a persistent undercurrent of dark sexuality in *Frankenstein* that makes Praz's remark seem like something more than a chance hit. Aside from internal textual evidence, there is the testimony of Marchand, who claims in his definitive biography of Byron: "We know for certain that Byron, at least, had a secret copy of *Justine* in his possession in April 1816, only a few months before he met the Shelleys in Geneva."[15]

Did Byron take his copy of *Justine* with him when he went to the Villa Diodati? If he did, he would most probably have shared it with the assembled guests during their terror sessions just as he read to them from the *Fantasmagoriana*. Ken Russell, the film maker, thinks Mary read *Justine* and makes this reading one of the central events of *Gothic*, his film about the party that gave birth to *Frankenstein*. In the film, during one of the nights following the terror seances, neither Byron nor Mary can sleep. Byron calls for his maid, interestingly named Justine, who disrobes partially to satisfy one of his fantasies. In the meantime, Mary in another room in the same house is seen paging through a book, whereupon she comes upon a page of eighteenth-century pornographic drawings. The book is clearly one of the illus-

trated versions of *Justine* that was published during the French Revolution, when censorship was a thing of the past.

Mary's epiphany in *Gothic* is wordless, and we are left to specu-
late what the eighteen-year-old English woman was thinking as she
viewed the scenes of sexual torture in *Justine*. In Sade's *Justine*, Mary
found all of the Enlightenment arguments espoused by her father in
*Political Justice* and Shelley in *Queen Mab* carried to their logical conclusion in the torture and death of young women her age.

As with all of Sade's works, *Justine* is a rambling juxtaposition of
pornography and rationalization, the latter taken primarily from the
lucubrations of *philosophes* like La Mettrie. According to Sade, every
impulse, no matter how hurtful or bizarre, is to be acted upon because
it is inspired in us by Nature. How do we know this? Because it exists.
Whatever *is* is right. Sade simply carries the same idea to its logical
sexual conclusion, which is to say, as a justification for committing
murder, which is not a sexual act at all but somehow invariably associated with sex as practiced by Sade's heroes.

> Man's pride alone erects murder as a crime. . . . [W]ere not mur-
> der one of the human actions which best fulfilled [Nature's] in-
> tentions, would she permit the doing of murder? Murder, in
> other words, is the most "natural" act there is: The man who
> moves in this direction, who plunges ahead with all possible zeal,
> will incontestably be the one who serves [Nature] best, since it
> will be he who most cooperates with the schemes she manifests
> constantly. . . . the person who most nearly resembles her, and
> therefore the most perfect being, necessarily will be the one whose
> most active agitation will become the cause of many crimes. . . .
> Therefore, crimes serve nature.[16]

With this point firmly established in the mind of the reader, Sade
describes the intermediary stages of the sex-horror trajectory as well.
Following La Mettrie's lead, Sade sees human beings as nothing more
than machines. This includes women, who, Sade adds, are "nothing
but machines designed for voluptuousness."[17] Once the premises of

the Enlightenment have been established—man is a machine, morals are culturally relative, murder is the rearrangement of matter—then pleasure becomes the highest good and man is free to use man (or, more usually, woman) in whatever way serves that pleasure, especially if pleasure and science coincide.

As part of her travels, Justine meets another unfortunate teenaged girl (in Sade's writings all teenaged girls are unfortunate) whose father is interested in science, specifically the science of anatomy, which, the reader is informed, "will never reach its ultimate state of perfection until an examination has been performed upon the vaginal canal of a fourteen- or fifteen-year-old child who has expired from a cruel death." "Everything suggests," says Rosalie, the object of these experiments, "that these monsters are going to use me in one of their experiments and that your poor Rosalie is doomed" When Rosalie and Justine are brought to the impromptu operating room, the heroine is confronted with her "appalling" sentence: "It is nothing less than a question of vivisection in order to inspect the beating of my heart, and upon this organ to make observations which cannot practicably be made upon a cadaver."[18]

The parallels between *Justine* and *Frankenstein* become obvious at this point. Sexual desire using science as a cover turns human beings into objects by promoting the notion that morals are either "unscientific" or are a mere epiphenomenon of the mechanism as yet not understood. As one of the science-loving monsters tells Justine in an ongoing attempt to corrupt her morals, "When the study of anatomy reaches perfection, they will without any trouble be able to demonstrate the relationship of the human constitution to the taste which it affects. . . . what do you do when we have arrived there? what is to become of your laws, your ethics, your religion, your gallows, your Gods and your Heavens and your Hell when it shall be proven that such a flow of liquids, this variety of fibers, that degree of pungency in the blood or in the animal spirits are sufficient to make a man the object of your givings and your takings away?"[19]

Once morals have been banished, man—especially if he is a male scientist—is free to do whatever he wants, because man—especially if it is a teenaged female—is nothing but a machine for voluptuousness, matter in motion with no transcendent purpose. But once morals have been banished from human consciousness, man finds himself bound to a trajectory which he does not choose and for the most part does not understand, one that moves from sexual pleasure to death in a remarkably short time.

Sade explains this trajectory as well as anyone, and certainly more completely than the naïve Enlightenment philosophes who preceded him. Egoism is nature's fundamental commandment. Since every desire is Nature's command, man, as the choosing subject, disappears and is replaced by man, the response to Nature's stimulus. So the more man succumbs to his desires, the less possible it is to call him a man. He is simply an obedient locus of sensations, which would satisfy the sexual libertine were it not that successive sensations never render the same pleasure. Sexual activity becomes insipid and can only be revived by mixing it with increasing doses of violence. If pleasure is reduced to mere sensation, then the more violent the sensation the greater the pleasure. So we arrive at the essence of sadism: pain gives pleasure. Father Clement, the lecherous priest, tells Justine,

> Voluptuous emotion is nothing but a kind of vibration produced in our soul by shocks which the imagination, inflamed by the remembrance of a lubricious object, registers upon our senses, either through this object's presence, or better still by this object's being exposed to that particular kind of irritation which most profoundly stirs us; thus our voluptuous transport—this indescribably convulsive needling which drives us wild, which lifts us to the highest pitch of happiness at which man is able to arrive— is never ignited save by two causes: either by the perception in the object we use of a real or imaginary beauty, the beauty in which we delight the most, or by the sight of that object undergoing the strongest possible sensation; now, there is no more lively sensation than that of pain; its impressions are certain and dependable; they never deceive as may those of the pleasure women perpetually feign and almost never experience and, furthermore, much self-confidence, youth, vigor, health are not needed in order to be sure of producing this dubious and hardly very satisfying impression of pleasure in a woman. To produce the painful

impression, on the contrary, requires no virtue at all: the more defects a man may have, the older he is, the less lovable, the more resounding his success.

Therefore,

> he who will cause the most tumultuous impression to be born in a woman, he who will most thoroughly convulse this woman's entire frame, very decidedly will have managed to procure himself the heaviest possible dose of voluptuousness, because the shock resultant upon us by the impressions others experience, which shock in turn is necessitated by the impression we have of those others, will necessarily be more vigourous if the impression these others receive be painful, than if the impression they receive be sweet and mild; and it follows that the voluptuous egoist, who is persuaded his pleasures will be keen only insofar as they are entire, will therefore impose, when he has it in his power to do so, the strongest possible dose of pain upon the employed object, fully certain that what by way of voluptuous pleasure he extracts will be his only by dint of the very lively impression he has produced.

When Justine protests that this leads to "the cultivation of cruel tastes, horrible tastes," Clement agrees, assuring her that "we can give ourselves up to our passions, whatever their sort and of whatever their violence, wholly sure that all the discomfitures their shock may occasion are naught but the desirings of Nature, of whom we are the involuntary instruments."[20]

Justine is quick to carry this train of thought to its logical conclusion. She argues, "if through atrocious principles of cruelty you love to take your pleasure only by means of causing suffering with the intention of augmenting your sensations, you will gradually come to the point of producing them with such a degree of violence that you will certainly risk killing the employed object."[21]

Justine here articulates the sex-horror trajectory in its entirety. "From his father," Justine tells us at another point in the book, describing another of her sexual tormentors, "Roland had inherited a fortune; very early on in his life he had become surfeited by ordinary pleasures, and begun to resort to nothing but horrors; these alone were able to revive desires in a person jaded by excessive pleasure." Once, in other words, sexual activity is wrenched from the moral order, which is to say from the matrix of life and love, its pleasures decline precipitously and can only be augmented by stimulation of a nonsexual sort involving pain. The libertine comes ever closer to murdering his victim, until finally he does. "The philosopher," Clement continues, "no longer fears to be selfish, to reduce everything about him, and he sates his appetites without inquiring to know what his enjoyments may cost others, and without remorse."

"But," Justine responds, "the man you describe is a monster."[22]

Mary had her own dealings with philosophers who behaved like monsters; in fact, it was becoming increasingly apparent after the summer at the Villa Diodati that she was now inextricably linked to someone who sated his appetites without inquiring what his enjoyments might cost others.

The problem for Mary was a remorse which she could not shake. "This," Mary would write of her dead husband later in life, "is neither the time nor the place to speak of the misfortunes that chequered his life. It will be sufficient to say that, in all he did, he at the time of doing it believed himself justified to his own conscience; while the various ills of poverty and loss of friends brought home to him the sad realities of life."[23] The sense of bewilderment exhibited here may have been part posture and part disingenuousness, but part of it is undeniably real. One of the reasons why Mary wrote horror stories and not moral tracts is that she was never quite able to state in a coherent fashion the chain of causality that led Shelley, the reformer in love with mankind, to cause unhappiness and death for so many of those close to him. The main barrier to any cogent explication of what happened was Mary's participation in the sin that suffused her with remorse.

Sade had a cure for remorse, of course: "Guilt is an illusion," Dubois tells Justine, "it is naught but the idiotic murmuring of a soul too debilitated to dare annihilate it."

"Annihilate it! May one?"

"Nothing simpler; one repents only of what one is not in the habit of doing; frequently repeat what makes you remorseful, and you'll quickly have done with the business; against your qualms oppose the torch of your passions and self-interest's potent laws."[24]  Making the guilt-causing crime a habit was strong medicine—toxic medicine, one might add—but neither Shelley nor Mary could make use of the cure Sade proposed.  Remorse loomed ever larger on the psychic horizon of both.

The monster in *Frankenstein* is largely remorse personified.  What began innocently when Victor "considered the improvement which every day takes place in science and mechanics," soon became "the birth of that passion, which afterwards ruled my destiny," namely, becoming the author of life on his own terms:

> It was with these feigns that I began the creation of a human being. . . . Life and death appeared to me ideal bounds, which I should first break through, and pour a torrent of light into our dark world.  A new species would bless me as its creator and source; many happy and excellent natures would owe their being to me.  No father could claim the gratitude of his child so completely as I should deserve theirs.  Pursuing these reflections, I thought, that if I could bestow animation upon lifeless matter, I might in process of time (although I now found it impossible) renew life where death had apparently devoted the body to corruption.[25]

Things, of course, turned out differently than was planned.  Victor's labors in his "workshop of filthy creation" create a monster, who appears to Victor during a flash of lightning: "A flash of lightening illuminated the object, and discovered its shape plainly to me; its gigantic stature, and the deformity of its aspect, more hideous than belongs to humanity, instantly informed me that it was the wretch, the filthy daemon to whom I had given life.  What did he there?  Could he be (I shuddered at the conception) the murderer of my brother?"[26]  Lightning, the force that was to set mankind free, now takes on the same coloring it took at the end of Sade's *Justine*.  Instead of begetting life, all lightning can do is illuminate the horror, causing Victor to see himself as "the author of unalterable evils," and to live in the "daily fear, lest the monster whom I had created should perpetrate some new wickedness." The "life which I had so thoughtlessly bestowed" returns to haunt Victor Frankenstein, its creator, and when it speaks, it sounds a great deal like Harriet Shelley speaking from the grave: "'Shall each man,' cried the monster, 'find a wife for his bosom, and each beast have his mate, and I be alone? Are you to be happy while I grovel in the intensity of my wretchedness? You can blast my other passions; but revenge remains—revenge, henceforth dearer than light or food! I may die; but first you, my tyrant and tormentor, shall curse the sun that gazes on your misery.'"[27]

Revenge and remorse become the two emotions that drive the novel to its conclusion, like Shelley's description of himself in *Epipsychidion*, into a "death of ice." Like Mary, Shelley is "seized by remorse" in spite of his benevolent intentions, because "life thoughtlessly bestowed" returns in the form of a nameless monster to remind them of the moral order they violated. Frankenstein's monster is, in this regard, Nemesis, the reestablishment of moral equilibrium; it is Harriet Shelley seeking vengeance from beyond the grave, and it is an uncanny premonition of things to come. Two years later, William, Shelley and Mary's favorite child, would die of fever in Italy in an uncanny parallel to the death of William Frankenstein at the hands of the monster.

For the rest of her life, Mary would be a prisoner of the remorse that she and Shelley had created by acting out Godwin's redaction of the Enlightenment: "I perceived, as the shape came nearer, (sight tremendous and abhorred!), that it was the wretch whom I had created."[28] Sexual liberation caused Harriet's suicide. Horror, as Sade predicted, is the fruit of lechery. The monster, spurned like Harriet, turns his "mind towards injury and death." Because she spurned Christianity and any possibility of repentance, Mary condemned herself to carry out Harriet's vengeance. "Look into your own heart," Beatrice says in Mary Shelley's novel *Valperga*, "gaze on mine; I will tear it open for your inspection. There is remorse, hatred, grief, misery." Shelley was haunted by the same remorse:

That time is dead for ever child!
Drowned, frozen, dead for ever!
We look on the past
And stare aghast
At the spectres wailing, pale and ghast,
Of hopes, which thou and I beguiled
To death on life's dark river.[29]

Horror involves both the result of those actions and the inability to face their moral cause. Terror is terrifying precisely for the latter reason, because its source is unknown, but unknown in the way Freud described in his essay on the uncanny, which is to say repressed, which is to say deliberately not known and yet at the same time compulsively presented anew because the repressed always returns. Mary wrote in *Perkin Warbeck*: "There is a terror whose cause is unrevealed even to its victim, which makes the heart beat wildly; and we ask the voiceless thing—wherefore, when the beauty of the visible universe sickens the aching sense; when we beseech the winds to comfort us, and we implore the Invisible for relief?"[30]

Terror is a function of bad conscience: "A bad conscience! yes, surely I had one," Victor says. "William, Justine, and Clerval had died through my infernal machinations. . . . Clerval, my friend and dearest companion, had fallen victim to me and the monster of my creation." Victor, like Shelley, chose to marry and thought he could accommodate that to his schemes to use others as objects. Eventually, his schemes caused the death of one woman, his first wife, and "horrors of remorse and guilt, which would pursue me [and his second wife] until death." The man who felt that he was master over good and evil finds that "for the guilty there is no peace. The agonies of remorse poison the luxury there is otherwise sometimes found in indulging the excess grief." In other words, both Shelley and Victor Frankenstein become prisoners of the very system they aspired to conquer. "If you had listened to the voice of conscience," Walton tells the monster, "and heeded the stings of remorse, before you had urged your diabolical vengeance to this extremity, Frankenstein would yet have lived."[31]

Mary, likewise, is consumed by remorse: "Polluted by crimes and torn by the bitterest remorse, where can I find rest but in death? For the bitter sting of remorse may not cease to rankle in my wounds until death shall close them forever."[32] But precisely because repression denies the possibility of repentance, she would go to her grave maintaining in one way or another that Shelley acted according to his conscience: "Many men have his opinions—none fearlessly and conscientiously act on them as he did—it is his act [leaving Harriet for her] that marks him." The statement leads one to believe that Mary felt Shelley was justified in leaving Harriet, a statement she contradicted later when she described Harriet as admirable and herself "torn to pieces by Memory. . . . Poor Harriet to whose sad fate I attribute so many of my own heavy sorrows as the atonement claimed by fate for her death. . . . One looks back with unspeakable regret and gnawing remorse to such periods fancying that had one been more alive to the nature of his feelings and more attentive to soothe them, such would not have existed."[33]

Mary never got over the sense that Shelley was a god or an angelic being from some celestial sphere. The myth she created around Shelley was almost as powerful as the *Frankenstein* counter-myth that revealed the truth about Shelley. Her creation of these two competing and contradictory myths was partially the result of pressure from Shelley's father and partially the result of remorse she felt at the life they led together. Either way, the romantic ideal as spilt religion comes across clearly in Mary's posthumous description of Shelley: "Inspired with ardour for the acquisition of knowledge, endowed with the keenest sensibility and with the fortitude of a martyr, Shelley came among his fellow-creatures, congregated for the purposes of education, like a spirit from another sphere."[34] Prevented from telling the truth about Shelley in an honest biography, Mary had to turn to fiction to portray the real Shelley. "This is not the time to relate the truth," Mary announced in her preface to "Queen Mab," "and I should reject any colouring of the truth."[35]

In the end, Mary was never able to make a clear break with the past. "O happy are you, dear Claire," she wrote to her sister late in her life, "not to be devoured by humiliating and remorseful thoughts." But Mary chose repression and respectability instead of repentance and truth. Shelley was apotheosized into a Victorian angel, but Mary always viewed him as a pagan god. He was Amor and she was Psyche, and his true story was transmuted into a myth that she and the age found palatable because it told the truth disguised as fiction. "I have done all that can be done with propriety at present," Mary wrote to Medwin, asking him not to write a biography of Shelley. "I vindicated the memory of my Shelley and spoke of him as he was . . . a celestial spirit given and taken away, for we were none of us worthy of him—and his works are an immortal testament."[36]

·  ·  ·  ·  ·

As the summer of 1816 turned to fall and the tale turned to a novel, Mary herself began to change. Emily Sunstein claims that "Mary shed a certain *jeune fille* provincialism this summer, thanks to Byron."[37] Whether she had Byron to thank, the change was unmistakable. One can trace it in the shift in the way she treats the Plainpalais, a public square of historic interest in Geneva.

When the bohemian Mary arrived in Geneva at the beginning of the summer, she described the Plainpalais with the most naïve and revolutionary fervor, a parody of something from the pre-Imlay Mary Wollstonecraft. In a letter to Fanny Imlay, Mary described Plainpalais park, wherein local revolutionaries had executed the city fathers and erected an obelisk "to the glory of Rousseau." Her letter quickly became a meditation on revolution and how, in good Illuminist form, the end justifies the means—specifically, how "the magistrates, the successors of those who exiled [Rousseau] from his native country, were shot by the populace during that revolution, which his writings mainly contributed to mature, and which, notwithstanding the temporary bloodshed and injustice with which it was polluted, has produced enduring benefits to mankind, which all the chicanery of statesmen, nor even the great conspiracy of kings can entirely render vain."[38]

"Temporary bloodshed" has a vampire-like ring to it, as does the concept of pollution flowing therefrom. It echoes the jaded vampire in *Justine*, who affirms of his young wife, whose blood he sheds for sexual pleasure, "Nothing equals the pleasure I experience upon shedding her blood . . . I go mad when it flows; I have never enjoyed this woman in any other fashion. Three years have gone by since I married her, and for three years she has been regularly exposed every four days to the treatment you have undergone."[39] Harriet Shelley would refer to her husband as a vampire before she committed suicide. Polidori drew on Shelley, specifically his seizure during the terror session at the Villa Diodati, for his own book, *The Vampyre*.

What cries out in Mary's letter from the early summer of 1816 is her lingering adherence to the revolutionary ideals of the Left, specifically the French Revolution, which in her mind still "has produced enduring benefits to mankind." But by the time she gets around to writing *Frankenstein* the Plainpalais has undergone a curious transformation. Now it is no longer a monument to men wanting to be free from tyranny. In *Frankenstein*, the Plainpalais becomes a monument to the miscarriage of justice. After killing Victor's brother William (*nomen est omen*: William is Mary's father, half-brother, and son, and the name seems to symbolize the sacredness of consanguinity), the monster plants a locket in Justine's pocket which leads, despite her innocence, to her arrest, conviction, and execution at the Plainpalais. "You are mistaken," Victor Frankenstein tells Elizabeth, "I know the murderer. Justine, poor, good Justine, is innocent." The place of revolutionary executions is now associated with the murder of innocents, no longer "enduring benefits to mankind."[40]

Throughout the past two hundred years, a predictable trajectory has invariably followed attempts at sexual liberation. Liberation has always been followed by mayhem, which was in turn has been followed by a reaction that has attempted to preserve the goals of liberation while at the same time limiting its bad effects. In each instance, the Enlightenment broke down into two factions: the idealists, who felt that sexual liberation could be made safe by more tinkering, and the nihilists, represented most effectively by people like Sade, who felt that once the moral order had been broken by Enlightenment science, nothing prevented the trajectory that led to torture and death. *Frankenstein* was the *locus classicus* of the Enlightenment attempt to avoid the sadist conclusion without the benefit of tinkering, that is, technology, available to later devotees of the Enlightenment.

In other words, horror is a kind of Enlightenment revisionism. Voltaire hoped for a society where religion and morals were abolished but where shopkeepers would still be honest. Sade showed the naïveté of that vision by carrying the premises upon which it was based to their logical conclusion. "Somehow," Leslie Crocker concludes, "all this was to be reconciled with the moral pretensions of 1789."[41] In his perverse but direct, nonrevisionist way, Sade reestablished the transcendent goal of human sexuality. It was meant for something more than just pleasure, as Sade's characters demonstrate by forever putting their sexual pleasures into the service of a transcendent, if demonic, ideal. Blasphemy presumes the existence of the God just banished from the mechanistic universe inhabited by men who are, it seems, more than machines after all. Sexual pleasure deliberately perverted from its connection to life will have to serve death instead in a perverse parody of sexuality as procreation: "I have been told this in confidence by an honourable murderer who kills women—in the course of rape rather than robbery. His sport consists in making his own spasm of pleasure coincide with the death spasm of the other party. 'In such moments,' he told me, 'I feel like a god creating the world.'"

On August 29, the party was over, ending one day before Mary Godwin's nineteenth birthday. The Shelley ménage started for home— if that is how London could be described—via Versailles, Le Havre, and Portsmouth. Once settled in, Mary started reworking, in novel form and with Shelley's help, on the tale about the student of the unhallowed arts that had appeared to her vision-like at the Villa Diodati. The work was interrupted by tragedy, and the trauma Mary Godwin endured would further transform her tale into a novel of the monstrous. The traumatic events of the fall of 1816 could be described, without too much exaggeration, as teratogenic.

On October 9, 1816, Shelley and Mary received a note from Fanny Imlay, a note whose tone of depression was alarming enough to send Shelley off on the next coach to Bristol, whence it had been postmarked, to prevent what seemed almost certainly an incipient suicide. Godwin received a similar note and set off on a similar mission. Both men arrived in Bristol, unbeknownst to each other, on October 10 and searched for Fanny in vain. On the night the note was sent, Fanny had arrived in Swansea, checked into a hotel, and after writing a note of farewell, had taken an overdose of laudanum and killed herself, in successful imitation of her mother's first failed suicide attempt. Fanny died wearing her mother's whalebone stays. The Godwins assumed she had killed herself over unrequited love of Shelley. What the note made clear, however, was that she was oppressed by her role as financial intermediary between the Godwins and the Shelleys and unhappy that the Godwins considered her a financial burden. Moreover, the Shelley-Mary-Claire escapades had rendered Fanny, who was not pretty to begin with, virtually unmarriageable. Fanny's note also mentions that she was "a being whose birth was unfortunate," an oblique reference to her recent discovery that she was illegitimate.[42]

This latter disclosure made a significant literary impression on Mary. Like Justine Moritz, Fanny seemed to die as a result of forces unleashed long before, in her case the illicit passion of her mother and Imlay. Mary was familiar with her mother's lighthearted comment about taking a husband for a while when she visited Paris to write about the French Revolution. Now she was struck by the disparity between the lighthearted and irresponsible way people could bring life into the world and the sad consequences that, out of all proportion to the emotion that begot them, flowed from those irresponsible actions.

When the monster finally confronts Victor Frankenstein, his creator, his speech is full of reproach: "How dare you sport thus with life?" he asks Victor, and Victor's response is to attempt to kill him.[43] The words the monster uttered could have come from the mouth of Fanny Imlay. In Mary's mind they probably did come from her half-sister, who was brought into the world as the result of "sport" by two quasi-revolutionary bohemians who felt that events in France had provided them with a holiday from the moral order. By the fall of 1816, Mary Godwin was coming to the opinion that violations of love and life, no matter how lightly undertaken, brought with them severe consequences, even if a generation removed. Nemesis was the Greek term for the restoration of moral equilibrium. Mary, who was familiar with the child's book of Greek mythology her father had written, saw the nameless monster in *Frankenstein* as a manifestation of Nemesis. She was learning, along with the other Prometheans in the League of Incest, that the moral order was not as chimerical as she had suspected.

The news of Fanny's death was, not surprisingly, suppressed by the Godwin family: "Go not to Swansea," Godwin wrote to Shelley, "disturb not the silent dead."[44] Shelley seems to have taken Godwin's admonition to heart, and to have repressed as well whatever moral the tale proclaimed. His diary seems to indicate that the round of his daily activities suffered no major changes after Fanny's death. It was only months later that the event made its way cryptically into verses, in which he describes himself as "A Youth with hoary hair and haggard eye" mourning "the names of kindred, friend and lover."

To make things even more dramatic in that fateful year of 1816, on December 10 the bloated body of Harriet Westbrook Shelley was dragged from the Serpentine. Harriet had watched helplessly as the influence of the Godwins, both the corrupting philosophy of the father and the sexual infatuation with the daughter, grew on Shelley. At the time Shelley was arranging the affair between Hogg and Mary, Harriet was writing to Mrs. Nugent that her son Charles "has been very ill" and that she herself is "truly miserable" and can "really see no termination to my sorrows. . . . Everything goes against me. At nineteen I could descend a willing victim to the tomb. How I wish those dear children had never been born. . . . Mr. Shelley has much to answer for. He has been the cause of great misery to me and mine."[45] Concluding that Shelley would relinquish neither, his lover or her father's philosophy, Harriet decided to kill herself. A series of unhappy love affairs may also have contributed to her depression. Shelley seized on the rumors and wrote a masterpiece of projection to Mary, blaming the Westbrooks for Harriet's suicide:

> It seems that this poor woman [Harriet]—the most innocent of her abhorred & unnatural family—was driven from her father's house, & descended the steps of prostitution until she lived with a groom of the name of Smith, who deserting her, she killed herself.—There can be no question that the beastly viper her sister [Eliza], unable to gain profit from her connection with me—has

secured to herself the fortune of the old man—who is now dying—by the murder of this poor creature. Everything tends to
prove, however, that beyond the mere shock of so hideous a catastrophe having fallen on a human being once so nearly connected with me, there would, in any case, have been little to regret.
Hookham, Longdill,—every one does me full justice; —bears
testimony to the uprightness & liberality of my conduct to her:
—There is but one voice in condemnation of the detestable
Westbrooks.[46]

In listening to Shelley whine about "the uprightness & liberality
of my conduct to her," it is hard not to conclude that he doth protest
too much. After the initial attempts at self-exculpation had worn off,
however, a more accurate vision emerged in his poem *Epipsychidion*,
where he mourns "from within a chaste cold bed" his children by
Harriet and Harriet herself:

> a sister and a brother
> The wandering hopes of one abandoned mother.

The deaths left the poet, like Victor Frankenstein at the end of Mary
Shelley's novel, immured in "a death of ice, immovable." The trauma
Mary suffered at the news of Harriet Shelley's suicide can only be
imagined. An indication of her remorse appears in *Frankenstein*, where
Harriet's death is portrayed symbolically as the monster's appearance
and the threat that followed therefrom: "I will be with you on your
wedding night."

On December 30, 1816, Shelley and Mary were married at St.
Mildred's Church on Bread Street. Once again, Shelley had reneged
on his commitment to free love. But this time he did it under threat.
"Of course you are free to do what you please," Mary told him, plac-
ing her hand on his shoulder, "and I am free to act as I like and I have
to tell you, dear Shelley, if you do not marry me, I will not live—I
will destroy myself and my child with me."[47] The two recent suicides
as well as the two suicide attempts of Mary's mother were sufficient
emotional blackmail to override even the strongest commitment to the
Godwinian system. Mary Godwin knew, notwithstanding the increas-

ingly hollow but still dominant principles her father and husband espoused, that without marriage, she was going to end up like Harriet.
And the summer and fall of 1816 had produced enough horror to convince Shelley that more was to come if he didn't marry her.

The marriage healed the rift with the Godwins. The Shelleys were
now allowed to dine with Mary's parents, but as the monster predicted
in *Frankenstein*, Harriet's death would cast a shadow over their marriage. Harriet's suicide seemed to Mary an attempt to wreak revenge
from beyond the grave. If so, it was remarkably successful; both Mary
and Shelley's lives would be blighted by remorse forevermore. Shelley
would describe his excruciating remorse in an occasional poem; Mary
poured out her own in *Frankenstein* and other books. "The consequences of our actions never die," Mary wrote in her novel *Lodore*.[48]

Shelley was pursued by furies which he unwittingly invoked by
the life he led and the philosophy he created after the fact to justify
that life. Shelley's life was a Molotov cocktail made up of all the toxic
elements that would prove lethal to the Enlightenment: materialist
science, revolutionary politics, sexual liberation, and psychological
manipulation of the sort that would be perfected by religious cults in
the late twentieth century. Add to this Shelley's penchant for dabbling in the occult, and it is not difficult to see that the modern genre
of horror sprang full-blown as a meditation on his life by those who
were lucky enough to escape his circle alive.

For her part, in creating *Frankenstein* out of the flotsam and jet-
sam of her years with Shelley and the ideas he attempted to forge into
a coherent revolutionary system, Mary Shelley created the myth of our
epoch—an epoch roughly coterminous with the Enlightenment.
Indeed, one of the indications that the epoch is with us still is the
fact that the Frankenstein story continues to be retold. And it will
continue to be retold as long as the Enlightenment, with its penchant
for manipulating humans according to the laws of "nature," continues
to hold its sway.

Kenneth Branagh, the British actor and filmmaker, makes the same
point—the obvious similarity between then and now—in explaining
why he remade *Frankenstein*: to plumb "whether brilliant men of science should interfere in the matters of life and death." "Since health

and medicine are already progressing," Branagh explains, "and the mind is learning to control the environment more effectively, the logic is inescapable—one day human beings will discover the secrets of the ageing process and learn how to halt it. If man is perfectible then man will one day become immortal."[49] Given such noble sentiments, we are always puzzled when the outcome is so horrific. As long as we cannot confront the Enlightenment on its own terms and refute it, the culture will crave Mary Shelley's makeshift solution, and remakes of *Frankenstein* will appear.

*Frankenstein* is in this respect the opposite of Nathaniel Hawthorne's *The Scarlet Letter*. *Frankenstein* is a mediocre novel that spawns first-rate movies, but it is also a myth; *The Scarlet Letter* is a great novel that spawns terrible movies because it is not a myth. Hester Prynne, Hawthorne's adulterous protagonist, is a great fictional character, but she does not embody the myth of her age in the way that Victor Frankenstein does his. Frankenstein is, in this regard, the myth of the Counter-Enlightenment. The story epitomizes the aspirations of the Enlightenment and explains, in its inchoate fashion, why they are doomed to failure.

The iconography of horror is about as fixed as that of any genre. By comparison, Chinese literature looks positively innovative. There is Frankenstein, and there is Dracula, and then there are various combinations of the two: Dr. Jekyll and Mr. Hyde, the Wolfman, and so on. Both icons made their appearance as literary tropes because of one event in Shelley's life—an extended house party at the Villa Diodati on the banks of Lake Geneva during the stormy summer of 1816. Frankenstein was modeled on Shelley by Shelley's second wife; the Vampire was modeled on fellow poet Lord Byron by Byron's physician John Polidori, who lived vampire-like for a while on Byron's reputation and finally himself committed suicide. The world would have to wait another eighty years for the definitive vampire story, which Bram Stoker wrote at the end of the nineteenth century when the Enlightenment was in another, less exuberant phase, but the concept came into existence over the summer of 1816. The concept was, of course, the monster in different form. Emily Sunstein calls *Frankenstein* "the first modern myth." With it, Mary Shelley "founded the genre we call science fiction." She goes on to quote Muriel Spark's verdict that Mary Shelley anticipated "the ultimate conclusions to which the ideas of her epoch were headed." "After a century and a half," as George Levine and U. C. Knoepflmacher write, "Frankenstein begins to look both inexhaustible and inexplicable."[50]

There is something obsessive about the repetition of themes and characters in horror films which lends itself easily to parody. That there is a Spanish film entitled *Dracula contra el Dr. Frankenstein* is not only unsurprising, it seems almost inevitable. That is because Dracula met Dr. Frankenstein at the Villa Diodati over a century earlier when Shelley introduced himself to Byron. Their lives recapitulated the trajectory of the Enlightenment in such vivid, meteoric form that we, who still live in the Enlightenment, cannot get them out of our imaginations. Since we have lived the trajectory of the Enlightenment, we have lived horror. Like Mary Shelley we too are the captives of two contradictory imperatives: we cannot disavow the Enlightenment, especially its commitment to sexual liberation; at the same time, we cannot deny that people get hurt when they act on its imperatives. We know that people die when they act on them, no matter how altruistic their intentions. Mary Shelley and Claire Clairmont had to learn this lesson the hard way; the other, more prominent members of that literary seance on Lake Geneva never learned the lesson at all.

Because of its mythic character *Frankenstein* always lent itself to transgeneric adaptations. Mary Shelley herself, along with her father, attended one of the plays based on her novel. Then the 1930s gave some indication that the novel could be adapted to film when James Whale used it as an allegory of the dangers of Nazi ideology and the master race that were just then appearing over the horizon in Germany. Forty years later, Andy Warhol created his versions of the Frankenstein-Dracula dyad as a metaphor for the cultural revolution of the 1960s with appropriately graphic sexual content.

The two monsters of the Enlightenment, now immortalized on cereal boxes, also portray two phases of the Enlightenment as it was actually implemented. *Frankenstein* epitomizes the first phase of the Enlightenment project—the early, ostensibly altruistic, optimistic phase, when the French Revolution, no matter how horrific its execution, still seemed plausible as a way of bettering mankind. This is the electricity phase, the phase of youthful energy, captured in Wordsworth's phrase,

> Bliss was it that dawn to be alive.
> But to be young was very heaven!

Dracula symbolizes the second phase of the Enlightenment—the syphilitic phase, the disillusionment phase, when blood has not only been shed but polluted, generally by venereal disease, as the logical consequences of sexual liberation. By the time the Enlightenment arrives in Germany during the Weimar Republic, revolution is seen as a draining of the blood of the innocent, and the revolutionary leader is seen as the scientific vampire, as Dr. Caligari and Nosferatu and the doctor in Dreyer's *Vampyr* were viewed at the time.

Furthermore, the two monsters so closely related yet distinct bespeak the fact that the history of horror is the history of foreign influence. The idea of the traveling monster is one of the images that remains constant throughout the genre. Dracula always arrives from elsewhere, usually by ship, in the form of a dog. Like the Black Plague, which arrived by ship, in the form of a rat, the vampire seeks new individuals to "infect." In *Lifeforce*, a film scripted by Dan O'Bannon, who wrote *Alien*, and directed by Tobe Hooper, who directed *The Texas Chainsaw Massacre*, the vampire arrives by spaceship in the form of a beautiful naked woman who breaks out of the laboratory where she is under quarantine and proceeds to infect all of London, drawing off the "lifeforce" of the men with whom she has sexual relations. Each infected person is in turn consumed by a "hunger" for someone else, spreading the plague throughout London, which NATO must now threaten with "nuclear sterilization." The film is firmly in the vampire genre, though heavily influenced by the sexual revolution of the 1960s. In the terminal phase of the Enlightenment, the female body is no longer considered attractive, but as a threat to civilization.

Vampirism and disease are ultimately metaphors for lust, which is a perversion of sexuality into something not life-giving but life-draining. The trajectory of the Enlightenment then has Frankenstein as its starting point and Dracula as its end point. The initial liberatory phase, symbolized by electricity, which Prometheans like Ben Franklin and Victor Frankenstein seize from the sky to aid mankind in its revolutionary struggle against tyrannical gods, is followed by the parasitic phase, symbolized by blood, where the power of the revolution draws life from the people it is supposed to liberate. What begins by promising liberation from the tyranny of outdated morals and religious superstition ends by draining its adherents of their life force.

Because it follows revolution and because revolution is inherently unstable, the monster is always on the move, traveling from one country to another. The country it leaves is the source of revolutionary ideology; the country where it arrives is the place that sees its true identity as a monster and suffers the consequences of the revolution. One could say that the Enlightenment was, in effect, the French reading of Newton, as facilitated by Voltaire, who visited England in 1728 and returned to apply Newton's *Principia* to the social order. If so, then Mary Shelley's *Frankenstein* was the sign that the monster had returned to England; Murnau's *Nosferatu*, the sign that the monster left England and went to Germany; and James Whale's *Frankenstein*, the sign that the monster was about to leave Germany and come to the United States. The film *Alien* is the sign that the cultural revolution put into practice what the Germans fantasized forty years earlier. Taken together, these voyages make up the trajectory of the Enlightenment as seen through the eyes of those who recognize the horrific outcome of a project that purportedly offers nothing but good for mankind.

PART II

THE MONSTER TRAVELS
FROM ENGLAND TO GERMANY

# 4

## Dracula and Sin

BRAM STOKER'S NOVEL *Dracula*, written in 1897 and perhaps the most blood-curdling book-length story in the English language, takes Mary Shelly's *Frankenstein* the inevitable step further. It marks the second phase of the history of horror because it marks a similar change in the history of ideas. By the end of the nineteenth century, the spiritual descendants of those who had invoked Newton to justify their utopian revolutionary schemes (Voltaire, La Mettrie, Godwin, and Shelley) were now invoking Darwin to justify a contemporary version of the same revolutionary ideology. But blood was now more important than electricity. Darwinian biology would provide what physics had failed to provide, namely, a metaphysics of man without God and thus, and more important, an infinitely malleable moral code appropriate to a world that lacked a creator. Stanley Jaki, one of the foremost contemporary historians of science, sees this as a principal reason for the "tremendous popularity" of Darwin's *Origin of Species*:

> That Creator and absolutes had no place in the vision presented in the *Origin* was a key to its tremendous popularity. The *Origin* supplied the already strong craving for the elimination of all metaphysics with a support which through its massive factuality

appeared scientifically unassailable. The objective of that craving, as articulated mainly by Spencer for the second half of the
century, was repose in the endless flux and reflux, a happy acceptance of the prospect that man and mankind were but bubbles
on unfathomable deep and dark waves, bubbles free of eternal
purpose and unburdened with eternal responsibilities. Bubbles—
racial and individual, commercial and political—could form and
burst with the ease of vagueness because evolution was a process
insensibly slow.[1]

In Spencer's endless flux and reflux, evolutionary bubbles replaced
the harder particles, the little billiard balls of Godwin and countless
other Enlightenment thinkers, but the result was the same. Man was
liberated from "eternal responsibilities" in general and the moral law
in particular because man was no different from animals, whose development was determined by the process of natural selection. Indeed,
natural selection was now the nineteenth-century version of gravity,
the all-encompassing "natural" explanation of human characteristics
that had replaced Christianity. Revolutionary gnostic science had
claimed that science would soon show that mind was simply a function of particles in motion, man nothing more than a machine made
up of electrical matter, and self-interest the universal human equivalent to Newton's gravity. But now, with the failure of the Enlightenment, it would assign the same mystical qualities to natural selection.
Evolution, not Promethean power, would usher in utopia. And since
the engine of progress was now biological rather than mechanistic in
the sense inspired by Newtonian physics, blood became the all-im-
portant vehicle for human progress.

Prometheus the revolutionary would be replaced, as J.B.S. Haldane
claimed, by Daedalus, the biologist, the eugenicist technocrat. There
is no fundamental antipathy between Prometheus and Daedalus, however. Daedalus is simply the revolutionary masquerading as a biologist, whereas Prometheus was the physicist or chemist functioning as
revolutionary. As Haldane put it, "The chemical or physical inventor
is always a Prometheus. There is no great invention, from fire to flying,
which has not been hailed as an insult to some god. But if every
physical and chemical invention is a blasphemy, every biological in-

vention is a perversion. There is hardly one which, on first being brought to the notice of an observer from any nation which had not previously heard of their existence, would not appear to him as indecent and unnatural."[2]

By the end of the nineteenth century, Prometheus had become passé (in England at least) precisely because he was so confrontational—assaulting the gods directly, stealing fire from the sky and giving it to man. The English needed a revolutionary suitable to their antirevolutionary culture. Darwin fit the bill—Darwin, who, unlike Shelley's Prometheus, showed himself to be "not concerned with gods." He was too busy being a "scientist," or at least giving the impression that he was one. From the morning after Christmas 1859, when T. H. Huxley launched Darwin's career by reviewing *The Origin of Species* in the *London Times*, the success of Darwin's revolutionary biology depended upon the persona of Darwin, the disinterested observer, just explaining how things were and, almost as an afterthought, kicking out the supports from underneath the notion of God as creator and nature as embodying a sense of purpose.

Darwin, of course, failed as definitively in his project as Newton had in his, for he was never able to give one instance of a species evolving, nor was he able to banish purpose from the world of biology without postulating miracles that demanded even more credulity than Christianity. But the legend persisted. John Tyndall declared in 1870 that a "mind like that of Darwin can never sin wittingly against either fact or law." John Dewey, representing the American branch of the Darwinian establishment, declared (without seeing his statement as contradictory) that "the *Origin of Species* foreswears inquiry about absolute origins and absolute finalities." "The French, for all their revolutionary scientism, caught the ideological spin of Darwinism, when the authors of the fifth volume of the *Encyclopedie française* concluded, after consulting that nation's leading biologists, that the theory of evolution was 'impossible.' 'Evolution,' they continued in a memorable phrase, 'is a kind of dogma in which its priests no longer believe but which they keep presenting to their people.'"[3]

The insult was especially galling coming from descendants of the Encylopedists, from the land that had bequeathed the term *revolution* to the modern world. The English, however, had chosen their way. Darwin was king, along with Herbert Spencer and the claque of journalist enthusiasts who spread the religion to the masses, who in turn accepted it with a credulity that made the faith of the Middle Ages seem tepid by comparison. "It must have been at a fairly early age that I decided that Mr. Darwin had a better explanation of my existence than God," wrote one devotee. "Dr. Himmelfarb knocks holes in his data and logic, but even if she took the bottom out of him altogether . . . I should still find him satisfying, even if not right."[4]

Satisfying and therefore right is how the Anglo-American academy found Darwin, as did the captains of industry who were financing the academy to suit their newly discovered intellectual interests. Uncannily like Marx but on the opposite end of the economic and political spectrum, Andrew Carnegie found Darwin so congenial that his discovery amounted to a sort of religious conversion, a flood of light that made all clear to him: "Not only had I got rid of theology and the supernatural, but I had found the truth of evolution. 'ALL is well since all grows better' became my motto, my true source of comfort."[5] Jaki, who cites Carnegie's conversion as one of the practical consequences of Darwinism, sees that, as "in countless other cases, the abandonment of the supernatural for the natural meant the espousal of a nature with powers that were vying with the supernatural."[6]

But the difficulty with a pseudo-metaphysics based on biology— in effect, one based on race and therefore on blood—is that contamination, impossible in a classical, Christian metaphysical system, is an ever-present possibility. This sense of simultaneous urgency and vagueness accompanies a blood metaphysics that Bram Stoker's novel *Dracula* conveys. Dracula, we should remember, was not a vampire until Stoker made him one.

· · · · ·

When Abraham van Helsing, the Dutch physician and metaphysician, is called in to diagnose Lucy Westenra, Dracula's first victim in England, he pronounces that she is being drained of her blood. At one point Van Helsing says that the blood is not contaminated, but at another he tells Mina Harker that Dracula may "have infect[ed] you."[7] Van Helsing, it seems, cannot make up his mind, an ambivalence that carries over into his handling of Dracula himself. Van Helsing is a scientist, but above all a devout *Catholic* scientist who makes liberal use of the crucifix and the consecrated host as weapons against Dracula. He is also steeped in peasant lore regarding the best way to deal with vampires: garlic wreaths figure prominently in his arsenal. Religion, science, superstition: you never know what is going to be effective and so you make liberal use of all three just to be sure.

Jonathan Harker is likewise "infected" with an ambivalence, but of a different sort. His ambivalence has more to do with the source of the malady affecting both Lucy Westenra and his wife than with its effects or its cure. In Murnau's *Nosferatu*, the classic film version of *Dracula*, the source of the malady is clearer: Jonathan is bitten by Dracula. But in the original novel, the cause is not so obvious. While imprisoned in Dracula's castle, Jonathan nicks himself shaving. Dracula throws Jonathan's mirror out the window, but never bites him.

Missing from the Murnau film is Jonathan's encounter with the three women, which gives some explanation of how the malady associated with Dracula travels from Transylvania to England. After a few days in his newfound prison Jonathan gets restless, and careless of the warning Dracula gave him to stay in his room, ventures to another part of the castle, where the "ladies had sat and sung and lived sweet lives." "I suppose I must have fallen asleep," he tells us in his journal entry after the fact. Sleep here is another cover for ambivalence. Falling asleep is, for the most part, an involuntary action and therefore not subject to the moral law. By establishing this as the reason he stayed in the room, Jonathan seems to want to set a nonmoral precedent for what follows, for before long he realizes that he "was not alone." In fact, "in the moonlight opposite me were three young women, ladies by their dress and manner. I thought at the time that I must be dreaming when I saw them, for, though the moonlight was behind them, they threw no shadow on the floor." The ladies are sexually attractive in the vampire manner that has become fashionable in the twentieth century. Jonathan is struck by their brilliant white teeth, but even more by the "ruby of their voluptuous lips."[8]

But here, even in the heat of sexual attraction, a note of ambivalence intrudes: "There was something about them that made me uneasy, some longing and at the same time some deadly fear. I felt in my heart a wicked, burning desire that they would kiss me with those red lips." "I lay quiet, looking out under my eyelashes in an agony of delightful anticipation. The fair girl advanced and bent over me till I could feel the movement of her breath upon me. Sweet it was in one sense, honeysweet, and sent the same tingling through the nerves as her voice, but with a bitter underlying the sweet, a bitter offensiveness, as one smells in blood." Stoker is giving here the classical description of sexual sin, the sin which begins in the sweetness of sensual pleasure but quickly degenerates into the bitterness of remorse.[9]

As the interlude with the three ghostly ladies continues, it becomes clear that Jonathan's guilt is over some sexual transgression:

> The girl went on her knees, and bent over me, simply gloating. There was a deliberate voluptuousness which was both thrilling and repulsive, and as she arched her neck she actually licked her lips like an animal, till I could see in the moonlight the moisture shining on the scarlet lips and on the red tongue as it lapped the white sharp teeth. Lower and lower went her head as the lips went below the range of my mouth and chin and seemed about to fasten on my throat. Then she paused, and I could hear the churning sound of her tongue as it licked her teeth and lips, and could feel the hot breath on my neck. Then the skin of my throat began to tingle as one's flesh does when the hand that is to tickle it approaches nearer. I could feel the soft, shivering touch of her lips on the supersensitive skin of my throat, and the hard dents of two sharp teeth, just touching and pausing there. I closed my eyes in a languorous ecstasy and waited—waited with my beating heart.[10]

Before the voluptuous lady can bite Jonathan's neck, Dracula appears and drives the three women away, ending their "ribald coquetry." Dracula wants Jonathan all to himself, but to assuage their disappointment, Dracula throws them a sack with a "half-smothered child" in it, which the three women proceed to devour.

The scene ends soon after, and the reader is left to wonder just what happened. Did Jonathan commit some sexual sin? Before he can explain further, he simply adds that "the horror overcame me, and I sank down unconscious." Horror draws a veil over Jonathan's conscience, and the reader is left to wonder whether the incident was more like a visit with prostitutes or like being bitten by a venomous snake. The first instance is morally significant, the second is not, and Jonathan's attempt to described the former experience in terms more appropriate to the latter indicates, surely, his desire to hide something. "Nothing," we are told after Jonathan regains consciousness, "can be more dreadful than those awful women, who were—who are—waiting to suck my blood."[11] But what Harker really means by "sucking my blood," an essentially amoral act, is a morally significant act so horrible that his guilty conscience will not allow him to mention it explicitly. Jonathan's "horror" is really a form of exculpation.

Jonathan's reticence in discussing what happened in Castle Dracula continues throughout the novel. The first thing he writes after his experience of the women and his desire for them concerns his wife-to-be Mina. "It is not good to note this down," Jonathan writes, adding another note of ambivalence by, in fact, noting it down, "lest someday it should meet Mina's eyes and cause her pain; but it is the truth." Mina rushes off to Budapest to be with Harker while he recuperates. When Mina finally gets to see him, she is struck by how his experience in the castle has changed him. Mina writes in her diary: "I found my dear one, oh, so thin and pale and weak-looking. All the resolution has gone out of his dear eyes, and that quiet dignity which I told you was in his face has vanished. He is only a wreck of himself, and he does not remember anything that has happened to him for a long time past. At least he wants me to believe so, and I shall never ask." Again the ambivalence intrudes. The loss of memory seems convenient from Harker's point of view, as Mina seems to recognize. She then adds her own excuses to his, suggesting that it might be bad for Harker's health were he to recall those unpleasant memories: "He has had some terrible shock, and I fear it might tax his poor brain if he were to try to recall it."[12]

Sister Agatha, the nun who has been treating Harker, is evidently privy to his secrets, but she considers it a matter of professional confidentiality not to tell: "Sister Agatha, who is a good creature and a born nurse, tells me that he raved of dreadful things while he was off his head. I wanted her to tell me what they were; but she would only cross herself, and say she would never tell; that the ravings of the sick were the secrets of God, and that if a nurse through her vocation should hear them, she should respect her trust."[13] With that statement the matter would seem to be settled with Sister Agatha, but she brings it up again the next day in response to the troubled look on Mina's face:

> She is a sweet, good soul, and the next day when she saw I was troubled, she opened up the subject again, and after saying that she could never mention what my poor dear raved about, added, "I can tell you this much, my dear: that it was not about anything which he has done wrong himself; and you, as his wife to be, have no cause to be concerned. He has not forgotten you or what he owes to you. His fear was of great and terrible things, which no mortal can treat of." I do believe the dear soul thought I might be jealous lest my poor dear should have fallen in love with any other girl. The idea of my being jealous about Jonathan! And yet, my dear, let me whisper, I felt a thrill of joy through me when I knew that no other woman was a cause of trouble.[14]

Once again the matter seems to have been laid to rest, though the dramatic irony is thick in the last line of this passage, for another woman—three, in fact—is indeed the cause of Harker's "brain fever."

However, the matter that has been laid to rest is resurrected yet another time—this time by Harker himself. The first thing he looks for upon waking is his notebook, which Mina sees as providing "some clue to his trouble." After reading it alone, Jonathan calls Mina to him and delivers a speech about "the trust between husband and wife":

> there should be no secret, no concealment. I have had a great shock, and when I try to think of what it is I feel my head spin around, and I do not know if it was all real or the dreaming of a madman. You know I have had brain fever, and know what it is to be mad. The secret is here, and I do not want to know it. I

want to take up my life here, with our marriage. For, my dear, we had decided to be married as soon as the formalities are complete. Are you willing, Wilhelmina, to share my ignorance? Here is the book. Take it and keep it, read it if you will, but never let me know; unless, indeed, some solemn duty should come upon me to go back to the bitter hours, asleep or awake, sane or mad recorded here.[15]

Just what is Jonathan trying to tell his fiancée? The passage is a series of contradictions in which he simultaneously attempts both to reveal and conceal something important. The ambivalent tenor of the passage has its source in the statement about his diary: "The secret is here, and I do not want to know it." The moment of revelation turns out to be a moment in which revelation is thwarted: "Are you willing to share my ignorance?" We have here an example of the ambivalence at the heart of horror, an ambivalence based on the guilty conscience that fuels the imagination that creates monsters. The chain of ambivalence goes on and on, reaching back in the end to one unspeakable secret.

What is that secret? Jonathan never says, but he cannot conceal the secret's effects, which show up as symptoms of an unknown malady in the novel's two main female characters. Lucy Westenra is affected first. Dr. John Seward notices "that she is somewhat bloodless, but I could not see the usual anaemic signs." Indeed, after testing a few drops of her blood, Seward concludes that the condition is not only normal but "shows . . . in itself a vigorous state of health." As a result of discovering no physical cause, Seward comes "to the conclusion that it must be something mental." Just to be sure, he decides to consult his friend from Amsterdam, Professor Abraham Van Helsing, "a philosopher and a metaphysician, and one of the most advanced scientists of his day." Once Van Helsing arrives, the two doctors realize that Lucy's healthy blood is being mysteriously drained away, and they arrange an impromptu series of transfusions to restore her to health. They also notice "a red mark on her throat." "Just over the external jugular vein there were two punctures, not large, but not wholesome looking. There was no sign of disease, but the edges were white and worn looking."[16]

Unable to stop the mysterious illness, Van Helsing and Lucy's three suitors (a parallel to Harker's three women) stand helplessly by as Lucy, in spite of the blood transfusions, weakens and dies. The boundary between life and death, however, seems more than a little ambiguous. In a journal entry dated September 10, Seward notes: "There on the bed, seemingly in a swoon, lay poor Lucy, more horribly white and wan looking than ever. Even the lips were white, and the gums seemed to have shrunken back from the teeth, as we sometimes see in a corpse after a prolonged illness."[17] And yet the closer Lucy comes to death, the more attractive she becomes. Arthur, one of her suitors, is almost drawn to kiss her but is saved at the last minute by Van Helsing's warning.

After her death Lucy seems more alive than she did before she died: "Some change," Seward writes, "had come over her body. Death had given back part of her beauty, for her brow and cheeks had recovered some of their flowing lines; even the lips had lost their deadly pallor." "She makes a very beautiful corpse," notes the woman who is called in to prepare Lucy's body for burial, and Seward is forced to concur: "All Lucy's loveliness had come back to her in death, and the hours that had passed, instead of leaving traces of 'decay's effacing fingers,' had but restored the beauty of life, till positively I could not believe my eyes that I was looking at a corpse."[18]

The transformation continues the longer Lucy remains dead. When, much later in the book, the four men return to her grave to kill her, they are struck by how her beauty has been transformed into terrible but alluring voluptuousness: "I could hear the gasp of Arthur," Seward writes, "as we recognized the features of Lucy Westenra. Lucy Westenra, but yet how changed. The sweetness was turned to adamantine, heartless cruelty, and the purity to voluptuous wantonness." Her lips "were crimson with fresh blood, and the stream had trickled over her chin and stained the purity of her long death robe." In spite of seeing "Lucy's eyes unclean and full of hellfire, instead of the pure gentle orbs we knew" Arthur finds himself still drawn to her: "[H]e seemed under a spell; moving his hands from his face, he opened wide his arms."[19] Lucy has been restored to life—"[T]he wounds on her throat had absolutely disappeared"—but it is a life that is worse than death. The beauty she regained is somehow both dangerous and un-natural.

Something similar happens to Mina Harker. She too has been "infected" by the monster, and as a sign of her infection she receives "the red mark upon my forehead." Seward mentions the scar to Van Helsing, and both come to the conclusion that "it is some of that horrid poison which has got into her veins beginning to work." Whenever Seward begins to doubt the reality of their situation, he need only gaze on the "red blotch on Mrs. Harker's forehead" to be "brought back to reality."

The red mark is the sign of some reality which remains cryptic, but is inescapable. It is the reminder of something that has been re-pressed—the physical reminder of what Jonathan Harker wanted for-gotten. It is the sign of the monster. Even Mrs. Harker herself seems to lose sight of her trouble for whole spells, but the "terrible scar" re-minds her that the trouble has not departed, no matter how easily she seems to forget about it.

In their vampire condition—that is, sick and near death yet in-creasingly alluring—Lucy and Mina are like Lady Arabella, the dan-gerous woman in Stoker's last novel, *The Lair of the White Worm*. Lady Arabella owns an English country estate of some antiquity, dating back to Roman times, that used to be known as Diana's Grove. At the center of Diana's Grove is a tower, and in the center of the tower a large hole, referred to variously as a "mysterious orifice" and a "dark orifice." In the hole lives a sort of dragon, which in the local jargon was called a worm, specifically the "white worm." The color, we are told, comes from the clay and has no "cryptic significance": "When the monster came to view in the upper world, it would be fresh from contact with the white clay. Hence the name, which has no cryptic significance, but only fact."[20]

That Stoker tells us the whiteness has no "cryptic significance" is a sure sign that it does. Its significance, however, can be gleaned only by indirection and a careful study of the life of Lady Arabella. Stoker tells us that "When still a young girl, Lady Arabella wandered into a small wood near her home, and did not return. She was found un-conscious and in a high fever—the doctor said that she had received a poisonous bite, and the girl being at a delicate and critical age, the result was serious. . . . All hope had been abandoned, when, to everyone's surprise, Lady Arabella made a sudden and startling recovery. Within a couple of days she was going about as usual! But to the horror of her people, she developed a terrible craving for cruelty, maiming and injuring birds and small animals—even killing them."[21]

Even the layman can see from the foregoing account, if he is attentive enough, that Lady Arabella has a disease similar to that which afflicts Mina Harker and Lucy Westenra. Lady Arabella becomes sick and then makes a miraculous recovery, after which all sign of the illness disappears, just as Lucy's wound disappeared before she died. Lady Arabella, once the innocent youngster, is reputed to be the cause of numerous murders, just like Lucy Westenra, the very definition of purity and gentleness, who in *Dracula* is nonetheless caught in flagrante delicto with a half-smothered child. "Several people have disappeared," Sir Nathaniel, the counterpart in *The Lair of the White Worm* to Professor Van Helsing in *Dracula*, tells the young Adam, "without leaving the slightest trace; a dead child was found by the roadside, with no visible or ascertainable cause of death—sheep and other animals have been found in the fields, bleeding from open wounds."[22]

All of this leads Sir Nathaniel to the following conclusion: "Putting together many small matters that have come to my knowledge, I have come to the conclusion that the foul White Worm obtained control of her body, just as her soul was leaving its earthly tenement— that would explain the sudden revival of energy, the strange and inexplicable craving for maiming and killing, as well as many other matters with which I need not trouble you now." As is the case with Lucy Westenra, "the once beautiful human body of Lady Arabella is under the control of this ghastly White Worm."[23]

By now, I suggest, one hardly needs a medical degree to draw the obvious conclusion: the white worm is Treponema Palladium, the pale treponema, otherwise known as syphilis. Reading the *Dracula-White Worm* connection the other way, therefore, Jonathan Harker's secret in *Dracula* is that he contracted syphilis while with the three ghastly women and, coming back to England, spread it to Lucy Westenra and to his wife.

Stoker's biography seems to confirm these suspicions. To begin with, Stoker died of syphilis. "Locomotor Ataxia" (LA) was the cause of death listed on his death certificate. But LA was another term for Tabes Dorsalis and General Paresis, also called GPI, General Paralysis of the Insane, the term generally used for the terminal stage of syphilis. Stoker, like Dracula, was a creature of the night, attending the plays of Henry Irving, for whom Stoker worked, and the plays of others, and then often celebrating afterward until dawn. As a creature of the night, he was exposed to the temptations of the night, and having succumbed to them, eventually suffered the disease of the night, syphilis, whose pains often render sleep impossible.

People suffering from this disease exhibit in its preliminary stage "a change in character" as well as an "unaccountable fatigue." In addition to mental and physical restlessness syphilis victims also suffer "unbounded egoism." The sequels are acute maniacal stages, obstinate sleeplessness, and blind, uncalculating violence. At the end, the syphilis patient, like Lucy Westenra, becomes bedridden, and like her dies of exhaustion. In writing the story of Lucy Westenra's death, and Lady Arabella's possession by the worm, Stoker, bedridden like Lucy in a fisherman's cottage that overlooked the sea, recorded a premonition of his own death.

Syphilis explains the moral ambiguity of *Dracula*, in which women, although innocent, can be contaminated. This moral ambiguity, however, is completely lost on film maker Francis Ford Coppola, whose remake of *Dracula* aspired to a faithfulness to the original that was superficially compelling, but vitiated by his misunderstanding of the role that syphilis plays in the book. For instance, Coppola has Van Helsing mention the word *syphilis*, which is the book's ultimate taboo, but the whole point of Dracula as monster is that neither Stoker nor Harker can mention syphilis. The monster is, in effect, the sign that neither Stoker nor Harker can bring themselves to face the true cause of their problems. As Harker says when describing the incident with the three ghastly women, "Then the horror overcame me, and I sank down unconscious." Horror means that the real cause of evil has been repressed and replaced by a monster who points to the true cause by indirection, revealing and concealing it at the same time.

"The secret is here," Jonathan tells Mina, "and I do not want you to know it." This contradictory admonition corresponds quite precisely to the guilt-ridden conscience.

The second deformation in Coppola's *Dracula* film is more significant from a cultural point of view. Coppola has transformed both Lucy and Mina into sexually liberated women. Stoker, though, goes out of his way in *Dracula* to stress Lucy's antecedent and subsequent purity. She has been infected with something that renders her unclean, but through no fault of her own. Coppola, on the other hand, has Lucy talking like the star in a porno film. "Oh, Quincy," she says to her Texan suitor, "it's so big. Can I touch it?" Whereupon she draws his Bowie knife out of its sheath. The same could be said of Mina. By making them wanton, sexually complicit, liberated women, Coppola destroys the real source of guilt which suffuses Stoker's novel, namely, the guilt of the philandering husband who infects his innocent wife with syphilis after consorting with prostitutes.

·  ·  ·  ·  ·

Syphilis made its first appearance in Europe at the end of the fifteenth century. Its arrival coincided with the discovery of the New World. In fact the latter event was the necessary condition for its arrival in Europe in the loins of Spanish sailors. It was war, however, that was responsible for the spread of syphilis throughout Europe.

On September 1, 1494, Charles VIII, king of France, invaded Italy at the head of an army of mercenaries drawn from all over Europe, including Spanish soldiers either recently returned from the New World, or infected by whores infected by other Spanish soldiers. Five months later, on February 22, 1495, the French army marched into Naples unopposed, followed by a horde of beggars and prostitutes. For the next five months, the army caroused and fraternized with the local population, behaving so badly that the tide of opinion among the Italian princes turned against the army they had previously declined to oppose. On July 5, 1495, Cumano, military doctor to the Venetian troops allied with Charles VIII, noticed a strange new disease afflicting the soldiers under his care, specifically:

several men-at-arms or foot soldiers who, owing to the ferment of the humours, had "pustules" on their faces and all over their bodies. These looked rather like grains of millet, and usually appeared on the outer surface of the foreskin, or on the glans, accompanied by mild pruritus. Sometimes the first sign will be a single "pustule" looking like a painless cyst, but the scratching provoked by the pruritus subsequently produced a gnawing ulceration. Some days later, the sufferers were driven to distraction by the pains they experienced in their arms, legs and feet, and by an eruption of large "pustules" [which] lasted . . . for a year or more, if left untreated.[24]

In one of the first cases of syphilis ever recorded, Gaspar Torella, physician to Pope Alexander VI, noted in Rome in 1496, in the case of a Nicolas Valentius, that "in six days the ulcer had partly healed over but the patient experienced dreadful pains, *especially at night*, in the head, neck, shoulders, arms and legs. After ten days the same areas became covered in scabby pustules." Juan Almenar, a Spanish doctor from Valencia, noticed the same thing a few years later. Syphilis begins with a primary ulceration, usually of the penis, followed by "sensations of heaviness in the head, and the pains in the cervix which soon affect the joints and which become worse at night."[25]

Charles VIII's Italian campaign ended in the summer of 1495, and with the demobilization of his troops, the disease was spread throughout Europe. It gave rise to the famous disputation about the disease's name, which seems to have followed contamination vectors and was named according to who got it from whom. As Claude Quetel wrote:

Each newly affected country lost no time naming the new disease after the neighbor which it suspected, usually with good reason, for having been the source of contamination. The following gives an idea of the variety of names: the Muscovites referred to it as the Polish sickness, the Poles as the German sickness, and the Germans as the French sickness—a term of which the English also approved (French pox) as did the Italians (which presented certain difficulties). The Flemish and Dutch called it "the Spanish sickness," as did the inhabitants of

Northwest Africa. The Portuguese called it "the Castellan sickness," while the Japanese and the peoples of the East Indies came to call it "the Portuguese sickness." Only the Spanish, oddly enough, did not call it anything.[26]

Like the Italians, who called syphilis Mal Franzoso, the English seemed to have settled on the French as the culprits and named the malady the French disease. In 1530 Girolamo Fracastoro, who studied medicine and philosophy with Copernicus at the University of Padua and later became physician to the fathers of the Council of Trent, wrote a poem which would confer on the pale treponema a less invidious name. Fracastoro called the poem *Syphilis*, after the poem's eponymous main character, a shepherd who was unfortunate enough to contract the disease. Lest anyone miss his drift, the full title was *Syphilis sive morbus gallicus (Syphilis, or the French Disease)*, so the French were named once again even in the poem that produced the term that would exonerate them.

Jean Fernel, a famous physician and equally famous mathematician and astronomer who lived during the first half of the sixteenth century, talked about hair loss stemming from syphilis and took this as the origin of wigs at the French court. But hair loss, no matter how disfiguring, was the least of the ills caused by syphilis. Nicollo Massa described the pain arising from the corruption of the bones causing disfigurement and lack of sleep, until the sufferer wasted away and died.

As syphilis spread all over Europe, the horror at its unprecedented virulence spread with it. It was the sexual version of the black plague. As the descriptions of the doctors who first diagnosed the disease make clear, the advent of syphilis had much to do with the iconography of horror. The horrible faces in horror movies have a long history. More often than not, those faces have been derived from the symptomology of syphilis.

As Ambroise Pare observed in the last third of the sixteenth century, syphilis caused those suffering from it to "lose an eye, and often both, or large portions of their eyelids, and even after they were cured the patients remained hideous to behold, on account of their scarred eyes; some lose their hearing, others their noses; others suffer from perforated palates and deterioration of the bones. . . . Some are unable to use their arms or legs, and drag themselves on wooden frames for the rest of their lives. Some suffer from permanently contracted limbs, and are left unable to do anything but speak, which in most cases involves shouting, lamenting, and cursing the hour that they were begotten."[27]

Writing in 1785, Antonio Sanchez thought that syphilis caused a revolution in Europe, "like that which happened in the fifth century when the Roman monarchy fell apart because of its weakness, luxury and moral depravity." The medical profession demanded that "the whole of society must unite its efforts to wipe out this great destroyer, this deadly enemy of the human race, to root out this foul leprosy, which is all the more dangerous because it strikes from the shadows. . . . Humankind has allowed this evil to multiply its stealthy attacks, and to spread its poisons into the veins of every nation, every family—I was on the point of saying every individual!" "Syphilis," according to the *Annale d'hygiene* of 1841 "is slowly and surreptitiously sapping the strength of succeeding generations. It does not kill outright, but it prevents people from living. It attacks the very essence of life, poisoning it at the source and grinding down the spirits. The more it infects individuals, the more it poisons families, the more it insinuates itself into the masses, the more it brings about the degradation and degeneration of the human race."[28]

In *L'Infamant*, a novel by Paul Verola written in 1891, the hero, Marc Favrot, is taken to the syphilitic ward of the Hopital du Midi as a prophylactic warning (he ends up infected anyway) and remembers "faces half-devoured by an indescribable evil": "One head in particular haunted him, a head of living death, without nose, without lips, with decomposed and greenish cheeks, a head straight out of a Danteesque nightmare."[29]

Laws were passed to deal with the problem of syphilis. The French tried centralized regulation of prostitutes. They also proposed laws that dealt specifically with recreant husbands. In a proposed regulation of prostitution in Paris in 1887, there is a note of indignation usually foreign to the French temperament in matters venereal: "[T]he husband who infects his wife is doubly vile, since his first victims are often their children. . . . Therefore, we would like this crime to be punished in all cases, and most severely."[30]

In 1911, the vice commissioner of Chicago had similarly horrific descriptions of the disease and the vice which was the main vector in spreading it: "Prostitution is pregnant with disease, a disease infecting not only the guilty but contaminating the innocent wife and child in the home with sickening certainty almost inconceivable; a disease to be feared as a leprous plague; a disease scattering misery broadcast, and leaving in its wake sterility, insanity, paralysis, and the blinded eyes of little babies, the twisted limbs of deformed children, degradation, physical rot and mental decay."[31]

The very foundation of the social order, marriage, was threatened by syphilis borne by prostitutes: "This man has inflicted the supreme insult on the woman he married; he has made her the victim of the most odious attack. He has debased her. He has, in a manner of speaking, forced her into contact with the streetwalker whose curse he has transmitted to her. He has created I know not what mysterious link between her and this woman who is used by everyone. It is the poisoned blood of this prostitute which poisons the child, and her too. This abject creature lives in us, it is in our family, he has brought it to sit at our hearth. He sullies the imagination and thoughts of my little one as he has sullied her body."[32]

Horror is another way of expressing this "mysterious link." An action undertaken in the heat of pleasure leads inexplicably to suffering and death for the man who commits it. This is bad enough, but, even worse, it spreads the same woe to innocent bystanders, in this instance the wife, the home, the children; as a result, the entire social order is threatened. The history of syphilis is in so many ways congruent with the history of horror that what needs explanation is why it took so long for the two traditions to coalesce, as they did in *Dracula*.

But we have already suggested the answer to this question. Only with the rise of Darwinian biology and its pseudo-metaphysics based on blood does the deadly contamination of the blood by syphilis become of supreme importance. That is, only with the concept of purity of blood raised to the level of metaphysical keystone does Dracula, the poisoner of blood, become the ultimate terror.

Stoker did not invent the connection between syphilis and vampirism. Quetel, for example, interprets as an allegory of syphilis the drawing of a prostitute by Stoker's French contemporary Felicien Rops: "Behind the heavy makeup and the already toothless smile stand the she demon, the death's head. . . . Between the thighs of this woman who offers herself outstretched slips death with the long wings of a vampire, avidly licking her sex with its red tongue." Given its connection with blood, it is also not surprising that syphilis would be associated with the vampire, the monster who needs fresh blood and yet contaminates the blood of those with whom he comes into contact. Indeed, given its effects, it is hardly surprising that syphilis would be described as a monster in a novel of the time: "a red and blood-spattered companion, like an unbelievably savage master. . . . He remembered its learned name: syphilis. Implacable science, which names and dissects our ills—it filled him with fear because it throws us into hospital, because it sees us for what we are, because it cuts up our lives with its words and instruments as if we were nothing but flesh, disease and death."[33]

Though he had not invented the link between syphilis and vampirism, Stoker summed up the link in unforgettable, indeed mythical, fiction. In *The Lair of the White Worm*, Lady Arabella, under the influence of the white worm, wants to ensnare Edgar Caswall, the wealthy but eccentric owner of Castra Regis, the estate next to the one Adam Salton, the novel's main character, is about to inherit. If Lady Arabella marries Caswall, their estates can be merged and her debts paid off. Stoker's description of the seduction is instructive: "She tore off her clothes, with feverish fingers, and in full enjoyment of her natural freedom, stretched her slim figure in animal delight. Then she lay down on the sofa—to await her victim! Edgar Caswall's life blood would more than satisfy her for some time to come."[35]

Lady Arabella, we are told at another point, "was clad in some kind of soft white stuff, which clung close to her form, showing to the full every movement of her sinuous figure. She wore a close-fitting cap of some fine fur of dazzling white." That and "the peculiar sinuous way in which Lady Arabella moves," which both Adam and Sir Nathaniel have noticed, leads Sir Nathaniel to conclude that "the white thing that I saw in the wood was the mistress of Diana's Grove!" This leads Adam to "dangerous" conclusions of his own: "If we followed it out, it would lead us to believe that Lady Arabella is a snake."[35] This is, of course, exactly what she is, but a very special kind of snake, one with a long literary heritage.

Lady Arabella is, on the one hand, a literary descendant of Coleridge's *Christabel*, the recitation of which prompted Shelley's breakdown at the Villa Diodati. But she is also, and more nearly, a descendant of Keats's *Lamia*, a mythological monster with the head and shoulders of a woman but the body of a snake, "said to allure youths and women in order to suck their blood." In other words, Lady Arabella, by being a lamia, is also a vampire. The syphilis worm that has taken over her body is also a Dracula.

The classical description of the lamia, like that of the sphinx and the satyr and other human-animal hybrids, is usually taken to symbolize man's dual nature as rational and animal. But in the present instance the lamia is a metaphor for male lust, the sexual attraction represented by the attractive human part, the physical disgust following consummation of that sexual desire by the loathsome reptile. And more than physical lust, too. The reptile-like scales became an image of the real disfigurement that accompanied secondary syphilis, which appeared most characteristically on the torso in the form of pustules normally covered by clothing but revealed, as in the case of the dangerous lady Geraldine in *Christabel*, by its removal.

The pustules or pox, from which syphilis got one of its names, would moreover rupture in the course of the disease to be replaced by scabs; this would give new meaning to the scales on the nether regions of the otherwise beautiful lamia. Keats gives credence to this interpretation of the lamia when he describes her transformation as follows:

> Left to herself, the serpent now began
> To change; her elfin blood in madness ran,

Her mouth foam'd, and the grass, therewith besprent,
Withered at dew so sweet and virulent.

The lamia's mania mirrors the syphilis of the victim.

A loathing of female nature rooted in venereal disease has been the mainstay of misogyny throughout the ages. It is a prominent feature of Shakespeare's problem plays, such as *Hamlet*. Hamlet's mother is guilty not only of adultery but of infecting Hamlet's father as well. Hamlet accuses the queen of "making love" with Claudius "in the rank sweat of an enseamed [that is, greasy] bed, Stewed in corruption" (*stew* invariably meant a whorehouse where syphilis was rampant). In marrying Claudius, Gertrude is applying an ointment to a sore, and thereby guilty of treating the symptoms but letting the disease go untouched and unchecked. "Hamlet's metaphor," Johannes Fabricius writes, "clearly refers to the Renaissance practice of applying mercurial unctions to ulcerous and usually syphilitic sores. Hamlet also voices the observation and fear, shared by many doctors that these ointments only healed the cutaneous lesions of syphilis, while the venereal disease itself spread invisibly and unchecked. . . . 'Rank corruption, mining all within' while 'infecting unseen' suggests that the same kind of poison which killed King Hamlet will spread everywhere."[36]

Like *Hamlet*, which was written shortly before *Troilus and Cressida*, is full of revulsion at faithless women who have poisoned the fountains of love. Pandarus, for example, is clearly syphilitic. Fabricius sees this misogyny in Shakespeare as having a long tradition thereafter. Schopenhauer, Baudelaire, and Maupassant, all of whom contracted syphilis as young men, gave expression in their writing to their misogyny as a form of projected self-loathing. Because of his connection with the English theater (being actor Henry Irving's agent), Stoker was familiar with Shakespeare, and because of his own syphilitic condition probably made the same connections that Fabricius and others made.

The other characteristics of Dracula the vampire can be derived from the folk wisdom of a culture whose main public health problem over a period of roughly 450 years was syphilis. Those who contract the disease are often overcome by a desire for revenge, a fact noted by

Erasmus in 1524 (*seu conjugium impar*) in a dialogue in which one of the characters notes, "And we will undoubtedly find that all those who have this sickness will never be happy until they have transmitted their leprosy to many others. And then those who have been banished can flee, they can pass on their infection at night, or to those who are unaware of their condition; from the dead, on the other hand, we would have nothing to fear."[37]

The term "living dead" arose to convey this horror. The great French doctor Alfred Fournier "had been so effective in spreading the fear of syphilis therefore set about gently reassuring those who had nonetheless fallen and might have been tempted to think that they were no more than living dead." From this and other related anecdotes came the sense that syphilis was "unending death." "But what is syphilis if not an unending death?"[38]

Unending also signifies that the disease may go away for a while, but it always returns. Syphilis, in other words, is eternal, a notion almost contemporaneous with its discovery. In 1597, a hundred years after its arrival in Europe, Fernel concluded that "unless God in his clemency destroys this scourge, or men moderate their unbridled lust, the venereal sickness will never die out and will, I believe, always be the companion of the human race."[39]

The sense that syphilis is a never ending scourge of humanity, prevalent during Stoker's time, has gained new credence in the post-1954 era. Antibiotics came close to eradicating the disease but failed to stem its resurgence with the sexual revolution of the 1960s:

> For a long time it seemed that the idea that the "pox virus" could lie dormant and reappear after a long period was based more on fantasy than on the facts of the matter. But the intuitive view now seems not to have been so far wide of the mark (if the disease is allowed to develop and is left untreated): the treponema might, it seems, be able to penetrate all cellular elements, including the nerve cells and the nuclei, just like a virus. Now it is not certain that the concentration of penicillin is as high in the tissues as in the external lesions or the blood. Consequently it is still possible to find treponemas in the tissues, and the cephalorachidian fluid and the lymphatic ganglions after treatment of

late syphilis which has resulted in a negative blood test and therefore a theoretical cure. These treponemas, which have lost a good
deal of their virulence, remain inactive in the tissues, but can
become pathogenic once more in circumstances which are not yet
fully understood.[40]

The issue of syphilis and its perduring unto the end of the race
is, at base, theological. As Van Helsing says,

> Let me tell you this, it is out of the lore and experience of the
> ancients and of all those who have studied the powers of the
> UnDead. When they become such, there comes with the change
> the curse of immortality; they cannot die, but must go on age
> after age adding new victims and multiplying the evils of the
> world; for all that die from the preying of the UnDead become
> themselves UnDead, and prey on their kind. And so the circle
> goes on ever widening, like the ripples from a stone thrown in
> the water. Friend Arthur, if you had met that kiss which you
> know of before poor Lucy die; or again, last night when you open
> your arms to her, you would in time, when you had died, have
> become nosferatu, as they call it in Eastern Europe, and would
> all the time make more of those UnDeads that so have fill us with
> horror. The career of this so unhappy dear lady is but just be-
> gun . . . but if she live on, UnDead, more and more they lose
> their blood and by her power over them they come to her, and
> so she draw their blood with that so wicked mouth. But if she
> die in truth, then all cease; the tiny wounds of the throats disap-
> pear, and they go back to their plays unknowing ever of what has
> been. But of the most blessed of all, when this now UnDead be
> made to rest as true dead, then the soul of the poor lady whom
> we love shall again be free. Instead of working wickedness by
> night and growing more debased in the assimilating of it by day,
> she shall take her place with the other Angels.[41]

Dracula, as the character Renfield makes apparent, is very much a
religious figure in this regard. The Count is the new Master, ready to
return and take control of his kingdom. In this, he is also the Anti-
Christ. In *Dracula*, the "zoophagous" Renfield "used to fancy that life

was a positive and perpetual entity, and that by consuming a multi-
tude of live things, no matter how low in the scale of creation, one
might indefinitely prolong life. At times I held the belief so strongly
that I actually tried to take human life. The doctor here will bear me
out that on one occasion I tried to kill him for the purpose of strengthening my vital powers by the assimilation with my own body of his
life through the medium of his blood—relying, of course, upon the
Scriptural phrase, 'For the blood is the life.'"[42]

Both Christ and Dracula deal with blood and eternal life. Vampirism is, as Renfield makes clear, the antithesis of Christianity.
Whereas Christ shed his blood so that his followers could have eternal life; Dracula shed his followers' blood so that he could have eternal life. Dracula is a reworking of Christianity according to the canons
of Social Darwinism. The monster is simply the inversion of Christianity that was taking place throughout Europe as once again the
Enlightenment was implemented through one of its pseudo-scientific
ideologies.

In a satanic way typical of the reversal of Christian order that the
vampire creates, man achieves immortality through immorality and by
infecting others—that is, through lust. Christianity exalts love; vampirism—Darwin's survival of the fittest pushed to its extreme—exalts
the hunger of desire. Man under the thrall of lust as epitomized by
this disease, loses his reason and becomes a zombie bound to do the
bidding of the pale treponema, the white worm. Man is thus made
a function of nature, much as the Marquis de Sade said he was.

Andrea Dworkin caught the underlying sense of Dracula as predatory sex in a book written long after the threat of syphilis as a fatal
disease had disappeared. In *Dracula*, she writes, "vampirism is . . . a
metaphor for intercourse; the great appetite for using and being used;
the annihilation of orgasm; the submission of the female to the great
hunter, the driving obsessiveness of lust, which destroys both internal
peace and any moral constraint; the commonplace victimization of the
one taken; the great craving, never sated and cruelly impersonal. The
act in blood is virtually a pun in metaphor on intercourse as the origin of life: reproduction; blood as nurture, the fetus feeding off the
woman's blood in utero."[43]

Dworkin is writing on the far side of sexual liberation, two decades after the 1960s, and drawing on a pool of sexual trauma so vast, including what Dworkin characterized as a wave of "throat rape," that she views the sexual act itself as evil. Furthermore, Dworkin sees a connection between unnatural sex and vampirism. Since there can be no completion of unnatural sexual acts, and since there can be no issue because the pseudo-act is unnatural, the participants become engaged in a mutually debilitating, unending round of sucking or being sucked that reminds Dworkin of vampirism: "And with the great wound, the vagina, moved to the throat, there is, like a shadow, the haunting resonance of the blood-soaked vagina in menstruation, in childbirth; bleeding when a virgin and f——. While alive the women are virgins in the long duration of the first f——, the draining of their blood over time one long, lingering sex act of penetration and violation; after death, they are carnal, being truly sexed. The women are transformed into predators, great foul parasites."[44] Like Dworkin, Stoker mentions the throat frequently as well as "voluptuous" mouths, which leads to the conjecture that he contracted his disease as the result of oral sex, an activity that would be transmuted into one vampire sucking on another.

Dworkin also notices that "The immersion in lust without restraint appears to create a burden of distress, the desperate feeling of craving and addiction. Augustine, living with a mistress, 'found by my own experience the difference between the restraint of the marriage alliance, contracted for the purpose of having children, and a bargain struck for lust. . . .' Using the women as he wanted, when he wanted, he felt 'sunk in death,' 'wallowing in filth and scratching the itching sore of lust.'" Citing the etymological meaning of *prurience*, an element of obscenity, which means "itch" in the context of lust, Dworkin sees its logical outcome not as pleasure but rather "the feeling of being dragged down, compulsive, obsessed." Lust is "experienced as a form of degradation or a form of suffering. Restless and driven, the men who have unlimited carnal power find themselves the opposite of free even though they are on top." "Its deadly pleasures," wrote Augustine of lust, "were a chain I dragged along with me, yet I was afraid to be freed from it."[45]

Lust, in other words, is parasitic, and as such, there exists between it and the blood parasite syphilis a natural affinity. This is expressed through a symbolic figure like the vampire, who infects his host and drains him of vitality—of blood.

. . . . .

In dealing with a Darwinian, blood-based horror like *Dracula* or *The Lair of the White Worm*, we are not dealing with simple allegory, nor with a venereal disease version of the *roman à clef*. The monster is not simply the pale treponema; it is a nexus of a number of unspeakable things, of which syphilis is merely one. Nevertheless, all these unspeakable things, whether physical disease, dementia, lust, or sexual violence, have as their root a violation of the moral law. The Darwinian move to ignore and thus violate the dictates of the moral law was portrayed, of course, as it had been a century earlier, as liberation from superstition. But in both instances, liberation led to fears so all-encompassing they could not be resolved; they could only be portrayed.

That Marx and Carnegie used Darwin as a justification of mutually contradictory social movements—the class struggle in history, on the one hand, or Social Darwinism, on the other (the "most beautiful rose results from cutting buds," according to Carnegie)—is irrelevant. Both men felt that might made right. By the end of the nineteenth century, both the Left and the Right were espousing Sadean moral systems justified by Darwin's biology. Blood replaced morals as the major concern of a secularized intelligentsia, and the result was blood, oceans of it. That this system should lead to the cataclysm of World War I is not surprising; the Darwinian system was nothing if not a glorification of war, the war of all against all. Of America's Civil War, Darwin said, "in the long run a million horrid deaths would be amply repaid in the cause of humanity."[46]

But even more than war, the logical outcome of the Darwinian reading of the ideology of Promethean science was horror. As with the Marquis de Sade, so with Darwin: If I can do this to them, they can do the same thing to me. The only thing that prevents exploitation is power, a power that, since it is divorced from morals, no one seems able to control. Hence, the dread, the angst, the horror, and the novels that acted as a psychic anodyne by giving form to the unknown anxiety.

The ultimate Darwinian creature is one with power but no morals, but a little reflection will show that that creature is of necessity grotesque. Sir Nathaniel discusses with Adam the size of the White Worm and its ability to evolve according to circumstances: "If such a creature were, by its own process of metabolism, to change much of its bulk for intellectual growth, we should at once arrive at a new class of creature—more dangerous, perhaps, than the world has ever had any experience of—a force which can think, which has no soul and no morals, and therefore no acceptance of responsibility. A Snake would be a good illustration of this, for it is cold-blooded, and therefore removed from the temptations which often weaken or restrict warm-blooded creatures."[47]

The monster, in other words, corresponds in an uncanny fashion to the Enlightenment project for man as articulated by La Mettrie and Sade: man understood as a "force which can think, which has no soul and no morals, and therefore no acceptance of responsibility," is a simple machine and, finally, a sadist. The lamia, and hence Lady Arabella, and Dracula are just the sort of creatures Sade portrayed in his pornographic novels.

"We must be careful not to confuse the physical and the moral," Sir Nathaniel tells Adam.[48] That statement could be taken as Stoker's warning about the Enlightenment, which revelled in that confusion, with disastrous—indeed, monstrous—effects. True, the horrors and their causes could be repented of, and Stoker's warning comes close to sounding a call for repentance—but not quite. After all, that route is closed by the very manner of thinking that brought forth the horrors. Repentance requires transcendence, something Darwinian ideology denied. The monster in horror fiction is a function of this bind.

The source of Count Dracula's strength lies in Jonathan's sexual sin and his inability to follow its pressing psychic effect back to its moral cause. The monster, Dracula, represents the unspeakable thing that, in defiance of transcendence that demands our repentance, has been repressed. The monster is eternal because unrepented sins are eternal.

By the time Stoker wrote *Dracula*, *Frankenstein* (the novel itself, as well as numerous stage adaptations) had long established itself as a myth. But as a vehicle to express the terrors of the age, which, as noted, had rejected Prometheus, *Frankenstein* was inadequate. One can intuit this from Stoker's treatment of electricity, the revolutionary element in *Frankenstein*. Van Helsing seems to hold views very similar to those of both Shelley and Frankenstein when it comes to electricity. "Let me tell you, my friend," he tells his protégé Dr. Seward, "that there are things done today in electrical science which would have been deemed unholy by the very men who discovered electricity—who would themselves, not so long before have been burned as wizards. There are always mysteries in life."[49]

There is a sense, of course, in which Dracula and Frankenstein are the same monster. Dracula is to the Darwinian ideal what Frankenstein's monster is to electrical mechanism. Dracula is strong; he feeds on the weak, absorbing their life force into his. People do not have to be good anymore; they only have to be racially pure. For a moment there is a sigh of relief. The prospect of "no eternal responsibilities" seems greatly promising until it becomes clear that the very release from the moral law which the culture so ardently desired has turned men into vampires who feed off each other. With no set of principles to guide his actions, man can only grow strong by draining his neighbor of his life force. It is either eat or be eaten in the world Darwin created, and Hitler only carried the aspirations of Darwin's world to their logical conclusion.

The transition from hope to fear takes place automatically when the premises are faulty, as they are in Darwinism. The transition takes place automatically because the premises do not correspond to any reality, and so when the hoped-for breakthrough does not occur, all that is left is the chaos that follows naturally when humans abandon the moral law as the guide for their actions. Biological premises of this sort always lead to racist phobias. The one necessarily begets the other, and the appearance of the vampire simply indicates that the transition from a Christian society based on the moral order to a racist one based on Darwin's pseudo-biology has taken place. The appearance of the vampire is the sign that the break with the moral order is complete and that a new and more terrifying Nemesis is on the scene, one which represents the materialist aspirations of Darwinism gone wrong.

One of the messages of *Dracula* is that electricity, in spite of the awe it still inspires in Van Helsing, is not what it was. It is not the secret *élan vital* soon to fall into the hands of Promethean revolutionaries. It had lost its place in the scientific hierarchy of values to blood. Van Helsing knows this. "The blood," Van Helsing tells Seward, quoting Scripture, "is the life."

By the time Stoker wrote *The Lair of the White Worm*, his final novel, electricity was only important as a way of showing the foolishness of the utopian schemes of his character, Edgar Caswall. Caswall, Stoker tells us, was closely associated with Mesmer in Paris and "took away with him a vast quantity of philosophy and electric instruments, [although] he was never known to use them again." As a result, people came to believe "that the Caswall family had some strange power of making the wills of other persons subservient to their own." Like a latter-day Ben Franklin, Caswall flies a kite from the tower of his ancestral home, where he also keeps Mesmer's electrical apparatus. It is difficult to communicate with him because of "the blustering of the wind and the perpetual cracking of the electricity." Caswall, in other words, is a typical Promethean in the Shelleyan sense. Like Frankenstein and Ben Franklin, Caswall flies his kite during electrical storms to steal the celestial fire from the gods because "electrical disturbance in the sky and the air is reproduced in animals of all kinds, and particularly in the highest type of them all—the most receptive—the most electrical," namely, man. Caswall the Promethean "felt the effect of the gathering electric force. A sort of wild exultation grew upon him, such as he had sometimes felt just before the breaking of a tropical storm."[50]

But Stoker's portrayal of Caswall suddenly turns negative and with it the whole Promethean project comes in for the sort of criticism that is a staple of the horror tradition. Caswall, precisely because he experiments with electricity, is like Captain Ahab trying to absorb the St. Elmo's fire into his body from the rigging of the *Pequod*, suffering from "the most usual form of monomania . . . an overlarge idea of self-importance." Stoker tells us that "Every asylum is full of such cases—men and women, who, naturally selfish and egotistical, so appraise to themselves their own importance that every other circumstance in life becomes subservient to it. The disease supplies in itself the material for self-magnification. When the decadence attacks a nature naturally proud and selfish and vain, and lacking both the aptitude and habit of self-restraint, the development of the disease is more swift. It is such persons who become imbued with the idea that they have the attributes of the Almighty—even that they themselves are the Almighty."[51]

The connection Stoker is making should by now be obvious. Caswall, who succumbed to the charms of Lady Arabella, who was herself under the sway of the white worm, has GPI. He is suffering from the delusions of grandeur common in the tertiary stage of syphilis. According to Stoker, the godlike delusions common to those who had GPI were also the distinguishing characteristic of the Enlightenment, especially its Promethean strain, and that is what is parodied in Caswall's kite-flying episode. That Caswall has Promethean delusions of grandeur, that he believes, like a god, that he can call down fire from the sky, shows not that the Enlightenment project has succeeded, but that he is experiencing the mental breakdown symptomatic of tertiary syphilis. Electricity has once again been contextualized by blood. The people who believe they can control the elements are really mad.

In this particular instance, Caswall is using the "experiments with the kite" as a way of seducing Mimi. In this he is not unlike Shelley. But Mimi, not afflicted with Caswall's decadence and the delusions of grandeur flowing therefrom, sees things differently: "She did not like to be left alone at such a height, in such a place, in the darkness, with a storm about to break."[52] Caswall, on the other hand, is the fulfillment of the Promethean aspirations of the previous century; he is the Enlightenment, not as victor over nature, but as victim of insanity:

The sky was now somewhat lighter than it had been. Either there was lightning afar off, whose reflections were carried by the rolling clouds, or else the gathered force, though not yet breaking into lightning, had an incipient power of light. It seemed to affect both the man and the woman. Edgar seemed altogether under its influence. His spirits were boisterous, his mind exalted. He was now at his worst; madder than he had been earlier in the night. . . . To him it seemed that these manifestations were obedient to his own will. He had reached the sublime of his madness; he was now in his own mind actually the Almighty, and whatever might happen would be the direct carrying out of his own commands.[53]

Stoker is proposing in the Caswall-GPI-Prometheus image an equation for us that signifies both the continuation of the horror tradition and a crucial turn therein as well. The Promethean scientist, like Frankenstein, thinks that he is like God because he can manipulate the forces of nature, whereas, according to Stoker's reading of the Enlightenment tradition, the Promethean delusion comes from a more prosaic source. He thinks he is God because his mind is deteriorating from syphilis caught, so to speak, from the Enlightenment, which first leads man to believe that he is above the moral law, and then leads him to act on that premise. As a result, he contracts syphilis, which turns him into the very thing he aspired to be in the first place—a being, like Lady Arabella, the snake woman, possessing force but no morals and, therefore, no mind. His Promethean aspirations to be like God have made him mad. "Come to me!" Caswall tells Mimi:

You shall see now what you are despising, what you are warring against. All that you see is mine—the darkness as well as the light. I tell you that I am greater than any other who is, or was, or shall be. When the Master of Evil took Christ up on a high place and showed Him all the kingdoms of the earth, he was doing what he thought no other could do. He was wrong—he forgot Me. I shall send you light, up to the very ramparts of heaven. A light so great that it shall dissipate those black clouds that are rushing up and piling around us. Look! Look! At the very touch of my hand that light springs into being and mounts up—and up—and up![54]

Caswall becomes in his monomania the ultimate Enlightenment figure, a Lucifer, a light-bearer, who brought so much woe to earth. Like Ahab, who is also a parody of Christ, Caswall feels that "even the wind and the sea obey him," when in fact the opposite is the case. Caswall by playing the Promethean is simply exposing himself to danger because the whole Promethean project is as dangerous as it is mad: "Kite flying on a night like this from a place like the tower of Castra Regis is, to say the least of it, dangerous. It is not merely courting death or other accident from lightning, but it is bringing the lightning into where he lives. Every cloud that is blowing up there—and they all make for the highest point—is bound to develop into a flash of lightning. That kite is up in the air and is bound to attract the lightning."[55]

Which is precisely what happens. The lightning travels down a wire and topples the tower at Castra Regis like "a house of cards." But its destructive force is not spent. "A blue flame fell downward from the tower, and with inconceivable rapidity, running along the ground in the direction of Diana's Grove, reached the dark silent house," thereby igniting the explosives which Adam and Sir Nathaniel had placed in the white worm's "mysterious orifice," causing a series of

> explosions that had thrown out from the wellhole, as if it had been the mouth of a cannon, a mass of fine sand mixed with blood, and a horrible repulsive slime in which were great red masses of rent and torn flesh and fat. As the explosions kept on, more and more of this repulsive mass was shot up, the great bulk of it falling back again. Many of the awful fragments were of something which had lately been alive. They quivered and trembled and writhed as though they were still in torment, a supposition to which the unending scream gave a horrible credence. At moments some mountainous mass of flesh surged up through the narrow orifice, as though forced by a measureless power through an opening infinitely smaller than itself. Some of these fragments were partially covered with white skin as of a human being, and others—the largest and most numerous—with

scaled skin as of a gigantic lizard or serpent. Once, in a sort of lull or pause, the seething contents of the hole rose, after the manner of a bubbling spring, and Adam saw part of the thin form of Lady Arabella, forced up to the top amid a mass of blood and slime and what looked as if it had been the entrails of a monster torn into shreds.[56]

The final result of Caswall's electrical experiments is an explosion in "the impenetrable gloom of the mysterious orifice." But in many ways, the final cataclysm in the novel is the Enlightenment fantasy that never was—namely, electricity as a cure for syphilis. That would have been the fulfillment of the Enlightenment's secret dream, a final conquering of "the Worm's hole [which] appeared to breathe forth death in its most repulsive forms." Eventually, this fantasy of the Enlightenment would be fulfilled, for a time at least, when penicillin became the "magic bullet," which along with the contraceptive allowed the advent of Shelley's heaven on earth in the 1960s. But even after a cure for syphilis had been found and a sure-fire preventative for pregnancy invented, a monster would appear after the revolution, as it did in 1979 with *Alien*, because the monster symbolizes the ineradicable nature of man's conscience. Technology can never kill it.

# 5

## Blood and Berlin

T HE TRAJECTORY OF THIS SECOND PHASE, the trajectory of blood, the trajectory of Dracula, would reach its culmination in the Weimar Republic, Germany's post-World War I government. On February 19, 1924, D. H. Lawrence wrote in his "Letter from Germany," "at night you feel strange things stirring in the darkness. . . . There is a sense of danger . . . a queer, *bristling* feeling of uncanny danger." Christopher Isherwood, author of *Goodbye to Berlin*, went to Berlin in the 1920s as a sexual tourist to savor the gay bars and noted the same thing five years after Lawrence. "There was terror in the Berlin air," Isherwood wrote in his autobiography, *Christopher and His Kind*. "The terror felt by many people with good reason—and Christopher found himself affected by it. Perhaps he was also affected by his own fantasies. . . . Now Christopher began to have mild hallucinations. He fancied that he heard heavy wagons drawing up before the house, in the middle of the night. He suddenly detected swastika patterns in the wallpaper. He convinced himself that everything in his room, whatever its superficial color was basically brown, Nazi brown."[1]

The passage from Isherwood's memoir has an eerie resemblance to the vision of another, earlier sexual tourist, Mary Wollstonecraft, who saw bloody hands at her window when she went to Paris to see the French Revolution. Isherwood and Wollstonecraft made their sexual pilgrimages precisely because revolutionary regimes sanction the violation of the moral order. But with the breakdown of moral order comes terror, both a real fear of bodily harm and a nameless dread that bad things are imminent and inescapable. Nemesis comes in many forms: in France, it came as the Terror; in the Weimar Republic, it wore a brown shirt.

The Weimar Republic was decadent because it was modern. As Paul Johnson observes,

> Throughout the war, the German ultra-patriotic press had warned that defeat would bring the triumph of Western "decadent" art, literature and philosophy, as though Lloyd George and Clemenceau could not wait to get to Berlin to ram Cubism down German throats. Now it had actually happened! Weimar was the great battleground in which modernism and traditionalism fought for supremacy in Europe and the world, because in Weimar the new had the institutions, or some of them, on its side. The law, too: the Weimar censorship law, though still strict, was probably the least repressive in Europe. Films like the *Blue Angel* could not be shown in Paris. Stage and night club shows in Berlin were the least inhibited of any major capital. Plays, novels and even paintings touched on such themes as homosexuality, sado-masochism, transvestism and incest; and it was in Germany that Freud's writings were most fully absorbed by the intelligentsia and penetrated the widest range of artistic expression.[2]

Germany's defeat in 1918 had created a cultural revolution even if the actual revolution had failed. The science that begot revolutionary ideology began in England with Newton and Bacon was taken to France by Voltaire and brought back to England by Wollstonecraft, Godwin, and their progeny, where it developed during the nineteenth century. In the early twentieth century, it was again on the move, and came to rest in Germany. What was once a semifeudal oligarchy presided over by Lutheran pastors and Prussian military men was changed almost overnight into a cabaret republic designed by Max Weber in which every form of decadence was celebrated. The Germans had a word for the transformation of authority and the transvaluation of values that took place after World War 1. They called the hegemony of modernism over all of the cultural institutions of the Weimar Republic "Kulturbolschewismus."

By far the worst of transformations in the Weimar culture war was on the sexual front. What Germans found most offensive was the lack of decency. They were led to feel that they were on the receiving end of something as culturally merciless as the bolshevists were militarily. In the struggle between *Zivilization* and *Kultur*, the cultural revolutionaries seemed willing to use any means to undermine the moral and social order, and the fact that they made such free use of sex only confirmed their ruthlessness in the popular mind. If Germany were "noble, helpless and suffering, stricken in defeat," as Paul Johnson puts it, "and jeeringly tormented by cosmopolitan riffraff who appeared to control all access to the platforms of the arts and, by secret conspiracy, were systematically replacing German *Kultur* by their own, accursed *Zivilization*," then the most sensitive area was sex. And it was just here that Hitler made his greatest inroads by pandering to the sense that German blood was being tainted by the sexual forces of a Jewish conspiracy that comprised both English bankers and Russian bolshevists. Many Germans were revolted by the art and culture of the 1920s because they quite correctly saw that art had become a vehicle for the subversion of morals. Johnson continues:

> The foxtrot and short skirts, the addiction to pleasure in "the imperial sewers of Berlin," the "dirty pictures" of sexologist Magnus Hirschfeld or the typical man of the times (the rubber cavalier on crepe soles with Charleston pants and pulled back Shimmy haircut) took on in the minds of the average citizen a repugnance that is difficult to recall in hindsight without some historical effort. In a number of highly celebrated provocations, the stage of the '20s dealt with topics like patricide, incest and other crimes and the deepest inclination of the times tended to self-mockery. In the final scene of the Brecht/Weill opera *Mahogonny*, the actors walked the boards holding placards calling "For the chaotic conditions of our cities," "In support of love

for sale," "For the honor of murder," and "For the immortality of meanness."[3]

It was this use of art as an assault on the moral order that convinced Oswald Spengler, the German philosopher, that the "Untergang des Abendlandes," the decline of the West, was at hand. It was time for Germans to wage war against what he called "das innere England."

As the 1920s progressed, the average German began to feel trapped. The threat of the revolution from the East was matched by the avarice of usurious bankers from the West who exacted ruinous reparation payments. Everything seemed to be manipulated by unseen powers, and nowhere were these fears portrayed more vividly than in the new medium of the film. The set of the film *The Cabinet of Dr. Caligari* is a good illustration of the disorientation that set in after the war. Nothing seems square; perspective has no relation to actual distance and proportion, and behind it all is the sinister figure of the scientist-doctor who, as Adam Weishaupt had predicted, rules men without them knowing it. Dr. Caligari embodied the socialist-scientific-modernist regime. He was either a sideshow barker at a traveling carnival or the director of a mental hospital. In the first instance, he ordered his zombie-like somnambulist to kill people and then let others take the rap. In the second instance, he had anyone who accused him of crime committed to a mental hospital run by other somnambulists in white coats. In both instances, something sinister and unseemly had taken the place of the straightforward authority exercised by the Prussian military. The man in the white lab coat with "Doktor" before his name was now proposing variants of human behavior that had previously been considered unnatural and disgusting.

During the 1920s the Germans made more films than anyone else in the world, and from the point of view of quality of execution and originality of thought, German films were also the best in the world. More often than not, they portray a world under the control of "invisible governors" and their scientific advisors. Fritz Lang's *Metropolis* portrays a world dominated by rich industrialists and their Frankenstein-like scientists such as Dr. Rotwang, who creates a female robot in the likeness of an underground religious leader. *M*, another Fritz Lang film, takes as its theme a then-famous murder case in Duesseldorf but soon becomes an expression of the revulsion that average people feel at the scientific theories that abrogate personal responsibility, especially in sexual matters. Siegfried Kracauer sees the Peter Lorre character as an updated version of Cesare, the somnambulist from *The Cabinet of Dr. Caligari*, a man who is reduced to subhuman status under the spell of scientists manipulating human nature to their own ends from behind the scenes.

Some of Germany's pornographic films attempted to wrap themselves in the mantle of science. *Es Werde Licht* (*Let There Be Light*) purported to be about syphilis, but the Enlightenment ambiance of the title gave it away as an exercise in titillation as well as an apologia for a "scientific" approach to sexuality, an approach in which morality was subsumed into hygiene. The abolition of censorship after the war was supposed to enhance political freedom; instead, notes Johnson, "now that they had nothing to fear from official supervision, they all indulged in a copious depiction of sexual debaucheries." Though films like these portrayed the fears of the common man and incited his revulsion, he seemed powerless to stop the trend.

Six years after the premiere of *Caligari*, Janowitz called on Count Etienne de Beaumont, who, expressing his admiration of *Caligari*, said, "Now the time has come for the German soul to speak, Monsieur. The French soul spoke more than a century ago in the Revolution, and you have been mute. . . . Now we are waiting for what you have to impart to the world."[4] When the Wehrmacht marched into Paris, the French would learn what the Germans had to impart .

· · · · ·

And then there was *Sexualwissenschaft*, or "sex science." As sexologist Erwin Haeberle pointed out, *Sexualwissenschaft* was a Jewish creation: "Much early sexological research, indeed the very concept of sexology, was the work of German Jews."[5] Adolf Hitler would exploit this fact, claiming that Weimar's degeneracy was the fault of Jews in general, Jews like Magnus Hirschfeld.

Born in 1869, before there was a Germany, Magnus Hirschfeld in many ways personified the sexual degeneracy of the Weimar Republic. A major figure in homosexual rights history, Hirschfeld followed in his father's footsteps as a physician. After he met the publisher Max Spohr in August of 1896, he brought out his book *Sappho und Sokrates oder Wie erklaert sich die Lieber der Maenner und Fraue zu Personen des eigenen Geschlechts?* (*Sappho and Socrates, or How to Explain the Love of Men and Women to Members of the Opposite Sex*). It was the first of a series of pro-homosexual quasi-scientific tracts that would establish him in the public mind, even more than Sigmund Freud, as Weimar's premier example of *Kulturbolschewismus*.

Less than a year later, on May 15, 1897, Hirschfeld, Spohr, the lawyer Eduard Oberg, and the writer Franz Josef von Buelow founded the world's first homosexual rights organization, the *Wissenschaftlich-humantaeres Komitee*. Hirschfeld, a homosexual, known in the gay milieu of Berlin as "Tante Magnesia," would head this committee for the next thirty-three years. He published a magazine for sexual research, called *Die Aufklärung*, or in English, *The Enlightenment*, an indication of its intellectual orientation and, beyond that, of the Enlightenment's hidden sexual agenda, which now espoused homosexuality as its *cause célèbre*. He also worked for the overturn of Paragraph 175, the law criminalizing sodomy, though for all its decadence the Weimar Republic never decriminalized sodomy. In 1930, in anticipation of the Nazis' rise to power, he went on a world tour—or less euphemistically, into exile.

A decade before his exile, in 1919, Hirschfeld founded in Berlin the *Institut für Sexualwissenschaft* (Institute for Sex Science), which became a mecca for homosexuals throughout Europe and America. During the 1920s he would periodically hold international congresses for sexual "reform." In January 1921, Hirschfeld was made an honorary member of the British Society for Sexual Psychology, with corresponding publicity, but "the greatest event of the year," according to Charlotte Wolff, his adulatory biographer, was the First International Conference for Sexual Reform Based on Sexual Science, which took place in Berlin from September 15 to September 20, 1921. When Hirschfeld addressed the conference, he reminded his audience that the term "sexual science" derived from Charles Darwin's *The Descent of Man* and Ernst Haeckel's *Natürliche Schöfungsgeschicte* (*Natural Creation History*). "Nothing which is natural," he told his audience, "can escape the laws of nature." The statement established Hirschfeld as the link connecting the Marquis de Sade to Alfred Kinsey in the Enlightenment's continuing attempt to destabilize morals and replace them with biology and hygienic technology. During the Weimar years, Hirschfeld's name was synonymous in the popular mind with the moral decline of Germany. He testified as an expert at high profile sodomy trials like the Eulenberg affair and participated in the Weimar Republic's decadent film industry.

Hirschfeld became a movie star on May 24, 1919, playing himself as a sympathetic, enlightened, sexually approving doctor in the Richard Oswald's pro-homosexual film, *Anders als die Andern*, based on the life of the violinist Paul Koerner (Koerner was played by Conrad Veidt, who would pay for his role with his forced emigration to Hollywood and would gain his revenge by playing the malignant Nazi officer in *Casablanca*). Koerner is courted by two women but is really in love with one of the women's brothers who is threatened with blackmail and about to commit suicide, when Magnus Hirschfeld appears on screen, *in persona propria*. Hirschfeld not only dissuades the young man from following in Koerner's footsteps by killing himself but, playing "the great doctor he was," as Charlotte Wolff put it, saved "the youth's life through his empathy with his predicament" and persuaded him to join in the crusade to overturn "the nefarious Paragraph 175" as well.[6]

Christopher Isherwood remembered seeing the film at the Institute:

> Three scenes remain in my memory. One is a ball at which the dancers, all male, are standing fully clothed in what seems about to become a daisy chain. It is here that the character played by Veidt meets the blackmailer who seduces and then ruins him. The next scene is a vision which Veidt has (while in prison?) of a long procession of kings, poets, scientists, philosophers, and other famous victims of homophobia, moving slowly and sadly with heads bowed. Each of them cringes, in turn, as he passes

beneath a banner on which "Paragraph 175" is inscribed. In the final scene, Dr. Hirschfeld himself appears. I think the corpse of Veidt, who has committed suicide, is lying in the background. Hirschfeld delivers a speech—that is to say, a series of subtitles—appealing for justice for the Third Sex.[7]

As films went, *Anders als die Andern* was an outrageous example of homosexual agitprop, and Wolff, in spite of her sympathy for Hirschfeld's goals and his claim that the film was part of the flowering of art and culture in Weimar, could not help noticing that the film evoked a powerful negative reaction.

On August 18, 1920, after making cinematic history in Germany, the film was banned by government censors, who saw it as an exercise in homosexual propaganda whose purpose was to undermine public morals. In addition to bringing the topic of homosexuality to the public, *Anders als die Andern* had as its other main effect an increase in anti-Semitic attacks against Hirschfeld and other Jews for being decadent purveyors of *Kulturbolschewismus*. "The Weimar Republic," Wolff observes, "which had promised a new freedom to the German people, had its roots in the air. The mass of the population, particularly the middle classes and the monarchists, resented the revolution. Anti-Semitism became more rampant than ever, as Jews were, as usual, made the scapegoats for discontent."[8]

Wolff's reading of the times overlooks that anti-Semitism was not historically a German phenomenon, but was fanned into a white heat during the Weimar Republic by the perception that Jews were in the forefront of the corruption of German morals through their stranglehold on the instruments of culture. No one was more responsible for giving this impression than Magnus Hirschfeld, who seemed to embody, in the eyes of the average German, everything wrong with the Weimar Republic.

Less than a month after *Anders als die Andern* had been banned, the newspaper *Das Hamburger Echo* called for a disruption of a lecture by Hirschfeld on September 16 in Hamburg. Hirschfeld gave his lecture anyway and escaped unharmed. But he was not so lucky when he tried to do the same thing in Munich, by then a Nazi stronghold. He was attacked and brutally beaten by a group of Nazi students, prompting the publisher of his autobiography to remark that the "Nazis had chosen him from the very beginning as a symbol over everything they hated, and it was Hitler himself, who, after the fascist students attacked Hirschfeld in Munich in 1920 and left him badly injured, declared him in many public speeches as the very epitome of the repulsive Jew and enemy of the German people."[9] If Hirschfeld had not existed, Hitler would have had to invent him.

In June 1926, as if determined to prove Hitler right, Hirschfeld accepted an invitation from the Soviet government and made the sexual version of the Potemkin tour of Russia. Like George Bernard Shaw, who toured Ukraine in the 1930s and determined that everyone was happy and well fed, Hirschfeld returned with nothing but praise for the sexual freedoms which the Russians enjoyed under Stalin. He hailed what he called "marital bolshevism" in the Soviet Union:

> We who have seen with our own eyes the consequences of the new marriage law in Russia, find the word "*Ehebolschewismus*" an affront. We in Germany are still ruled by the inequality of the sexes and material conditions in allowing a marriage. I think it right that men and women in Russian need no banns, but can just register their marriage. And either the woman or the man is allowed to register divorce when the marriage is at an end, either because the partners do not love each other any more, or find the menage unsuitable. A so-called "concubinage" is not punishable in Russia either. The Soviets have also nothing against marriage on the basis of friendship [*Kameradschaftsehe*], but the partners have to inform each other about venereal and mental diseases in either family. False reports would be punishable, not with prison sentences, but work in a factory, or a fine of 1000 rubles. This strictness in a *Kamdreaschaftsehe* seems to me unbelievably out of place. The prescription would be more suitable for a "real" marriage, where apparently it is not demanded.[10]

We have here the fulfillment of Shelley's dream in *Queen Mab*. That it should be advocated by a homosexual is not surprising because it amounted to the homosexualization of marriage. Marriage would be reduced to the level of couplings at the Cozy Corner, one of Isherwood and W. H. Auden's favorite gay bars in Berlin.

Thus, in addition to *Kulturbolschewismus*, Hirschfeld was now promoting *Ehebolschewismus* direct from the capital of the garden variety *Bolschewismus*. In doing so, he undoubtedly provided ammunition for Hitler, who in *Mein Kampf* wrote, "Deutschland ist heute das nächste grosse Kampfziel des Bolschewismus" (Germany is bolshevism's next big target).[11]

Christopher Isherwood, whose *Goodbye to Berlin* was eventually made into the musical *Cabaret*, described Hirschfeld as "notorious all over Western Europe as a leading expert of homosexuality. Thousands of members of the Third Sex, as he called it, looked up to him as their champion because, throughout his adult life, he had been campaigning for revision of Paragraph 175 of the German Criminal Code." Isherwood not only visited Hirschfeld's Institute, he lived there for a while as part of his pilgrimage to the holy land of sexual liberation, as Berlin then was for sodomites in the know. Isherwood's reaction to living at the Institute is a complex mixture of prurience and disgust. Referring to himself in the third person, he writes: "Christopher giggled because he was embarrassed. He was embarrassed because, at last, he was being brought face to face with his tribe. Up to now, he had behaved as though the tribe didn't exist and homosexuality were a private way of life discovered by himself and a few friends. He had always known, of course, that this wasn't true. But now he was forced to admit kinship with these freakish fellow tribesmen and their distasteful customs. And he didn't like it. His first reaction was to blame the Institute. He said to himself: How can they take this stuff so *seriously?*"[12]

Such was the reaction even of homosexuals to the "sexual science" popularized by Hirschfeld. The Institute, as Isherwood and others would learn, was in reality simply a scientific cover for a homosexual bordello. Isherwood makes this point in his memoir:

> Live exhibits were introduced, with such comments as: "Intergrade. The Third Division." One of these was a young man who opened his shirt with a modest smile to display two perfectly formed female breasts. [French novelist and homosexual André] Gide looked on, making a minimum of polite comment, judiciously fingering his chin. He was in full costume as the Great

French Novelist, complete with cape. No doubt he thought Hirschfeld's performance hopelessly crude and un-French. Christopher's [Isherwood's] Gallophobia flared up. Sneering, culture-conceited frog! Suddenly he loved Hirschfeld—at whom he himself had been sneering, a moment before—the silly solemn old professor with his doggy mustache, thick peering spectacles, and clumsy German-Jewish boots. . . . Nevertheless, they were all three of them on the same side, whether Christopher liked it or not. And later he would learn to honor them both, as heroic leaders of his tribe.[13]

Hans Blüher, another homosexual rights activist of the time, also discovered that science was Hirschfeld's cover for desire. Blüher describes meeting Hirschfeld at the Institute "sitting on a silk covered fanteuil, legs under him like a turk." Hirschfeld introduced Bluher to a beautiful young man. "A Hermaphrodite," said Hirschfeld. "Why don't you come to me during my office hours tomorrow; you can see him naked then." During the same meeting, an older gentleman in his sixties recited a poem to a sixteen-year-old youth full of yearning. This  and the rest of the "scientific" goings-on at the Institute convinced Blüher, that he was "in the middle of a brothel."[14]

Hirschfeld's appetites were insatiable, and everything he did was a way of justifying them both to himself and to the world at large. Guenter Maeder, a colleague of Hirchfeld's, told Charlotte Wolff that Hirschfeld's "sensuality was such that he could not keep his hands off attractive youths." Hirschfeld had two long-term sexual relationships in addition to the numerous anonymous encounters typical of the homosexual lifestyle. One was a boy he met in China, the other a German youth by the name of Karl Giese, who became his assistant at the Institute. Isherwood remembers Giese as having a "long handsome face" that was melancholy in repose: "But soon he would be giggling and rolling his eyes. Touching the back of his head with his fingertips, as if patting bobbed curls, he would strike an It girl pose. This dedicated earnest intelligent campaigner for sexual freedom had an extraordinary innocence at such moments. Christopher saw in him the sturdy peasant youth with a girl's heart who, long ago, had fallen in love with Hirschfeld, his father image. Karl still referred to Hirschfeld as 'Papa.'"[15]

Hirschfeld liked to be called Papa by his homosexual friends, rather than Tante Magnesia, because in some intuitive way he understood that he could expand his sexual gratification by appealing to the qualities these young men sought but could not find in their own fathers. Giese was also drawn into other forms of perversion. Wolff writes that "Karl Giese . . . loved Hirschfeld, but needed masochistic satisfaction in the form of flagellation which he could not get from him. Hirschfeld apparently did not mind. Erwin Hansen, a sturdy communist, supplied the need by beating him."[16]

Indeed, as all this attests, Berlin between the wars eclipsed Paris as the capital of European decadence. The *Fauves* and *Blaue Reiter* and the *Bruecke* and dada and jazz and nudism were unleashing anarchy, arbitrariness, and formlessness, from which flowed a general sense of anxiety. In many ways, the cultural revolutionaries saw the Berlin intelligentsia as the successors of the French revolutionaries of a century before, but the average German was not impressed. If a scurrilous cartoonist like Otto Dix could be made a professor of art in Berlin, something was not right. Gradually this pool of resentment grew to the point where it could be manipulated by someone with political acumen. That man was Adolf Hitler.

. . . . .

After the 1923 Munich beer hall putsch failed, Hitler had time to think things over in prison, and the fruit of those lucubrations was *Mein Kampf* (1924) and the realization that if he wanted to come to power, he would have to do so as a democratic politician, one who could mobilize to his own ends the anxieties that plagued the Weimar Republic.

In *Mein Kampf,* he captured the German sense of resentment, attacking "the Bolshevism of Art" as "outgrowths of insane and degenerate men that we came to know under the general term of cubism and dadaism at the turn of the century." But, Hitler added, it was also during the time the communists ruled Bavaria that posters and other propagandistic drawings proclaimed, in his view, nothing but signs of political and cultural decay. "Sixty years ago," Hitler continued, "an exhibition of so-called dadaistic 'experiences' would have been considered impossible, and its organizer would have been thrown in a mental institution, but now this same person presides as the head of an arts council." Being a good Darwinist in a Darwinist world, Hitler fell back on biological images to get his point across: "Everywhere we come across germs that cause the beginning of tumors, which will sooner or later case the death of our culture."[17]

Prometheus did not disappear as a literary symbol with the rise of Darwinian evolution which so enthralled Hitler, but was transformed by it nonetheless, as the following passage makes clear: "He is the Prometheus of humanity, from whose illuminated brow the divine spark of eternal genius leaped, a spark . . . that illuminated the tacit secrets of the night and empowered mankind . . . to conquer every other form of Life on earth."[18]

The "he" in question here is the Aryan. Hitler has racialized Prometheus and turned him from an expression of Shelley's revolutionary will to an expression of pure Aryan blood. Hitler, in other words, Darwinized Prometheus. A biological determinist, Hitler learned his Darwin through Haeckel, Darwin's disciple, and by mixing that pseudo-science with Wagnerian myth and Weimar horror films, he created what he and many other people felt was a bulwark against the Russian-Jewish bolshevism ready to pounce on Germany.

If race and German blood were the highest good, then Western decadence, with its penchant for equality, parliamentary procedure, and internationalism, was seen by Germans like Hitler as no less contrary to the law of nature than the communist threat from the East. In the middle lay beleaguered Germany, defeated in 1918, wracked with revolution, saddled with the unjust reparations payments exacted by the Versailles Treaty, and finally, and most gallingly, threatened with the contamination of its culture. "Now it's still morning," Hitler wrote, slipping into the horror genre, "but again and again the powers of darkness are stretching forth their polyp-like arms in our direction to suck us dry at a hundred different places and draw us back into the darkness."

Hitler's solution to this cultural crisis was to make the Jew responsible for the Enlightenment and the *Kulturbolschewismus* that followed from it. Hitler, perhaps the most complete Darwinist ever, attacked the Jew who embodied the Enlightenment because Hitler's racial ideology made human beings incapable of transmitting ideas except through blood. The transformation of the attack from cultural decadence to the Jews was made plausible because Jews dominated the instruments of culture. Paul Johnson believes that Hitler was wrong in seeing the Jews backing Soviet bolshevism, for by the late 1920s bolshevism had taken a decidedly anti-Semitic turn under Stalin's direction. But concerning decadent culture, Johnson feels that Hitler's charge against the Jews was plausible:

> There is nothing more galling than a cultural tyranny, real or imaginary, and in Weimar culture "they" could plausibly be identified with the Jews. The most hated of them, Tucholsky, was a Jew. So were other important critics and opinion formers, like Maximilian Harden, Theodor Wolff, Theodor Lessing, Ernst Bloch and Felix Salten. Nearly all the best film-directors were Jewish, and about half the most successful playwrights, such as Sternheim and Schnitzler. The Jews were dominant in light entertainment and still more in theatre criticism, a very sore point among the Easterners. There were many brilliant and much publicized Jewish performers: Elizabeth Bergner, Erna Sack, Peter Lorre, Richard Tauber, Conrad Veidt and Fritz Kortner, for instance. Jews owned important newspapers, such as Frankfurt's *Zeitung*, the *Berliner Tageblatt* and the *Vossische Zeitung*. They ran the most influential art galleries.[19]

The Jew, according to Hitler, enthuses about "the necessary progress of humanity," insinuating himself into the circulatory system of national production by buying stocks and thereby robs business of its basis in personal ownership. He fights for religious tolerance using above all the corrupt instrument of Freemasonry. He uses terms like "enlightenment," "progress," "freedom," "humanity," and so on, when all the Jew really has in mind is protecting the integrity of his race. "He poisons the blood of others," Hitler wrote, again Darwinizing the general sense of resentment that characterized Weimar, "but preserves the purity of his own. The Jew hardly ever marries a Christian, but the Christian marries a Jew." The Jew, in short, is "a parasite in the body of other nations. . . . His ability to reproduce is typical of all parasites; he is always on the lookout for new hosts for his race." He rants on: "The Jew is and remains the eternal parasite, a freeloader, who like a destructive bacillus, spreads more and more as long as he is provided with a favorable nurturing environment. The net result of his existence, however, resembles that of all parasites: wherever he appears, the host people dies sooner or later."[20]

More than once Hitler refers to the Jew as a leech: "a real leech, that attaches itself to the body of this unfortunate people and can't be gotten rid of until the princes themselves are again in need of money and personally drain that blood off from it themselves."[21] German culture is based on blood, not language; Jewish influence is something that "contaminates" art, literature, theater, and "drags mankind down under its spell into its own lower form of life." As Hitler put it, "this lost purity of blood destroys our inner happiness forever and the consequences can never be removed from either body or soul." This same impurity of blood leads to "the impotence of nations and their senility." If Germany's enemies could have waged clandestine biological or chemical warfare against it, their goal would have been German blood, the essence of the German *Volk*.

Here as elsewhere in *Mein Kampf*, we have a conflation of images, all of which have some connection to blood, the ultimate value in a Darwinian universe. And the major threat to German blood was the Jew, a parasite who drained the German people of its vitality and ultimately its life by polluting its blood. The Jew, in other words, was a vampire. All the threats radiate from the meaning of blood, as explicated by the horror genre in general and *Dracula* in particular.

Hitler's description of the Jew in *Mein Kampf* could have been taken directly from Bram Stoker's novel or from Murnau's 1922 film version of that novel:

> The blackhaired Jewboy lurks for hours waiting with a satanic joy on his face for the unsuspecting girl, whose blood he violates, thereby robbing the girl's race as well. With all of the means at his disposal he attempts to corrupt the racial basis of the people he plans to subdue. Just as he systematically violates women and girls, so also does he not shy away from contaminating the blood lines of others as well. It was Jews who brought the Negroes to the Rhine, always with the same ulterior motive and clear goal, to destroy the hated white race by the subsequent and necessary bastardization and to topple that race from its cultural and political heights and then to place themselves over them as their rulers.

Lest he prove too subtle for his German reader, Hitler makes the connection explicit a few lines later when he refers to the Jew specifically as a vampire: "After the death of its victim, the vampire also dies sooner or later." ("Nach dem Tode des Opfers stirbt auch früher oder später der Vampir.")[22]

Distilled, the fears of the Weimar Republic boiled down to fears about blood, since blood in a biological-determinist universe was the source of all health and value. Once all value is placed in one source, the thing that threatens that source becomes the ultimate threat—the monster which embodies those fears. In short, since the Jew threatened to contaminate the purity of German blood, he was a vampire, a parasite.

Joachim Fest, a biographer of Hitler, describes the components of Hitler's ideology as *Ideenfetzen*, idea scraps:

> Darwinism and anti-Semitism ("I consider the Jewish race the sworn enemy of all that is pure and noble in humanity"), the idea of German power and the liberation of barbarism, the mysticism of blood purification from *Parsifal*, above all the dramaturgic artistic world of the theater, in which good and evil, the pure and the corrupt, master and slave confront each other in crude dual-

ism. The curse of the gold, the subterranean burrowing, inferior race, the conflict between Siegfried and Hage, the tragic genius, the brave and meaningful world of streaming blood and slaying dragons, lust for domination, betrayal, sexuality, heathens, and at the end of it all Salvation and clanging bells in a theatrical Good Friday—that was the ideological milieu which corresponded to Hitler's anxieties and his need for vindication.[23]

For Hitler, the vampire was the symbol that explained the Weimar Republic. In a Darwinist universe, the vampire was the only logical explanation for a world where progress had stopped, where things were going wrong, and where everyone knew that things were going wrong: the situation in Germany after its defeat in World War 1. If blood was the source of all virtue, something was contaminating the blood of the German nation. And that something was a vampire. Since candidates had to be of another race or "blood" (Aryans could not contaminate themselves) and since there were no blacks in Germany at the time (other than the Senegalese troops the French had sent into the Rhineland) and no Asians, the most likely candidate for vampire was the Jew from the East (even though the culturally prominent Jews were not newly arrived). Hence, the Jew (even though he was not racially distinct) must be a vampire. This last step, conflating Darwinism and anti-Semitism through the image of the vampire, was Hitler's contribution to Weimar culture.

Hitler was an avid reader of trashy horror fiction, but there is no evidence that he read Stoker's novel. He did go to the movies, which means he no doubt saw Murnau's *Nosferatu*. This film, a takeoff of *Dracula*, is more than another of Fest's *Ideenfetzen*—more than just another ingredient in the stew of ideas that made up National Socialism. Hitler knew the fears that pervaded the Weimar Republic had been given form in *Dracula* and a whole host of other Frankenstein-like characters from Dr. Caligari to Dr. Rotwang in *Metropolis*.

Paul Johnson describes the concern about blood that dominated Germany between the wars as an irrational phobia, akin to the ecological fads of the 1970s:

The Germans, on the other hand, had been "poisoned." That was why they lost the First World War. Even he was poisoned: that was why he occasionally made mistakes—"all of us suffer from the sickness of mixed, corrupt blood." Race-poisoning was a comparatively common obsession in the time of Hitler's youth, rather as ecological poisoning became an obsession of many in the 1970s and 1980s. The notion of ubiquitous poisoning appealed strongly to the same type of person who accepted conspiracy theories as the machinery of public events. As with the later ecologists, they thought the race poison was spreading fast, that total disaster was imminent.[24]

What Johnson fails to mention is the role syphilis—which with *Dracula* had come to full public view in England—played in the phobia of race-poisoning that haunted the Weimar Republic. Even a cursory reading of *Mein Kampf* will show that Hitler made the connection repeatedly. In fact, Hitler saw syphilis as the physical manifestation of the "corruption of customs and morals": "Parallel to the political and moral corruption of the German people there has been for many years an equally horrible corruption of the health of the body politic. Syphilis began to spread in the big cities at the same time tuberculosis was reaping its deadly harvest in the country."[25]

Quetel sees the hysteria surrounding syphilis in the period following World War I as the result of "two horribly complementary catastrophes, both fatal: on the one hand the catastrophe of healthy men mown down by the war, and on the other that of the heredos—the genetically defective rejects—who were to populate, or rather depopulate, the France of the future."

In a Darwinian world with no penicillin, with a demobilized and syphilitic army returning home and spreading disease to sexually liberated women throughout the land, the disease took on fearsome contours in the public mind, fanned, of course, by the popular press, which kept syphilis continually in the news. "In 1926 alone," Quetel writes, "15,000 articles in the popular press were recorded, not to mention the numerous scientific journals; these latter added to the number of medical articles relating individual cases."[26]

If this caused consternation in France, which had been on the winning side in World War I, it caused widespread panic in Germany, which had lost the war and now saw the spread of syphilis as one of the consequences. This sense of syphilitic subversion was further exacerbated by Germany's internal enemies, the cultural bolshevists, who spread decadence and disease through their perverted art. Syphilis, in fact, became the word that symbolized the peace. Fest thinks it significant that the *Voelkische Beobachter* called the Versailles Treaty a "syphilis peace," which "like a plague born of desires that were not too long ago taboo begins with a small hard ulcer and gradually infects all limbs and joints until every bit of the sinner's flesh including the heart and brain succumb."[27]

If Versailles was a syphilis peace, then the Weimar Republic was a syphilis regime. The idea recurs in *Mein Kampf* repeatedly. Hitler made political capital from the spread of syphilis in two ways: first, as an indictment of the ineffectiveness of the Weimar regime in dealing with what everyone conceded was a serious health problem; and secondly, as a way of getting to the heart of the matter, which entailed a "contamination of love," or corruption of morals. "The moral devastation alone," Hitler wrote of syphilis, "which brings with it corresponding degeneration, should bring the people to their senses."[28]

Taking Weimar's decadence and the common people's resentment as his starting point, Hitler gave his indictment additional urgency by stating that the cause of the disease threatened not only the health of the nation but the well-being of future generations. He made the Jews responsible for everything, and then proposed himself as the man to deal with them. Weimar's decadence, with Hitler's spin on it, had gone a long way: "[T]his Jewing down of our psychic lives, and the mammonization of our need to unite sexually will sooner or later spoil our progeny for generations to come."[29]

Hitler felt that Germany could "mock nature" in matters sexual for a while, but that nature would eventually take its revenge, and that when it did the signs of that revenge, however obvious, would come too late for effective action: "No, the fact that the population of our large cities is having its love life prostituted more and more and as a result ever wider circles are succumbing to the syphilitic plague cannot be denied; it is a simple fact. The most visible results of this mass contamination can be seen on the one hand in our insane asylums, and on the other, unfortunately, in our children. They especially bear the sad mark of suffering of this unstoppable corruption of our sexual lives; in the sicknesses of the children the vices of the parents are laid bare."[30]

Hitler's obsession with syphilis has been noticed by more than one writer. Walter C. Langer in *The Mind of Hitler* writes that "Throughout *Mein Kampf* [Hitler] comes back to the topic of syphilis again and again and spends almost an entire chapter describing its horrors." Langer gives this obsession a psychological interpretation, though the "phobia" need hardly have been irrational given the horrors syphilis produced and that there was still no cure. Robert G. L. Waite, in *Adolf Hitler, The Psychopathic God*, concludes, "There is no persuasive evidence that Hitler ever had syphilis." Nevertheless, "Of all the infections to which mortal flesh is prone, Hitler most feared—and was most fascinated by—syphilis. As a young man he talked about the disease by the hour. Years later, when he wrote his memoirs, he devoted page after passionate page to the evil power of the disease, insisting that it was the true reason for Germany's defeat in 1918 and proclaiming that the struggle against syphilis was the most important single task confronting statesmen."[31]

Waite evidently ignored the rapid degeneration of Hitler's health toward the end of his life; that and his increasing egomania and megalomania bring Edgar Caswall to mind and may have been symptoms of GPI. Fest notes that Hitler suffered from a *Waschzwang,* or washing compulsion, that became more noticeable as he got older, and traces this complex to "his often expressed fear of contracting a venereal disease." "The microbes are going to get me," he would say repeatedly, and gradually he began to forge a connection between the invisible germs that caused syphilis and threatened the health of both present and future generations of Germans, and the obsessive fear the Austrian Germans had of the "locustlike migration of Russian and Polish Jews" as well as the "niggerization of the German people." In the *Voelkische Beobachter*, he had a French poem reprinted with the line "Germans, we will possess your daughters."[32]

Samuel Igra claims that Austrian Chancellor Engelbert Dollfuss was murdered, not solely for political reasons, but because Dollfuss planned to bring a certified affidavit to the attention of European governments and the Vatican stating that Hitler "had been a male prostitute in Vienna at the time of his sojourn there, from 1907 to 1912, and that he practiced the same calling in Munich from 1912 to 1914."[33] If Hitler was a male prostitute, either he escaped syphilitic infection only by sheer luck—or he did not escape infection. His obsession with syphilis in *Mein Kampf* is explicable either way, as is his need to project his self-loathing onto others, the Jews, who became identical in his mind with the threat of syphilitic infection, the loss of bodily integrity, and the political equivalents of those ills, best expressed in the film industry.

All of this was forged into a political campaign that aspired to reform Germany and save it from the "contamination of our youth" and the "syphilization of the body politic which resulted therefrom," wrote Hitler. This all-out struggle, one demanding "ruthless measures," was necessary because "the sin against blood and race is the original sin of this world and the end of any humanity who succumbs to it." It is along such intellectual vectors that the Final Solution began to appear on the horizon, following step by step from the fear of syphilis fanned into panic by the eugenic movement's adoption of biological determinism as popularized by the Darwinian school.

·  ·  ·  ·  ·

Hitler was hardly alone in seeing syphilis as a scourge that demanded radical measures. He was merely latching on to, for perhaps personal as well as political reasons, a hysteria that had most of Europe in its grip. France, which had lost large numbers of its fittest youth to the war and even greater numbers to venereal infection, was haunted by the prospect of the "heredo," the genetically defective reject, who, to fill the vacuum, would procreate and determine the future of the French people. Soon fears began to feed on themselves, and students who failed to do their homework were seen as evidence of the decline in intelligence that flowed from hereditary syphilis.

The obsession with the intelligence quotient (IQ), the eugenics movement, curbs on immigration—all of these were traceable to Darwinism driven mad by the prospect of syphilis polluting the blood and future racial stock of the nation. (In this regard, it is interesting to note that Francis Galton, Charles Darwin's cousin—both were grandsons of Erasmus Darwin, whose experiments, according to Mary Shelley, inspired *Frankenstein*—and the father of the eugenics movement, was syphilitic.) Fear of syphilis was the monster that returned to haunt a world that had exchanged Darwinian ideology for Christian morals.

There were even heredo novels in which the heredo himself gives voice to the fears of the culture that created him. Marc Vanel, the main character in the eponymous novel by Jean Moye, published in 1939, goes to the Beaux Arts where he finds "many people who, like him, combined elegance of spirit with physical decrepitude—in a word, heredos." In Louise Hervieu's novel *Le Crime*, the heredos themselves give a speech on the eugenic threat they pose: "How can we escape the heredity of our Species? We are heredos. . . . In the white races the disease concentrates on the most vulnerable parts, the overworked and enfeebled nerve centers. It produces people who are mad, half-mad, quarter-mad, unbalanced, obsessed."[34]

The heredos were signs that the treponema, syphilis, had triumphed over Enlightenment optimism. They were synonymous with decadence and "living symbols of a past transgression (a curse on two generations), or rather, their perverse behavior is both a sign of the punishment and a reminder of the crime." As a result, Quetel finds it "not surprising . . . that the whole interwar generation was literally obsessed with the fear of syphilis." The novelist Julian Green gives a good illustration of the terror regnant at the time:

Syphilis—the disease was the terror of our youth in the twenties. He saw it everywhere. Nowadays it is difficult to imagine the dread which the mere mention of this scourge struck into young men's hearts. The awful consequences of this ever-present

contagion, the brain affected, one's entire life ruined in a shame-
ful way. . . . These notions were idiotic, but they nevertheless give
an idea of the latent panic into which we were thrown as soon
as the subject of physical love came up. There was a curse on
carnal pleasure outside wedlock, and yet. . . . The notion of the
punishment of sin inevitably entered the minds of some of us.[35]

In other words, syphilis resulting from the expulsion of the moral
order takes on the character of Nemesis, which is the manifestation
of the moral order restored in the form of a monster. The statistics
released by the French Ministry of Health's Commission for Prophy-
laxis against Venereal Diseases in 1925 were "astounding" and only
confirmed the widespread fear that a monster was loose, one that
threatened the future existence of France as a nation: "[F]our million
Frenchmen infected (one-tenth of the population), 20,000 children
killed each year (and twice the number of abortions), 80,000 deaths,
not to mention the indirect consequences of syphilis. In 1929 the
number of syphilitics in France was put at eight million, and it was
calculated that syphilis had killed 1,500,000 Frenchmen in ten years,
as many as the war in four years. The situation was judged to be even
worse amongst the troops and the indigenous population in the colo-
nies (in Senegal a doctor estimated that eight out of ten of the native
population were syphilitics)."[36] The figures on venereal infection in
Senegal released at the time that Senegalese troops were sent to oc-
cupy the Rhineland, gives some indication of what was fueling
Germany's racial fears, and how Hitler could so easily capitalize on
them politically. The statistics amounted to a direct attack on the
purity of German blood, to use the terms of the time, a kind of biological warfare with syphilis as the main weapon.

The French fear of syphilis was so pronounced, in fact, that after
the Nazi invasion, the Nazi regime in France gave as its raison d'être
combatting syphilis. The Pétain government hoped that this would
lend legitimacy to an obviously unpopular regime. Vichy France became the logical extension of what Hitler had done in Germany by
appealing to the same fears. And the same fears would allow Hitler

to pacify the countries he had conquered throughout the rest of Europe as well. The threat was exploited by Nazi propaganda in France, which in 1943 claimed: "Syphilis alone kills 200,000 Frenchmen each year. . . . peoples the asylums with madmen and the terminally ill, empties cradles and robs town and country of more than 300,000 births per year because it condemns to celibacy or childless marriage a huge number of procreators who have been badly deformed because they have not received proper treatment. Even so, this has not prevented us from being inundated with degenerates."[37]

Louise Hervieu dedicated her book *Le péril vénérien* to "those people who have reconquered their youth and include those who have punished us." The Nazi cloud, in other words, had a silver lining for France because the Germans "had first purified themselves of the venereal scourge" and would now do France the same favor. Sounding a little like Renfield in *Dracula*, Hervieu, who suffered from congenital syphilis, looked forward to the time when "in the bosom of a France which has been restored and healed, children will grow up beautiful and free from syphilis, the old hereditary enemy, will have been vanquished for ever. . . . Master, you and those like you are preparing for the coming of a new world."[38]

Others expressed a hope similar to Hervieu's in a less perfervid tone. Hitler is good for France, goes this argument, because he will combat venereal disease here as he did in Germany: "Under the aegis of the Marshal who has so courageously undertaken to regenerate our country we shall, we hope, also succeed in eliminating most of the factors in the propagation of the venereal disease which have just been enumerated. . . . We are conscious of the fact that, having supported to the utmost the organization of the anti-venereal struggle in this country, we have made a substantial contribution to the work of rebuilding and regeneration of France, to which Marshal Petain has dedicated himself with so much courage and self-denial."[39]

If the argument was at all convincing to Frenchmen, who had to accept the cure at the hands of a conquering army, then it was a fortiori appealing to the Germans. The eugenic solution to syphilis was Hitler's ticket to power. Eugenics was a model Darwinian concept.

J. B. S. Haldane described the eugenics movement as comprised of "a number of earnest persons [who], having discovered the existence of biology, attempted to apply it in its then very crude condition to the production of a race of supermen, and in certain countries managed to carry a good deal of legislation." In "Sexually Transmitted Diseases between Imperial and Nazi Germany," Paul Weindling sees Hitler's fear "that the spread of syphilis in Germany before 1914 was poisoning the health" of the German nation as "a response to a widespread public debate on the prevalence of such diseases that had been raging since the 1890s."[40]

. . . . .

The decadence in Germany that accounted for the "prevalence of such diseases" was personified in such sexually disordered people as the Englishman Christopher Isherwood. When Isherwood first passed through German customs, the thought occurred to him, still referring to himself in the third person, that "This might even become an immigration. When the German passport official asked him the purpose of his journey, he could have truthfully replied, 'I'm looking for my homeland and I've come to find out if this is it.'" His new homeland *in potentia* was exciting precisely because of the possibilities it offered for engaging in anonymous sex. Isherwood was specific in his memoir about the need to have sex outside his class and found it even more exciting when he was unable to speak the language of the person he had sex with. "Christopher," he writes after returning to Germany with a greater facility for the language, "found it very odd to be able to chatter away to him in German—odd and a little saddening, because the collapse of their language barrier had buried the magic image of the German Boy."[41]

There was magic in the image of the boy because it seemed to possess what Isherwood lacked, namely, a sort of masculine self-confidence. Hence, sex fulfilled a very special need in Isherwood's life, one that made it pointless to seek sexual gratification with women, because—and this is the gist of homosexual activity—there is nothing of value he can "draw off" from women. They are not "romantic." Isherwood askes himself: "Do I now want to go to bed with more women and girls? Of course not, as long as I can have boys. Why do I prefer boys? Because of their shape and their voices and their smell and the way they move. And boys can be romantic. I can put them into my myth and fall in love with them. Girls can be absolutely beautiful but never romantic. In fact, their utter lack of romance is what I find most likable about them. They're so sensible."[42]

Joseph Nicolosi, in his book *Reparative Therapy of Male Homosexuality*, sees homosexuality as essentially a "male deficit" that results from family problems, specifically, an estrangement between father and son at a crucial stage of the son's psychic development. Having failed to receive the father's approval, the son seeks his sense of masculinity from sexual contact with men who seem to embody what he feels he lacks. "After years of secrecy, isolation and alienation," Nicolosi writes, describing the psychic odyssey of one of his patients (his description is just as appropriate in describing Isherwood's odyssey from Victorian England to decadent Berlin), "most young men find the gay world powerfully alluring, with its romantic, sensual, outrageous and embracing qualities."[43]

This psychological need for the father's approval is transferred, generally through seduction by an older man, to sexual behavior, which quickly becomes compulsive and self-destructive. The homosexual, according to Nicolosi, is attracted to "Mysterious men . . . those who possess enigmatic masculine qualities that both perplex and allure the client. Such men are overvalued and even idealized, for they are the embodiment of qualities that the client wishes he had attained for himself." Nicolosi adds that "the homosexual carries a sense of weakness and incompetence with regard to those attributes associated with masculinity, that is power, assertion and strength. He is attracted to masculine strength out of an unconscious striving toward his own masculinity. At the same time, because of his hurtful experience with father, he is suspicious of men in power. Homosexual contact is used as an erotic bridge to gain entry into a special male world."[44]

Women, on the other hand, represent neither beauty nor pleasure, as they do to normal men, but a strange sense of heteronomous duty. Women are a challenge to which the homosexual does not feel adequate, and with that comes the sense that liking them and going out with them and having sex with them and marrying them are duties imposed from without by forces alien to the "real self." Whenever Isherwood thought of "girls," he

> would become suddenly, blindly furious. Damn Nearly Everybody. Girls are what the state and the church and the law and the press and the medical professional endorse, and command me to desire. My mother endorses them, too. She is silently brutishly willing me to get married and breed grandchildren for her. Her will is the will of Nearly Everybody, and in their will is my death. My will is to live according to my nature, and to find a place where I can be what I am. . . . But I'll admit this—even if my nature were like theirs, I should still have to fight them, in one way or another. If boys didn't exist, I should have to invent them.[45]

Since sex for the homosexual is essentially an attempt to appropriate the masculinity that he feels lacking in himself from someone who seems to embody it, sex with girls has no purpose, since girls do not have what he lacks. Once construed in this way, sex becomes, essentially, vampirism. It is either sucking the desired object to obtain its male essence, or being sucked for the same purpose. Isherwood makes this point but in a slightly veiled manner when he talks about Bubi, the first object of his homosexual attentions in Berlin: "Christopher wanted to keep Bubi all to himself forever, to possess him utterly, and he knew that this was impossible and absurd. If he had been a savage, he might have solved the problem by eating Bubi—for magical, not gastronomic, reasons"[46]

Isherwood again refers to magic, this time to a magic form of cannibalism that will allow him "to keep Bubi all to himself forever, to possess him utterly," in other words, to appropriate forever from Bubi what Isherwood himself lacks. Cannibalism, as the case of Jeffrey Dahmer showed, is nothing more that an extreme form of homosexuality. Both actions involve a "magical" ingestion of the desired characteristics of the other. In this regard, cannibalism is but one in a series of psychic linkages that radiate from the vampire—the prime representative of Weimar culture. (Hirschfeld, by the way, in his *magnum opus* listing all the sexual variants, includes vampirism as one and cites the specific case of a man who could not reach orgasm without first ingesting the blood of his spouse. The Marquis de Sade lists a similar instance in *Justine*.) In either case the point of the act is to assuage the feeling of hunger, the physical manifestation of the deficit nature of homosexuality, as well as lust. As one of Nicolosi's clients explains about his sexual involvement with a male, "That power and control—I've always wanted to draw off of that, to be so together."[47]

Like a vampire, the homosexual "draws off" that power by sucking, by draining the desired object of its life force and absorbing it into himself in some ritualistic "magical" banquet. But this magic never works; it only exacerbates the loneliness and inadequacy that drove the homosexual to this form of sexual activity in the first place. What arises in place of the "magic" is a compulsive, addictive sort of vicious circle: the homosexual tries to compensate for his sense of masculine inadequacy by engaging in homosexual activity, which, once it is over, only enhances his sense of inadequacy: "Immediately after every homosexual experience," one of Nicolosi's clients explains, "it feels like something is missing. The closeness I wanted with another man just didn't happen. I'm left with the feeling that sex is just not what I wanted."[48]

And once again the vampire provides the best explanation of the cyclic nature of this pseudo-sexual activity. There is the depletion of death, the craving, the hunger for what is lacking, which is temporarily alleviated by the sucking of fresh blood, but the transformation is eternally temporary, forcing the vampire, or in this case the homosexual, to engage in a neve-ending search for new partner-victims so that he can draw from them a momentary relief from his feeling of isolation and inadequacy. "Considering the habit-forming nature of sexual behavior," Nicolosi writes, "the more homosexually active the client is, the more difficult the course of treatment."[49]

Dr. Van Helsing in Stoker's *Dracula* discovered the same truth in treating Lucy Westenra. What the Weimar Republic discovered through the film *Dracula* is that everything Stoker had to say about lust applied a fortiori to lustful behavior between two men—all homosexual activity is essentially vampirism, a fact that emerges repeatedly in the testimony of Nicolosi's clients: "This week I made a list of all the guys I've ever had sex with. I wondered, what was I attracted to? I realized it had to do with exterior traits of masculinity and an appearance of self-assuredness. Some of the guys had this hypermasculinity—they were body builders and so on. Looking back, I realize this attraction to masculinity had to do with my not being confident in myself. I also realize now that most of them were actually as insecure as I was." Writing about his own life as a homosexual, author William Aaron states that "since part of the compulsion of homosexuality seems to be a need on the part of the homophile to 'absorb' masculinity from his sexual partners, he must be constantly on the lookout for [new partners]."[50]

That vampires are predatory is axiomatic; that they are essentially homosexual is not. It is rather a cultural development that has to do with the trajectory of sex disconnected from procreation, and perhaps, the demise of syphilis as sexually significant after World War II. By the time the film *Interview with a Vampire* was made in the late 1980s, the predominate significance of vampirism was homosexual.

*Interview* is a homosexual melodrama. Tom Cruise, the older homosexual, is jilted by his younger, and more attractive protégé, portrayed by Brad Pitt. "This movie is not just about vampires," Anne Rice, the author of the novel, announces to viewers of the film. "It's really about us." Or at least about us heterosexuals, who live today in a culture where vampires have been portrayed as the ideal citizens of the republic because of the close affinity their behavior has with homosexuals. And homosexuals have become cultural heroes because their rebellion against nature is more intimate and their sexual activity more machine-like than that of the average monogamous citizen. Homosexuals are just like us, the enlightened contraceptive culture exclaims, only more so.

When, at the end of *Interview*, Armand rescues Louis from "the terrible dawn," after Parisian vampires have immured him upside down in a niche in the cellar of the Theater of the Vampires, he tells him that as a vampire and, therefore, a monster, "the first lesson is that we must be powerful, beautiful, and without regret." Which is another reason why the movie is really about "us"—that is, it portrays the deepest aspirations of Enlightenment culture, the desire to be a monster like that of the *Alien* films, a being that possesses power but no morals, and is therefore not subject to remorse. The fact that these films are popular entertainment indicates the huge pool of sexual guilt that motivates the people who make them and those who pay money to see them. Absence of regret also ensures that the machine-like vampire sexual activity will continue, especially among homosexuals. According to Nicolosi, "A man who is depressed may gain a temporary sense of mastery though anonymous sex because of its excitement, intensity, even danger—followed by orgasmic release and an immediate reduction of tension. Later he is likely to feel disgusted, remorseful and out of control. Through repentance he regains control and is all right again. But where there is nothing to feed that healthy state, it is a matter of time until he gets depressed, feels powerless and out of touch with himself and seeks anonymous sex as a short-term solution to getting back in touch and feeling in control again."[51]

The "terrible dawn" in vampire culture is repentance, which like the sun makes moral reality apparent, but it is always painful for those whose conscience is troubled with sin and who therefore, like vampires, they prefer the darkness. "O sink hernieder, Nacht der Liebe" ("Descend, O night of love.") was Wagner's way of expressing the same feeling in *Tristan und Isolde*.

The Enlightenment eventually and paradoxically led to a fear of the light, with the vampire as its ultimate expression. The vampire—as the essence of compulsive sexual behavior in love with yet hating its own addiction—fears the light because the light causes it to die. Just as being born to the night symbolizes the conversion to sexual compulsion, fear of the light expresses the panic that facing reality causes in those habituated to sexual compulsion. Because repentance is the ultimate admission of the light of reason into a life darkened by these same sexual compulsions, it too is seen as a kind of death, the mirror image of the death that began with giving in to those compulsions.

·  ·  ·  ·  ·

In Germany, signs showing that destiny was catching up to Enlightenment depravity multiplied. "[T]here was terror in the Berlin air," Isherwood said, "the terror felt by many people with good reason— and Christopher [Isherwood] found himself affected by it."[52] Isherwood felt that he may "have been affected by his own fantasies," or stated with more psychological coherence, perhaps his fantasies brought on the terror. He started hearing heavy wagons drawing up to the house late at night and seeing swastika patterns in the wallpaper. Everything was beginning to look brown, Nazi brown. Once again, Nemesis appeared to be just over the horizon, and this time his name was not Robespierre but Adolf Hitler.

While in exile in France, Hirschfeld thought back on his days at the Institute, remembering a day, three years before the Nazis came to power, when the Institute treated a patient who had had a sexual encounter with SA chief and NSDAP founder Ernst Roehm. "We were on good terms with him," Hirschfeld wrote of this patient, "and he told us quite a bit of what happened in his circle. But at that time we hardly took notice of his accounts. He also referred to Adolf Hitler in the oddest possible manner. 'Afi is the most perverted of all of us. He is like a very soft woman, but now he makes great propaganda in heroic morale.'" Guenter Maeder described the conversation as "Tuntengeschwaetz," or queer gossip, but Hirschfeld was obviously having second thoughts, as did Maeder, who wrote that "after careful reflection about the matter, and in the view of prominent psychologists, Hitler had something feminine about him. He was perhaps sadomasochistic, with some homosexual inclinations. These instincts did not seem strong enough to resist repression and sublimation through an iron will."

And therein hangs a tale. Scott Lively and Kevin Abrams in their book, *The Pink Swastika*, attempted to uncover the homosexual roots of the Nazi Party. They discovered that far from persecuting homosexuals, the Nazi leadership was almost exclusively homosexual, and on their reading, struggles in the Weimar Republic during the 1920s amounted to a battle between two groups of homosexuals: the "butch" faction under SA leader Ernst Roehm and the "femmes" under Magnus Hirschfeld. When the courts referred violators of Paragraph 175 to him for treatment, Hirschfeld came into possession of a great deal of incriminating information on the sex lives and homosexual proclivities of prominent Nazis. Hirschfeld, apparently no respecter of professional confidentiality, worked hand in glove with the Social Democrat Party (SPD) in Germany during the Weimar Republic and released to its newspapers selected details about the perverted sex lives of Nazi luminaries.

Since the major parties of the Left—the SPD and the communists—espoused gay rights and came close to abolishing Paragraph 175 in the late 1920s, Hitler had only one way to exploit the average German's revulsion of the Weimar's rampant homosexuality. Hence, he embarked on an anti–gay rights campaign that focused obsessively on Hirschfeld and quickly shaded over into smearing all things modern as Jewish, foreign, internationalist, and racially degenerate.

On May 14, 1928, in response to a request for a formal statement from a German homosexual rights organization, the Nazi Party issued a statement which, among other things, averred: "Might makes right. And the stronger will always prevail against the weaker. Today we are the weaker. Let us make sure that we will become the stronger again! This we can do only if we exercise moral restraint. Therefore we reject all immorality, especially love between men, because it deprives us of our last chance to free our people from the chains of slavery which are keeping it fettered today."[53] Everything, it seemed, needed a Darwinian justification ("might makes right") in the Weimar Republic—homosexuality, as justified by Hirschfeld's appeal to Darwin at the first Congress for Sexual Reform in 1921, and anti-homosexuality, as promoted by Hitler. But the fact that Hitler called Roehm, who had fled to Bolivia, back to Germany one year later to suppress a rebellion in the SA ranks gives some indication that Hitler's rejection of homosexuality was merely cynical.

In 1935, the Nazis amended Paragraph 175 by including a provision criminalizing any type of behavior that might indicate homosexual inclination or desire. The results of, as well as the intention behind, this change in the law, which not coincidentally dropped reference to homosexuality as unnatural, are easy enough to fathom. The Nazis, in the name of upholding sexual morality, could now eliminate, without judicial restraint, anyone who disagreed with them. It will never be known how many heterosexuals were charged under this law, but the Nazis indisputably used false accusations of homosexuality to justify the detainment and imprisonment of many of their opponents. "The law was so loosely formulated," writes James D. Steakley, "that it could be, and was, applied against heterosexuals that the Nazis wanted to eliminate . . . the law was also used repeatedly against Catholic clergymen." Eugen Kogon concurs: "The Gestapo readily had recourse to the charge of homosexuality if it was unable to find any pretext for proceeding against Catholic priests or irksome critics."[54] The largely homosexual Nazi leadership could now eliminate its opponents by charging them with the crime of homosexuality, which also served to defame their character. If any actual homosexuals ended up in concentration camps, it was simply because they happened to be at the wrong end of the political equation, not because they were homosexuals. History shows that homosexuals who were helpful to the Nazis were unmolested.

Five years later, on December 4, 1930, Magnus Hirschfeld addressed the American Society for Medical History on the topic of sexology, a lecture arranged by Dr. Harry Benjamin, who played a pivotal role in bringing Hirschfeld's ideas to America. Hirschfeld was introduced by Victor Robinson, son of Hirschfeld's friend, Dr. William Robinson, who, like Benjamin, became an early supporter of Alfred Kinsey. And Kinsey, in his turn, established the American version of the *Institut für Sexualwissenschaft* at Indiana University and published the famous Kinsey reports on human sexuality in 1948 and 1953.

The most pressing reason for Hirschfeld's lecture tour was, of course, the increasingly dangerous political situation in Germany. His one lecture in New York expanded into a lecture tour throughout the country. When it came time to leave, Hirschfeld decided to go home the long way and embarked on a lecture tour in China, which led him to other ports in the Far East. He ended up living as an exile in France.

In his biography of Hitler, Joachim Fest talked about "an overwhelming sense of anxiety" pervading Europe at the time. "It was," he concluded, "above all and immediately, fear of the revolution, that 'grande peur,' which had haunted the dreams of the European bourgeoisie from the time of the French Revolution throughout the entire nineteenth century."[55] Isherwood had talked about it in his memoir. Mary Wollstonecraft had mentioned the same thing. Now it was stalking the streets of Berlin, wearing a brown shirt.

On May 6, 1933, Nemesis arrived at the doors of the *Institut für Sexualwissenschaft*. Erwin Hansen, the "sturdy communist" who used to beat Karl Giese to fulfill his masochistic needs, was at the institute when the Nazis arrived early in the morning. Since the arrival of the truck loads of Nazi students was accompanied by a brass band, in keeping with Hitler's penchant for public theater, Hansen went down to open the door for the invading army, but the Nazi youth broke it down anyway.

Isherwood, who describes the raid in his memoir, was struck that the Nazis seemed to know what they were looking for. The point of the raid was not so much the destruction of Hirschfeld's Institute and his dirty pictures but rather the removal of the incriminating evidence of the homosexual behavior of leading Nazis. Ernst Roehm was a prime suspect, but Roehm would pay the price for his homosexuality when, a year later, he and his homosexual friends were gunned down at a German resort on Hitler's orders. Hitler, for his part, was not only responding to pressure from Mussolini and others, but saw the raid as a opportunity to consolidate his power.

With the dissolution of the institute and the arrival of the Nazi Nemesis at the pinnacle of power, *Kulturbolschewismus* began to fold its tents and disappear, heading more often than not to the West, and ending up in the United States in general and, for people like

Isherwood, Schoenberg, Thomas Mann, Franz Werfel, Peter Lorre, Conrad Veidt, and Berthold and Salka Viertel, in Hollywood in particular. Isherwood's ticket to Hollywood had a German connection. He went there as Berthold Viertel's assistant and because he spoke German. He escaped Germany unharmed by either disease or the police, who were now hunting down foreigners.

Karl Giese was not so fortunate. He escaped to France with much of the Hirschfeld archival material, only to commit suicide there in 1938. But the archival material did not remain in France. It ended up at the Kinsey Institute in Bloomington, Indiana.

The monster was on the move once again.

PART III

# The Monster Travels
# from Germany to America

# 6

## *The Difference Between Us and Them*

ONE OF THE IRONIES of intellectual history is that the country that was conceived in revolution was a bulwark against the very thing that inspired its imitators. The American Revolution and the French Revolution may have shared a common name, but on deeper inspection, it is evident that the term *revolution* had no shared meaning. As with *revolution*, so with *liberty*: the Americans had one idea and the French had another, though they used the same word. The dichotomy between the French and American revolutions becomes nowhere more apparent than in the works of John Adams. Adams, though he was in the American sense of the term a bona fide revolutionary, could hardly be considered a Jacobin.

In the course of reading the Marquis de Condorcet's *Progress of the Human Mind*, Adams became so exercised at Condorcet's views that he felt compelled to write in the margins of the book. Condorcet believed that "no bounds have been fixed to the improvement of the human faculties, that the perfectibility of man is absolutely infinite," and that priests had become dupes of religious "fables" that enslave man. Adams was of another, equally forceful opinion. "Just as you and yours," he wrote in the margin, "have become the dupes of your own atheism and profligacy, your nonsensical notions of liberty, equality, and fraternity. . . . Your philosophy, Condorcet, has waged a more cruel war on truth than was ever attempted by king or priest." Later in the book, when Condorcet proposed the natural equality of mankind as the foundation of morality, Adams wrote, "there is no such thing [as morality] without the supposition of a God. There is no right or wrong in the universe without the supposition of a moral government and an intellectual and moral governor."[1]

The prime difference between the two revolutionary regimes, the American and the Jacobin, had to do with the moral law, a fact noted by Alexis de Tocqueville, one of the most perceptive observers of American mores. He also had the French Revolution fresh in his mind when he came to America to see whether democracy was indeed salvageable as a principle of social order. After touring the country and taking into account the peculiarities of government, geography, and mores, Tocqueville concluded that the uniqueness of the United States as a successful democracy, as opposed to the failed democracies of the classical world, had to do with American customs and their congruity with the moral law. Like Adams, but unlike Condorcet, Tocqueville saw religion and morals not only as compatible with democratic liberty, but as its sine qua non. Unlike the Jacobins, who saw religion as the enemy of "science" and progress, Tocqueville saw religion as the guardian of morals, which in turn became the guarantor of social order.

The distinction Tocqueville draws between revolutionary America and revolutionary France was a striking application of the same classical politics which Abbé Barruel drew on for his *History of Jacobinism*. Ethics, economics, and politics are three concentric circles radiating out from the good; they are, respectively, the way man achieves the good as an individual, as a member of a family, and as a member of the state. Tocqueville is at first struck by the absence of religion in public life in America, but concludes that appearances can be deceiving: "In the United States religion exercises but little influence upon the laws and upon the details of public opinion; but it directs the customs of the community, and, by regulating domestic life, it regulates the state."[2]

In this respect America is the antithesis of revolutionary France, where the revolutionary "tries to forget his domestic troubles by agitating society." In America, on the other hand, the average citizen "derives from his own home that love of order which he afterwards carries with him into public affairs":

> I do not question that the great austerity of manners that is observable in the United States arises, in the first instance, from religious faith. Religion is often unable to restrain man from the numberless temptations which chance offers; nor can it check that passion for gain which everything contributes to arouse, but its influence over the mind of woman is supreme, and women are the protectors of morals. There is certainly no country in the world where the tie of marriage is more respected than in America or where conjugal happiness is more highly or worthily appreciated. In Europe almost all the disturbances of society arise from the irregularities of domestic life. To despise the natural bonds and legitimate pleasures of home is to contract a taste for excesses, a restlessness of heart and fluctuating desires. Agitated by the tumultuous passions that frequently disturb his dwelling the European is galled by the obedience which the legislative powers of the state exact. But when the American retires from the turmoil of public life to the bosom of his family, he finds in it the image of order and peace. There his pleasures are simple and natural, his joys are innocent and calm; and as he finds that an orderly life is the surest path to happiness, he accustoms himself easily to moderate his opinions as well as his tastes. While the European endeavors to forget his domestic troubles by agitating society, the American derives from his own home that love of order which he afterwards carries with him into public affairs.[3]

If America is different—and Tocqueville thinks it is—the reason is simple: "There is no country in the world where the Christian religion retains a greater influence over the souls of men than in America." Liberty, as defined by the Enlightenment in France, was both a consequence of and an excuse for immoral behavior, and social chaos and terror were the results. In America, liberty and democracy succeeded because "every principle of the moral world is fixed and determinate." Social innovation and political adventurism find a natural brake in America because the tenets of the moral order are deeply ingrained in the mores of its citizens. A certain stability in the social order, therefore, necessarily follows: "Thus, the human mind is never left to wander over a boundless field; and whatever may be its pretensions, it is checked from time to time by barriers that it cannot surmount. Before it can innovate, certain primary principles are laid down, and the boldest conceptions are subjected to certain forms which retard and stop their completion." Moreover,

> The revolutionists of America are obliged to profess an ostensible respect for Christian morality and equity, which does not permit them to violate wantonly the laws that oppose their desires; nor would they find it easy to surmount the scruples of their partisans even if they were able to get over their own. Hitherto none in the United States has dared to advance the maxim that everything is permissible for the interests of society, an impious adage which seems to have been invented in an age of freedom to shelter all future tyrants. Thus, while the law permits the Americans to do what they please, religion prevents them from conceiving and forbids them to commit what is rash or unjust.[4]

Democracy, according to classical political theory, is the lowest form of government—and the last, because the unrestrained passions of "free" men invariably create so much social chaos that tyranny is the consequence. Put another way, because men could not impose order on themselves, as the ancients thought was invariably the case with democracy, order had to be imposed from without. Hence, tyranny is always the natural consequence of democracy. America proved this ancient maxim wrong by regulating freedom at its source. Self-government is saved from its own excesses by government of the self or, as Tocqueville demonstrated, because America's citizens adhere to the moral law, making dictatorship unnecessary.

Writing roughly 130 years after Tocqueville, John Courtney Murray, a Jesuit priest, made the same point in his seminal work, *We Hold These Truths*. Like Adams and Tocqueville, Murray saw a "radical distinction between the American and the Jacobin traditions" because America, although it has "its share of agnostics and unbelievers

. . . has never known organized militant atheism on the Jacobin, doctrinaire socialist or communist model; it has rejected parties and theories which erect atheism into a political principle." Freedom without morals is a contradiction in terms, one that was lived out to its horrific end in the French Revolution, the Weimar Republic, and the Soviet Union. The American experience, according to Murray, has been the very antithesis of the French Revolution: "Part of the inner architecture of the American ideal of freedom has been the profound conviction that only a virtuous people can be free. It is not an American belief that free government is inevitable, only that it is possible, and that its possibility can be realized only when the people as a whole are inwardly governed by the recognized imperatives of the universal moral law."[5]

Murray wrote those words in 1960 and died before the decade was out. He did not live to see the American experiment come crashing down around him, as though the culture he loved had taken his prediction as a dare. Murray made clear that the American "exception" had one cause: the moral order had been incorporated into American mores and allowed to flourish unimpeded by the American Constitution because it establishes a limited government. Adherence to the moral law was, in Murray's view, the sine qua non of freedom:

> The American experiment reposes on Acton's postulate, that freedom is the highest phase of civil society. But it also reposes on Acton's further postulate, that the elevation of a people to this higher phase of social life supposes, as its condition, that they understand the ethical nature of political freedom. They must understand, in Acton's phrase, that freedom is "not the power of doing what we like, but the right of being able to do what we ought." The people claim this right, in all its articulated forms, in the face of government; in the name of this right, multiple limitations are put upon the power of government. But the claim can be made with the full resonance of moral authority only to the extent that it issues from an inner sense of responsibility to a higher law. In any phase civil society demands order. In its highest phase of freedom, it demands that order should not be im-

posed from the top down, as it were, but should spontaneously flower outward from the free obedience to the restraints and imperatives that stem from inwardly possessed moral principle. In this sense democracy is more than a political experiment; it is a spiritual and moral enterprise. And its success depends upon the virtue of the people who undertake it. Men who would be politically free must discipline themselves. Likewise institutions which would pretend to be free with a human freedom in their workings must be governed from within and made to serve the ends of virtue. Political freedom is endangered in its foundations as soon as the universal moral values, upon whose shared possession the self-discipline of a free society depends, are no longer vigorous enough to restrain the passions and shatter the selfish inertia of men. The American ideal of freedom as ordered freedom, and therefore an ethical ideal, has traditionally reckoned with these truths, these truisms.[6]

"Men who would be politically free must discipline themselves." This is not only the essence of the American experiment, a political experiment based on a moral foundation, it is the antithesis of the Illuminist concept of Adam Weishaupt, who proposed, in the same year that Americans declared their independence, a way of governing men without their knowledge, first by ascertaining, and then by gratifying, their illicit passions. We have already shown how the Illuminist tradition was embraced by Shelley and his band of revolutionaries. *Frankenstein* was not only the chronicle of its failure, but the formula that would explain all future events based on its premises. *Frankenstein* was Mary Shelley's explanation of how the Illuminist notion of liberation invariably ended in horror.

Weishaupt's theory, however, did not die with Shelley. It was given new life by Freud and his band of psychoanalytic Illuminati. Psychoanalysis was simply a "scientific" way of ascertaining the passions. But the Illuminist tradition did not stop with Freud or his school, either. The intellectual equivalent of a venereal disease, it traveled from France to England, from England to Germany, and from Germany to the United States, following on the heels of revolution, ready to sap the vitality of the nation it would inhabit.

. . . . .

The vectors connecting Germany and the United States or, to be more specific, the Weimar Republic and Hollywood, were plentiful. After his stay in Berlin, Christopher Isherwood was drawn to Hollywood through his connection with Berthold Viertel. The immigration of prominent Weimar Republic refugees became so great that, during World War II, Hollywood harbored, if it did not become, a colony of German expatriates, sheltering in addition to actors like Conrad Veidt and Peter Lorre, novelists Thomas Mann and Franz Werfel (whose novel *The Song of Bernadette* became an Oscar-winning film in 1943). Arnold Schoenberg, the composer, was also in Hollywood. Schoenberg and his music became the inspiration for Mann's diabolical music novel *Doctor Faustus*. Mann collaborated with Theodor Adorno, whose musical theories were incorporated into *Doctor Faustus* as well. Adorno was part of the Frankfurt School, just about all of whose members made it to the United States. Herbert Marcuse ended up teaching in California and being a philosophical apologist for the cultural revolution of the 1960s. Paul Tillich, who was also at Frankfurt, carried his predilection for pornography and liberal theology to the Union Theological Seminary and eventually to Harvard University. There he was a colleague of Walter Gropius, who was expelled from Germany because of his advocacy of *Kulturbolschewismus*.

In general what happened to Gropius happened across the board in the post–World War II era. Whatever the Nazis called *Kulturbolschewismus* and, therefore, bad, became ipso facto good in the hands of cultural politicians like Adorno, who used the financial resources of the *Bundesrepublik* to promote Schoenberg, the twelve-tone system, and some of the most grating pieces of sonic torture devised by man.

The Illuminist concept was carried to the United States in attenuated form by all of these men, but in its most virulent form by Freud's nephew, Edward L. Bernays, the father of "public relations." In his early writings, Bernays was less linguistically astute. In 1928, he called public relations "propaganda," or "the conscious and intelligent manipulation of the organized habits and opinions of the masses."

"Those who manipulate this unseen mechanism of society," Bernays wrote in his book *Propaganda*, "constitute an invisible government which is the true ruling power of our country."[7] As time went on and Bernays' stature grew, he seemed to take a page from his own book and omit references to this invisible government, so redolent with Illuminist associations. The message, however, remained the same: the world is run by "invisible governors." He asserted that "in our social conduct or our ethical thinking, we are dominated by the relatively small number of persons—a trifling fraction of our hundred and twenty million—who understand the mental processes and social patterns of the masses. It is they who pull the wires which control the public mind, who harness old social forces and contrive new ways to bind and guide the world."

Compared to the refugees of the Weimar Republic, Bernays came early to the United States, before World War I, in time to work on the Committee on Public Information (CPI), the United States equivalent of a ministry of propaganda. There, as he later wrote in *Public Relations*, he "realized . . . as did others who had been engaged in various wartime promotional activities for the government," that "the publicity methods they had learned during the war" could be put to use on the civilian population after the war by "refining their methods and broadening the scope of their operations as the expanding postwar economy and the increasing complexity of their publics demanded." "When I left the CPI in 1919," Bernays concluded, "it was logical that, with my prewar experience in publicity and press agentry and my wartime CPI experience, I should follow a similar pattern of activity. With Doris E. Fleischman as my associate, I began working in the public relations field. We called our activity 'publicity direction.'"[8]

Although he used terms like democracy with ever-increasing frequency, it was soon apparent that what Bernays was proposing was the antithesis of democracy. The manipulation of pubic opinion had been around as long as men had had opinions, but it had come of age with the French Revolution, which began as a conscious manipulation of the instruments of culture. Bernays was merely exploiting something old that had been given new life by technological advances whose political implications no one quite understood until the outbreak of World War I.

"With the printing press and the newspaper, the railroad, the telephone, telegraph, radio and airplanes," Bernays wrote, "ideas can be spread rapidly and even instantaneously over the whole of America." What he did not mention is that those who control the new media also control the flow of information and the political power it confers. Thus, what on its face looked like an advance for "man" and "democracy" turned out to be especially advantageous for those who control the media of communication, since they form the opinions that become the invisible constitution of the republic.

Bernays tried to put a happy face on this development, but the iron fist of control kept appearing beneath the velvet glove of democracy and science. Literacy had increased, Bernays conceded, "but instead of a mind, universal literacy has given [man] rubber stamps, rubber stamps inked with advertising slogans, with editorials, with published scientific data, with the trivialities of the tabloids and the platitudes of history, but quite innocent of original thought."

"These examples," Bernays continued, trying to back away from his own conclusions, "are not given to create the impression that there is anything sinister about propaganda. They are set down rather to illustrate how conscious direction is given to events, and how the men behind these events influence public opinion." Propaganda, in other words, does nothing more than focus and organize public opinion, a task "necessary to orderly life."[9]

But whose order are we talking about? Order, for Bernays, was pretty much what the orderers say it is, a vicious circle of legal and technologically-driven positivism. Those with the power create the order because they have the power to create it. We have, in other words, the standard moral theory of the Enlightenment. Might is right because morality is nothing but the justification of the hegemony the powerful have over the weak. "Propaganda," according to Bernays, "is the executive arm of the invisible government": "There are invisible rulers who control the destinies of millions. It is not generally realized to what extent the words and actions of our most influential public men are dictated by shrewd persons operating behind the scenes. . . . In some departments of our daily life, in which we imagine ourselves free agents, we are ruled by dictators exercising great power. A man buying a suit of clothes imagines that he is choosing, according to his taste and his personality, the kind of garment which he prefers. In reality, he may be obeying the orders of an anonymous gentlemen tailor in London."[10]

As if again made uneasy by his own frankness, Bernays hastened to add that the public-relations counsel's "business is not to fool or hoodwink the public. If he were to get such a reputation, his usefulness in his profession would be at an end." Just why this is so, Bernays never explained. He also said that "if we accept public relations as a profession, we must also expect it to have both ideals and ethics," both of which turn out to be "pragmatic": "the ideal of the industry is to eliminate the waste and the friction that result when industry does things or makes things which its public does not want, or when the public does not understand what is being offered it."[11]

The ethics of the profession is even more vague, though it "compares favorably with that governing the legal and medical professions." It consists in refusing "a client whom he believes to be dishonest, a product which he believes to be fraudulent or a cause which he believes to be antisocial." Overall, Bernays tended to emphasize the power of the public relations man over his ethical responsibility, claiming that "in public opinion, the public relations counsel is judge and jury, because through his pleading of a case the public may accede to his opinion and judgment."[12]

Bernays's defense of his profession was more negative than positive. Public relations is not omnipotent, although it is very powerful. Ultimately the desires of the public act as a check on its power because you cannot get people to do or to buy something they do not like: "The public has its own standards and demands and habits. You may modify them, but you dare not run counter to them. You cannot persuade a whole generation of women to wear long skirts, but you may, by working through leaders of fashion, persuade them to wear evening dresses which are long in back. The public is not an amorphous mass which can be molded at will, or dictated to."[13]

Bernays seems here to step back from claims he made earlier. Public relations can manipulate opinion, but it cannot recreate human nature. Yet, when Bernays describes man, he is talking about nothing more than the locus of desire. A public relations counsel, according to Bernays, can no more create a desire than an artist can create a color. Men will only buy what they want. The public relations man cannot create this force, he can only direct its course. Herein lies man's freedom from the conditioners: the "invisible governors" cannot manufacture desires; they can only manipulate desires. Man is ultimately in control because his desires are ultimately his.

Left out of Bernays's discussion is the Illuminist realization that if passions control the man, he who controls the passions controls the man. What Bernays assumes is a most important point: some desires are licit, some are not. Those which are not are much more likely to become controlling passions because they have transgressed the bounds of reason and thus have no internal control. Passions are in need of a tyrant precisely because they are incapable of self-control. Weishaupt turned this truth into an instrument of political and social control.

Bernays is never as frank as Weishaupt, but Bernays's disingenuousness becomes apparent more than once. What he proposes is not a vehicle that promotes the smooth functioning of democracy, but rather something that subverts democracy at its very roots. "Men," Bernays tells us, "are rarely aware of the real reasons which motivate their actions." This lesson he learned from his Uncle Sigmund: "It is chiefly the psychologists of the school of Freud who have pointed out that many of man's thoughts and actions are compensatory substitutes for desires which he has been obliged to suppress. . . . This general principle, that men are very largely actuated by motives which they conceal from themselves, is as true of mass as of individual psychology. It is evident that the successful propagandist must understand the true motives and not be content to accept the reasons which men give for what they do."[14]

Bernays never really ponders the implications for democracy of his theory of public relations. Or if he does, he does not make the implications clear. The reason is not surprising, because at the heart of Bernays's theory is an antidemocratic irrationalism, the antithesis of republican self-government. Essential to self-government is the idea of man as a reasonable being, that is, one capable of discerning his own good and acting in a coherent fashion on what he discerns. For Bernays, on the other hand, man is a concatenation of desires that he himself does not understand. The only people who really understand are the Freudian-Illuminist hierophants, who rule men through the manipulation of their desires. Passion is essentially heteronomous—subject to external control—and therein lies its potential as an agent of control. "Human desires," Bernays says at another point, "are the steam which makes the social machine work. Only by understanding them can the propagandist control that vast, loose-jointed mechanism which is modern society." "Ours," he says, giving the clearest sense of what he means by democracy, "must be a leadership democracy administered by the intelligent minority who know how to regiment and guide the masses." Mass man, in other words, is not a reasonable being; he is the thrall of his own misunderstood desires, which can be manipulated at will by those, like Bernays, who really understand them, and thus maximize the wealth and power of the "invisible rulers." As to mass man himself, when he follows the command of the manipulators, "It will come to him as his own idea."[15]

We have here, in other words, the complete subversion of the American experiment brought about by turning man the reasoning being into man the locus of desire. The control of passion is much easier than the control of reasonable behavior. We have in Bernays the fulfillment of the Illuminist idea, which aspired to *the arts of knowing men and of governing them without constraint*." Or, in Weishaupt's words, to "teach the adepts the art of knowing men" but more than that, "to govern them without their perceiving it."[16]

Speaking for the countertradition, John Courtney Murray argued that "since a rational soul is the proper form of man, there is in every man a natural inclination to act according to reason; and this is to act according to virtue. To act against reason is to act against nature, that is, to sin."[17] It was precisely this fallen side of human nature, this propensity to "act against reason," this propensity to sin, that the Illuminist tradition was to exploit in the interest of expanding their control over men and the social order. Advertising is a systemization of this exploitation. That its appeal has become more and more overtly sexual over the course of the twentieth century only emphasizes the role that passion played as the steam for this engine of control.

Sexual liberation, from this point of view, simply assured that the manipulation of passion could proceed with maximal effect and bring profits and control to the manipulators. Sexual liberation meant that reason would be exposed to the disrupting influence of passion unhindered by law or customs, both of which were abolished by publicity campaigns run by people like Bernays, or people who had learned from Bernays, following World War ii. These campaigns would appeal to individuals seeking liberation, but they would be promoted by those who had the most to gain financially—the "invisible rulers" Bernays mentions in his book.

Given Bernays's essentially Illuminist notion of desire and the role it plays in the state, it is not surprising that sexual liberation would be fostered, not only by commercial entities, but also by the state which is ever interested in "governing [men] without restraint." But, again, some desires are licit; some are not. Those that are not tend to become addictive, and those who succumb to them more easily controlled. But they will not be conscious of the action of the instruments of control, but rather will think that they are acting on their own. Pandering to illicit desire becomes then the perfect vehicle for subverting democracy, because democratic man feels that he is acting out his own will in the very act of enslaving himself to the manipulators of his desire. The sinister nature of this control became apparent to those with sufficient intelligence to understand what was going on. In *Brave New World*, Aldous Huxley wrote about the substitution for love of sex as an instrument of control. For those who were still not satisfied there was soma, a drug that overwhelmed resistance with pleasure.

· · · · ·

It was inevitable that the fear of control would manifest itself in the movies because the movies, an instrument of mass culture, would inevitably have to deal with the fears of the masses. But the movies were also one of the prime instruments of control, as Bernays himself made clear when he claimed that "the American motion picture is the greatest unconscious carrier of propaganda in the world today. It is a great distributor for ideas and opinions": "Motion pictures can standardize the ideas and habits of a nation. Because pictures are made to meet market demands, they reflect, emphasize and even exaggerate broad popular tendencies, rather than stimulate new ideas and opinions. The motion picture avails itself only of ideas and facts which are in vogue. As the newspaper seeks to purvey news, it seeks to purvey entertainment."[18] Film is a medium rife with ambivalence: to purvey is not to analyze. That means film is ripe for horror, because horror is the expression of ambivalence: we do not know the cause of what is going wrong, for we *are* the cause of what is going wrong.

The Enlightenment, Murray makes clear, citing Perry Miller, did not arise in this country with the American Revolution. It came much later through the universities. And it did not affect the culture at large until after World War II, when the influence of German *Kulturbolschewismus*, their Enlightenment, began to make inroads, largely through the de-Nazification and subsequent dissemination of the thought of Nietzsche at American universities. When the Enlightenment arrived in America, it had the same effect on the American mind as it had had on the German mind during the Weimar Republic; it was perceived as a monster at the beck and call of the scientist who manipulated him—and who invariably spoke with an accent, usually German. In many respects, Hollywood adopted the same monsters. There was no Dr. Caligari or Dr. Mabuse, but we did have Dr. Frankenstein, who embodied the general perception that the Enlightenment was now a German phenomenon and its main vectors were Germans.

Once the war broke out, the enemy, until then a nameless dread, was named, and as a result horror films all but disappeared during the 1940s. That is paradoxical because the 1940s was a decade filled with horror, but then again, the horror of war is not the horror that drives the horror genre. Horror thrives only when the distinction between good and evil has been lost—indeed, the presence of horror is the sign that the distinction has been repressed and forgotten. All of the details that might contribute to a sense of horror—blood and gore, mutilation and dismemberment—all take place during wartime, but since World War II was a war that Hollywood almost unanimously saw as a struggle between good and evil, none of these horrific details fueled the horror genre. Knowing how a particular death or injury fits into the context of the moral order deprives it of its usefulness for a horror movie. Boris Karloff, Lon Chaney, and Bela Lugosi continued to make their kind of film during the 1940s, but this had more to do with Hollywood's penchant for sequels than anything else. These films were holdovers from an earlier, less morally polarized period, a period when neither the forces of good nor evil had coalesced.

Along with the reemergence of the moral in the 1940s came a parallel reemergence of the distinction between "us" and "them." In Hollywood in the 1940s, "we" were good, and "they" were bad. The Nazis thought the same about their cause, of course. But the Nazis felt that they were good because of what they were, that is, members of a certain race. Hollywood, on the other hand, felt that we were good because of how we acted. America was different precisely because our mores were congruent with the moral order, as Adams and Tocqueville had said, and not because of our blood or some other mystical characteristic. Someone with relativist proclivities could portray the conflict as one of "conflicting moralities," but that simply does not do justice to the conflict. The major difference between America and Nazi Germany had to do with the moral law. In an increasingly tenuous and inchoate way, perhaps, America was America because it was moral; Nazi Germany was Nazi Germany because of race and blood. Americans could say that they represented the good in a nonrelativist way and without embarrassment.

As long as moral causality remained in view, there was no need for horror. Good people act one way; evil people, another. The distinction precludes horror because it contextualizes human suffering by keeping the purpose of that suffering in clear view. We follow the law; they do not. We respect innocent human life; they do not. They participate in atrocities; we prevent atrocities. Alfred Hitchcock attempted to articulate these differences in his collaboration with John Steinbeck in *Lifeboat*.

Perhaps more than any other top director to come out of Hollywood, Hitchcock is the name most commonly associated with horror and the macabre. *Psycho* is probably his most famous film, as well as the most famous horror film ever made. But during the 1940s, Hitchcock was not associated exclusively with horror films. In fact, that he ended his career that way is more an indication of the cultural trajectory I am trying to describe than any predilection on his part. Hitchcock could not have been so successful a director without a clear understanding of what was on the public's mind, and in 1942 a trans-Atlantic shipwreck was a bigger concern than a psychotic motel owner. Which is why Hitchcock collaborated with John Steinbeck on *Lifeboat*. If *Psycho* was the image of our culture's fears in 1960, *Lifeboat* was that image in 1942. *Psycho* was a horror movie, and *Lifeboat* was not, even though there is more death and carnage in the latter than in the former.

*Lifeboat* begins with Tallulah Bankhead, playing a wealthy writer, Constance Porter, sitting alone in a mink coat in the lifeboat of a ship just sunk by a Nazi submarine. Before long the ship's other survivors make their way to the boat, and in so doing create what the lifeboat genre has always created, namely, a microcosm of our society. As C.D. Rittenhouse, a rich factory owner, explains, "Now we're all sort of fellow travelers in a small boat on one mighty ocean." The boat is our culture reduced to its most basic elements, allowing a type of analysis to see what makes it tick. The first problem the survivors have to solve is whether they are different from the people they are fighting.

After comforting a woman with a dead baby, the survivors are given a more difficult assignment: what to do with a Nazi survivor, the captain of the attacking ship who created the carnage in the first place—what to do, in other words, with the baby killer. The initial reaction of the survivors is instinctive and violent. They want to throw the captain overboard; they want to kill him just as he killed so many of their compatriots. But the reaction is not universal. War becomes a mitigating factor. Miss Porter claims that the captain, who says that he is an ordinary seaman, was only following orders. The excuse carries no weight with the other survivors, however. Certain actions are wrong no matter what the circumstances, and those who have been ordered to take the lives of innocent people should simply refuse.

Kovac, one of the survivors, is a communist, and therefore the survivor who is most inclined to action and least inclined to be bound by the moral law. His solution is to "throw the Nazi overboard." But the rest of the survivors object, sensing immediately and intuitively that that sort of action would put them on the same level as the Nazis they are fighting. The captain is guilty of a crime, but the lifeboat society is not competent to assume the functions of the state and punish the crime. A debate ensues. Kovac asserts that since the circumstances are extraordinary, they can consider themselves not "against the law," but the authors of the law: "Whose law is it?" Kovac wonders. "In the middle of the ocean, we're the law." The rest of the survivors find the argument unpersuasive.

Kovac eventually wrests command of the lifeboat from the hands of the ineffectual Rittenhouse. What Kovac cannot do, though, is convince the survivors that they are the ultimate arbiters of right and wrong. When Kovac attempts to bully his way into executing the German captain, claiming that "the boat's too small for me and the German," the majority holds its ground against him. "I'm perfectly willing to abide by the tactics of the majority," says Rittenhouse, "but if we harm this man we're guilty of the same tactics they are." The United States, as is made obvious by the composition of the lifeboat crew, is a multiracial, multiethnic society. The lifeboat survivors could not make use of the Nazi principle of social unity based on blood even if they wanted to. Instead of killing the captain, Rittenhouse suggests that "we might be able to convert him to our way of thinking. That's the Christian way."

As the debate rages back and forth, it becomes clear that survival has a dual meaning. The activist party wants to throw the Nazi captain to the sharks partly out of a desire for revenge, partly because they think this will guarantee their survival. The party of reason, however, claims they have not got the right to do this. "He's a prisoner of war," says one of the men, "and according to international law" the survivors have to take him "alive to the proper authorities." But the deeper threat has to do with the crew's spiritual survival. The same group of people might make it to land if they killed the captain, but in the process they would have destroyed their identity as a group somehow different from the Nazis. They would no longer be distinguishable from "them," from the other. They would cease to exist as soon as they adopted the tactics of their enemies. It is the insight of this film, albeit suppressed perhaps in the interest of the war effort (we now know that the communists were virtually indistinguishable from the Nazis in their brutality and contempt for morals), that those who behave in an immoral manner are indistinguishable from each other. No matter what our faults, "we" do not act in such a manner. The whole concept of "us" is bound up with that fact. If we cease to distinguish ourselves from the enemy in terms of the moral law, then "we" have in effect ceased to exist because we are no different from "them." Hollywood's version of the moral law puts a premium on action, specifically the moral quality of the action, as the prime distinguishing mark between "us" and "them."

Eventually the conflict is resolved dramatically as the two poles are brought together. The woman with the dead child suddenly comes to her senses and realizes that her child is dead and that the captain, the killer, is right in front of her. As the other survivors watch, she pushes the dead baby into the captain's arms, as if to confront him with the enormity of what he has done, and begins to beat him with her fists. It is the dead baby, in other words, that brings the survivors to their senses. If they kill the captain, they are the moral equivalent of baby killers, which in the vocabulary of the film is the most heinous crime imaginable. Their solution is to bury the baby at sea, with a recitation of Psalm 23, and to allow the captain to stay, even if that jeopardizes (and it does) their chances for survival.

The German proves less than willing to adopt the values of the majority of the lifeboat survivors, but not before he has provided some valuable services. He amputates one of the survivors' gangrenous leg after informing them that he was a surgeon in civilian life. The comment prompts Kovac to reply that the only operations he ever performed were probably illegal, a veiled reference to abortion. The

German captain is also the only one on board with a compass and as a result assumes virtual and, before too long, actual command of the boat as he rows it alone toward a rendezvous with a Nazi supply ship. The captain, it turns out, also speaks English and French. He is, in other words, a cultured person, a man skilled in science, and a magnificent physical specimen as well, able to row for hours on end, singing away. He is, as the crew members note, a striking example of the master race.

But what distinguishes the master race from us is their failure to adhere to the canons of civilized behavior. The German's strength comes from the water and food he has hidden and refused to share with the others. His surgical skills save a life, but when his patient becomes delirious with thirst after having drunk sea water, the Nazi not only refuses to share his water, he encourages him to jump overboard, adding euthanasia to his other crimes.

When confronted by the survivors, the Nazi captain can only mouth the quality-of-life ethic that allowed him to commit his crimes against humanity in the first place. "You can't imagine how painful it was for me," he tells the crew by way of self-justification. "All night turning and suffering. There was nothing I could do for him. The best way to help him was to let him go. I had no right to stop him, a poor cripple dying of hunger and thirst. What good could life be to a man like that? He's better off dead." The explanation is too much for the others. When the flask of water the Nazi has been hiding falls to the floor of the boat and breaks, the crew falls on him as one man and throws him overboard. They then relapse into stunned silence, contemplating what they have done. The master race, it seems, is insensible to kindness and scorns conversion.

Hitchcock and Steinbeck make a number of points about ourselves, our system of government, and our differences with our enemy. But when the war ended this sense of moral distinction faded, and with the fading of moral clarity, the uncanny started to reappear. Like the 1930s, the 1950s saw the resurgence of horror films. The culture was aware that some new evil was afoot, but the evil had not yet been defined in any clear way. Horror, again, was an indication of confusion. One enemy had been defeated, but another enemy had taken its place. The threat of communist subversion lent itself more to the horror film because it was much less overt. The communists, it turned out, were no more bound by the moral law than the Nazis, but they differed from the Nazis in the means that they employed to attain their ends. Unlike the Nazis, whose military conquest had been repelled, the communists achieved their ends while appearing to be our friends. Instead of overpowering us with force, the communists relied on subversion, on tunneling secretly through our institutions.

*Them!* is a science fiction-horror film of the early 1950s that addresses precisely these fears. It begins, as horror films tend to do, with things going wrong and no one able to explain why. A little girl is found wandering alone in the desert; her family's trailer nearby has been shredded by something, a something that has not bothered to take her parents' money or valuables. The only thing missing is sugar. Later, the same sort of destruction befalls the local grocery store not far away. Again, nothing is missing but sugar. A policeman who stays behind to investigate the circumstances surrounding the break-in is mysteriously killed.

Solving the mystery requires the collaboration of both science and the military, neither of which has an easy time understanding the other's language. James Arness, the FBI agent assigned to the case, is just as perplexed at hearing scientific terminology as Edmund Gwenn, the scientist, is when he is expected to communicate by radio while flying over the desert in a helicopter. The message is clear: In America, no one group can combat this new evil alone. Science is helpless without military force; and military force cannot be applied in an effective manner without the expertise of science.

But behind both science and the military stands something more important still that gives them their reason for being, namely, the defense of innocent life. When giant ants are discovered to be the culprits and are tracked to a sewer in Los Angeles, one of the military men suggests that "we pour gasoline in the drain and light it," only to be reminded by James Arness, the FBI agent, that "we need to find out if the kids are in there." (Two children are missing.) The general immediately takes the utilitarian approach to this moral dilemma: "Are we supposed to jeopardize the lives of the people in this city for two kids who may already be dead?" he asks.

The film provides no answer to that question, if by an answer we mean a refutation of the consequentialism it implies. This lack of an answer can be construed as either good or bad: good in that the culture felt intuitively that the suggestion was wrong and did not need an answer; bad in that when the question was posed explicitly roughly twenty years later, the culture had no answer. All that the FBI agent can do is counter with another question: "Why don't you ask their mother that question, mister?" "Yeah, she's right over there," says James Whitmore, who plays a policeman. "I see what you mean," says the utilitarian, and the discussion ends with the right answer, even if there was no reasoning leading to it.

The military then enters the sewer, James Whitmore finds the children, and in getting them out of harm's way dies in the mandibles of one of the giant ants. The message is obvious: the purpose of science and its collaboration in the creation of technology and military might is the preservation of innocent human life, particularly of children and the family.

The only essential difference between *Them!* and *Lifeboat* is the nature of the enemy. In *Lifeboat*, the enemy is understood from a moral point of view; in *Them!* the enemy is a "monster," which is to say something that we do not understand. Edmund Gwenn describes the ants as "savage, ruthless and courageous fighters." They are "the only other creatures on earth that make war"; they are "chronic aggressors, and make slaves of their captives"; they have "an instinct and talent for industry, social organization, and savagery that make man look feeble by comparison." It could be the communists, or it could be us, but the fear is in the future tense in *Them!* We might become insects if we acted as they do.

．　．　．　．　．

*Them!* was released in 1954. In the history of sexual toleration, 1954 was truly an *annus mirabilis,* because in that year syphilitic contamination reached the lowest point since its introduction to Europe in 1496. In 1928, a Scottish doctor by the name of Alexander Fleming had discovered that the mold *Penicillium notatum* had as one of its properties the ability to kill bacteria. After a team of Oxford researchers purified the mold of toxic qualities in 1939, penicillin became a viable medicine that showed conclusive clinical results on humans by 1941 and almost immediately went into industrial production. Penicillin became the "magic bullet" that killed syphilis.

As a result, the aftermath of World War II was quite different from that of World War I, especially for the victorious Americans. If Dracula films were made in America after World War II, they were strictly parody and carried none of the psychic import that Murnau's *Nosferatu* had for the Weimar Republic. World War II was every bit as destructive of sexual morals for the millions of soldiers involved, but the disease they contracted now had a cure, and so the terror-inspiring specter of syphilis began to fade. In 1951, the U.S. Public Health Service published a report declaring that after six years of treating early syphilis with penicillin, 98 percent of those treated were cured.[19] Moreover, pregnant women with syphilis who were treated with penicillin before the fifth month of pregnancy did not transmit the syphilis to their children. The heredo was now a thing of the past.

The success of penicillin as a treatment for syphilis was so spectacular that it created the sense that the disease was no longer a threat, and this perception contributed to the sexually liberated morals of the 1960s—and a resurgence of the disease. The sudden evaporation of this terror just after World War II, thanks to the miraculous new antibiotics, is an astonishing social phenomenon. There was an instantaneous shift from an almost insane fear of to a complete lack of concern about the disease. From that point, all that was required to destroy the fragile treponema (so fragile that it is impossible to produce a laboratory culture of it, and, therefore, a vaccine) was a few hefty doses of penicillin. Syphilis became no more than a unpleasant memory, and folks could resume their depravities without fear.

This is not to say that the decline in sexual morals did not have consequences, but the consequences were not the same as those following World War I. In America, the main sexual fallout from the war was not venereal disease, but a skyrocketing divorce rate. Hollywood, sensitive to the new sexual freedom, did not make films about the horrors of sexual desire, but began behaving much like the returning soldiers. Having done its patriotic duty by providing a steady stream of propaganda films for the war effort, Hollywood now turned its attention to something more galling than the Nazis and considerably closer to home, namely the Production Code, which among other things prohibited nudity and profanity in films. Hollywood got a foretaste of the profits it might enjoy when Jane Russell, or certain parts of her, caused *Esquire's* circulation to jump by 186,000 copies. When Russell appeared—clothed, it should be noted—in *The Outlaw*, it outdrew *Gone With the Wind* in Atlanta, and grossed three million dollars—a sum unheard of at the time.

The situation became especially critical as the 1950s progressed. Films began to feel the competition of newer media like television, which filled the airways with refugees from vaudeville and Hollywood. William Bendix, after having his leg cut off in *Lifeboat*, went on to get his own television series, *The Life of Riley*, as did Ward Bond and Alfred Hitchcock. Hollywood was forced to rethink its way back to the glory days. One strategy was the expensive spectacular that television could not afford to produce. Rome became a movie boom town because it was less costly to make movies there, and films like *Ben Hur* and *Cleopatra* were the result.

But why, the Hollywood moguls must have wondered, build elaborate and expensive sets, when God had done the work for you, in a manner of speaking, by creating some well-endowed female who could be induced to remove her clothes in front of the camera? Were it not for the obstructive and antiquated morality of the Hays office, Hollywood could have been beating the brains out of television and making money hand over fist. And thus the war against the Production Code began.

This was another reason why many horror films were made in the 1950s. The feeling that we could not identify the enemy was mixed in with and gradually succeeded by an even more dreadful feeling that we ourselves were the enemy; that we, by making some of us—well-endowed women—instruments of pleasure for others, were in effect doing to ourselves the things that we had fought the war to prevent other people from doing to us. The distinction between "us" and "them" was getting progressively more blurred. Nowhere is this sense of confusion and ambivalence stronger than in the Don Siegel film, *Invasion of the Body Snatchers*. Siegel would go on to do *Dirty Harry*, one of the seminal films of the 1970s. Both films portray the fear that the country is being taken over, or has been taken over, by alien forces that look just like us but are intent on destroying us. In the case of *Dirty Harry*, the alien beings were the members of the Warren Supreme Court, who rendered the *Escobeda* and *Miranda* rulings which hamstrung police. Siegel said the idea of doing *Invasion of the Body Snatchers* came from Walter Wanger, the film's producer, who had read Jack Finney's novella *Body Snatchers* when it appeared in serialized form in *Collier's* magazine in 1954. Finding something especially appealing in the Finney story, something that spoke to the spirit of the times, Siegel immediately agreed.

"Many of my associates are pods," Siegel said later, "people who have no feeling of love or emotion, who simply exist, breathe and sleep. I thought the picture exposed that very well." "To be a pod," according to Siegel's interpretation of the story, "means that you have no passion, no anger, that you talk automatically, that the spark of life has left you." As such, the best possible spokesman for the new race of pod people who are taking over the country without a struggle would be a "pod psychiatrist," which is to say an Americanized version of the Freudian school. In Siegel's view, "He speaks with authority, knowledge. He really believes that being a pod is preferable to being a frail, frightened human who cares. He has a strong case for being a pod. How marvelous it would be if you're a cow and all you had to do is munch a little grass and not worry about life, death, and pain. There's a strong case for being a pod. That's why there are so many of them. The pods in my picture and in the world believe they are doing good when they convert people into pods. They get rid of pain, ill health, mental anguish. It leaves you with a dull world, but that, my dear friend, is the world in which most of us live."[20]

Siegel expressed the concern that "conformity" was threatening to subvert the values that characterized American life during the 1950s. When framed in terms like this, it is not surprising in the 1990s that most people would fail to see the threat. But that is precisely why the idea got cast as a horror film, because the danger, though present, was not clear in the 1950s. Hence the need in the film to stay awake at all costs. Siegel related the fear of sleep to his own chronic insomnia: "One of the reasons insomniacs are afraid to sleep is that they fear they won't wake up. The parallel is there. . . . I have suffered so much from chronic insomnia that I would have like to have turned into a pod."[21]

Siegel, like Dr. Miles Binnell in *Body Snatchers*, knows that something is going wrong but cannot quite put his finger on the cause. (In this he a typical protagonist of a whole genre of Hollywood films that might be called alienated-white-guy films.) Missing from Siegel's *Body Snatchers* is the sexual element, specifically divorce, the principal sexual issue in 1954. This is a surprising omission, in a way, since it figures so prominently in Finney's novella. Within moments of meeting each other, the topic arises in Miles's conversation with Becky Driscoll, whom he dated in high school:

"I said, 'Becky, I heard about your divorce, of course, and I'm sorry.'

"She nodded, 'Thanks, Miles. And I've heard about yours. I'm sorry too.'

"I shrugged. 'Guess we're lodge brothers now.'

"We had both married, neither had been able to make it work, and now we were back in our staid little home town."

Binnell is twenty-eight years old, a medical doctor in the state of California for one year, who plays golf and swims whenever he can, "so I'm always pretty tanned." Binnell's father had been a medical doctor before him. Since his divorce, Miles has been living in the family home, "a big old-fashioned frame house with plenty of big trees and lots of lawn around it." The dichotomy between the small town and divorce is introduced right away and developed throughout the story. The opposition between divorce as the 1954 stand-in for sexual liberation and the mores of the American small town drives the story: "I feel at ease with you, Miles," Becky says at one point. "I suppose it's because we've been divorced. . . . In Santa Mira it does make a difference."

The two young divorcees find each other sexually attractive, and the more the attraction grows, the more the pods proliferate. In the inchoate manner typical of the horror genre, there is a causal connection here that never is expressed causally. In horror films, the closest thing to causality is what logicians call the *post hoc ergo propter hoc* (after this, therefore because of this) fallacy. If Miles (or Finney, for that matter) could establish moral causality, then neither of them would be involved in the uncanny, and *Body Snatchers* would not be a horror story. The moral connections are all established by temporal juxtapositions, which seem like coincidences, but only add to the uncanny sense that pervades the work. The very thing Miles fears is always the very thing that happens, precisely because his fears are the cause of everything that happens. But also because at the root of his fear there is a desire that he is unable to relinquish—the sexual desire, the desire for sexual experience beyond the moral order typified by Santa Mira, the staid American small town where everyone knows everyone else. "In Santa Mira, divorce makes a difference," says Becky. "Well, of course that was it," Miles responds, "and now I realized it."

The root of the uncanny in this story is Miles's ambivalence about sexual morality. Miles wants it both ways: he wants the nice homey small-town atmosphere, but he is also divorced, something which he tries to render harmless ("It just didn't work out"), but which he knows entails more that something that just happened to two innocent bystanders. He wants something that he knows is impossible—sexual liberation—but he also wants the tight-knit social fabric that can only be based on the inviolability of the marriage bond. In his ambivalence, Miles mirrors the nation at the time. Imbued with an awe of Enlightenment-scientist ideology as a result of victory in war, the nation was ready to tinker with the social fabric in accord with premises which, as John Adams, Alexis de Tocqueville, and John Courtney Murray could have told them, were completely antithetical to the American experiment.

The Enlightenment was about to arrive in America for the first time, and as always it would appear as a monster, in this instance as pods descending from the sky to colonize the country in a way that would be invisible to most of its citizens. The engine for social subversion is the sexual impulse, which, by means of divorce, had now been cut off from the social order. When Miles brings Becky home from their first date he engages in sexual banter that ends with the suggestion that he tuck her into bed, causing Becky to respond by citing Shakespeare: "That way lies madness." Miles, however, continues to be the obtuse white guy and asks, "What's wrong with madness?" To which Becky replies, "Madness." Libido, in other words, is the fuel that causes the pods to proliferate, even though Miles never seems to realize it. As soon as the scene ends, the pod of Jack Bellicec opens its eyes.

In part two of the novella, the sexual pursuit continues. Miles finally kisses Becky and discovers "four giant seed pods in the basement" after giving us a reading of his own libido: "I wanted this kiss very much. I felt her lips, soft and strong, felt my hands pressed hard against her back and the terrible thrill of her body against mine. I'd never in my life experienced anything like this." Why, at this point, was the thrill of holding Becky's body described as "terrible" if not because its gratification is linked in some uncanny way with the proliferation of the pods? The thing he desires the most is linked to the thing he fears the most in a way that he cannot explain or understand. So Becky was right. Pursuing libido on these terms, that is, outside of marriage, leads to madness. At both the beginning and end of the film, Miles finds himself in a psychiatrist's office.

Miles knows that there is something seriously wrong with the country. He tells Bellicec, "I have a terrible urge to call the President at the White House, or the head of the Army, the FBI, the Marines or something." What he cannot face is the fact that his own behavior is the cause of the problem, nor for that matter could the country at that time, as divorce proliferated and slowly shaded over into other forms of sexual liberation with even more deleterious social consequences. "The local or state police can't do it," Miles continued, "they haven't the authority—this is a national emergency. The Army, the Navy, the

FBI, I don't know who or what, but somebody has to move into this town as fast as we can get them here. And they'll have to declare martial law, a state of siege or something—anything! And then do whatever has to be done." his voice dropped. "Root this thing out, smash it, crush it, kill it."

Santa Mira is faced with a big problem, and the biggest part of the problem is that no one understands its source in the libido, the pleasant sensation that gradually overwhelms them and lulls them to sleep. Certainly the average citizen, who eventually gets absorbed by the alien force, does not understand. But in his way, Miles does not understand either, even though he states over and over again the juxtapositions necessary to understanding it.

When the line goes dead on a call to the FBI in San Francisco, Miles is seized by panic, the sense that "something impossible, terrible, yet utterly real, was menacing us in a way beyond our comprehension or abilities." As long as he confronts the monster as something from out there, Miles remains helpless against "this unknown enemy."[22] Only when the discussion returns to divorce, which seemingly has nothing to do with the monster menacing Santa Mira, does a solution loom on the horizon.

Upon returning to Santa Mira, the couple has a long talk with a Professor Budlong, who, as a typical representative of the Enlightenment, does nothing more than restate the moral problem in "scientific" terms, making the situation mystifying and hopeless. The pods come from an ancient planet that is slowly dying. As a result, the pods' creatures have to seek life elsewhere because "the function of life everywhere [is] survival": "What happens when an ancient planet slowly dies? Well, the life forms on it must prepare. For what? For survival, for leaving that planet. To arrive where? and when? There can be only one answer . . . universal adaptability—to any and all other lifeforms, under any and all other conditions it might possibly encounter. . . . These pods have achieved it. They are completely evolved life, its ultimate form. For they have the evolved ability to reform and reconstitute themselves into perfect duplication, cell for living cell, of any lifeform they may encounter, in whatever conditions that life has suited itself for."[23]

The pod creatures, though cleansed now of any association they had with blood or syphilis, are the same Darwinian monster that infected the Weimar Republic. Because of that, there seems to be nothing negative associated with them; their takeover is seen as benign even by the people who get taken over. They are "the parasites of the universe," but unlike Dracula and syphilis seem to produce no deleterious side-effects, no hideous red marks, no GPI, nothing but a sense of eerie calm. The streets seem "dead" calm.

The more Miles and Becky talk with the professor the more hopeless the situation becomes because the professor, as representative of the first institutions in the United States to convert to the Enlightenment, is "one of them." Becky knows that the professor "wasn't what he seemed" because "he had no emotions . . . no real feelings any more, but only the memory and pretense of them." When confronted by Miles and Becky, Professor Budlong can only admit that they are right: "Emotion, you say. Hope and ambition. Well, I don't miss them; I really don't. And neither will you." The confrontation with Professor Budlong convinces Miles that the situation, at least as Budlong describes it, is hopeless: "And now I knew what a terrible mistake we had made in coming back to Santa Mira, how helpless we were against whatever was running this town."[24]

At this point, the film begins to differ significantly from the original novella. In the film, Becky becomes "one of them" and Miles escapes, only to be thought insane—"That way lies madness"—but vindicated by a chance traffic accident when a truck carrying the pods overturns on the highway. The novella is more sophisticated in a way. Becky does not become one of them; in fact, the turning point comes when Becky and Miles decide, after listening to Professor Budlong's Darwinian mumbo jumbo, to get married. "I wish we'd been married, Becky," Miles says almost as an afterthought, in reality bringing the plot of the novella back to its main theme. "Miles," Becky answers, "why didn't we?"[25]

The question forces Miles to rethink his own failed marriage from a new perspective: "I thought," he says to himself, "the fact that we had both been divorced somehow made us different, but now I knew it didn't. We were the same as everyone else, making mistakes, seeking happiness." "Miles," Becky says, "we had a better chance than most. We knew what failure was like, something of what caused it, and a little of how to guard against it." The sudden realization that marriage is a possibility for both of them fills Miles with a new sense of purpose in life and a strengthened resolve to defeat the pod creatures: "Suddenly, I was as determined as I've ever been in my life. I was going to marry Becky! I was going to defeat those pods single-handed if I had to. Nothing was going to stop me."[26]

The juxtaposition is significant—"I was going to marry Becky! I was going to defeat those pods"—because it reiterates the juxtaposition of seemingly unrelated events that created the crisis in the first place. If divorce had created the monsters, then marriage would defeat them. But the passage is not without ambivalence. Is marriage, in this instance, a repudiation of divorce as the thing that caused the problem, or is marriage a celebration of divorce as a way of giving people who have made a mistake a second chance? There is no way to resolve this ambiguity in this particular fictional universe. As with most cases of ambivalence, the solution in *Body Snatchers* is probably consistent with the ambivalence that drives the horror tradition—the solution involves mutually contradictory alternatives.

Whatever its status, Miles's sudden understanding of marriage frees him from the lethargy and befuddlement that Budlong's Darwinism induced, and frees him, if not to think clearly, at least to act decisively. After soaking the field where the pods are growing in gasoline, he sets them on fire and feels "a wave of terrible exultation" spread through him as the "great pods were leaving a fierce and inhospitable planet . . . for I knew what I had done in simply refusing to give up." Suddenly, "a war-time speech of Churchill's" comes to Miles's mind: "'We shall fight them in the streets, we shall fight in the hills, we shall never surrender.' True then for one people, it was true always, and for the whole human race, and I understood now that nothing in the whole vast universe could ever defeat us. And I knew that Becky and I had provided the final demonstration of that last unchangeable fact."[27]

But in spite of all the talk about gasoline and Churchill and the war, the key to understanding the defeat of the pods lies in understanding the role that "Becky and I" played. A little later, Miles says,

"We're together, Becky and I, for better or worse." The reference to marriage is again unmistakable, as is the reference to divorce, which is a repudiation of the marriage vow. So perhaps the final message is a repudiation of divorce. But since both Miles and Becky are themselves divorced, the ambivalence remains, which is why *Body Snatchers* remains part of the horror genre.

. . . . .

*Body Snatchers* was one film that expressed Hollywood's ambivalence at the sexual liberation which was just over the horizon in the late 1950s. *Forbidden Planet* was another.

Released in 1956, directed by John Milius, and starring Walter Pidgeon and Leslie Nielson, *Forbidden Planet* begins in outer space, which is to say, the realm of subconscious conflict, in this instance Hollywood itself. Billed as a remake of Shakespeare's *Tempest*, it is about the "brave new world" in both senses of the term. It is about America, the "new world" and American innocence. But it is also about the advent of a "brave new world" in Huxley's use of the term, the soft totalitarianism of the sexually liberated Illuminist regime where the drug soma is the ultimate solution to every problem.

As the spaceship approaches the planet Altair, one of the crew says, "The Lord sure makes some beautiful worlds." *Forbidden Planet* was in this regard a throwback to the Hollywood that represented American values (the commander of the spaceship is named John Adams)—the Hollywood of *Lifeboat*. The breaking of the decency code was still nine years away. But the sense of imminent sexual transgression pervades the film. Morbius, the scientist who is the lone survivor of the initial voyage to the planet and has no desire to return to earth, has a nineteen-year-old daughter, Altaira, who immediately catches the eye of the officers of the newly arrived space ship. Morbius and his daughter, like Prospero and Miranda, live in a paradise of wild animals who act tame in their presence. But once Altaira begins to show sexual interest in the crew's commander, the animals are no longer tame. Passion has a disruptive force on paradise, and Altaira loses her innocence. Soon people start dying—crew members are killed in their sleep by something that no one can see, either with the naked eye or its electronic enhancements.

In trying to solve the murders, the commander has to solve the mystery surrounding the original crew's disappearance, and this leads him to the history of the planet, which was inhabited long ago by a superior race of beings known as the Krell. The Krell possessed technology immeasurably superior to Earth's and were on the verge of some dramatic cultural breakthrough when they all mysteriously died off, leaving only the underground artifacts of their culture behind, which Morbius discovered and appropriated to his own use. Gradually, it becomes clear that the disappearance of the Krell, the death of the first crew, and the new murders have one and the same cause. After the ship's scientist attempts to increase his intelligence by taking the Krell "brain boost," a misguided attempt that proves fatal, it becomes apparent that the monster in question is not something "out there." "The Krell forgot one thing," Doc says, just before he dies, "monsters from the Id." The monster, in other words, is simply Morbius's "own subconscious desire for lust and destruction," projected by means of Krell technology onto anyone who threatens his outer space idyll.

*Forbidden Planet* is, in other words, a warning. Like the Krell and their "brave new world," America has achieved unprecedented technological heights, all of which are now threatened by "monsters from the Id." The term is at root Freudian; it refers primarily to libido or sexual desire, but recognizes in its way that sexual desire unmoored from the moral order becomes almost automatically destructive to both individuals and their culture. Libido becomes, in other words, the Achilles' heel of any culture that puts Enlightenment beliefs into practice. Science becomes the justification for jettisoning the moral order, and at that point the very same technologies cease to provide protection against the forces they have unleashed.

When Morbius's daughter throws in her lot with the spaceship's commander and decides to return to earth without her father, Morbius can no longer contain his rage, which now, thanks to Krell technology, becomes a monster with a being all its own, stalking not only his daughter and the ship's commander, but Morbius himself. Robbie the Robot, programmed to defend Morbius, goes into a state of shock at this point because it recognizes in its way that the monster he has to destroy and the master he has to defend are in reality the same person. Thus technology is helpless in defending Enlightenment culture because the monsters who threaten it are "monsters from the Id," that is, the desires of the very people controlling the technology in the first place.

When Robbie short-circuits, Morbius, his daughter, and the crew's commander flee to the Krell lab, which is protected by a door of solid Krell metal twenty inches thick. In a scene that was reprised in *Aliens*, the first *Alien* sequel, the monster starts to melt the Krell door. It is impossible to keep him out because he is already inside in the subconscious of Dr. Morbius. At this point, Altaira informs Morbius that "your twin self is in the tunnel," but more importantly that "we're all part monsters in our subconscious" which is why "we have laws and religion."

Like the Krell, America is on the verge of destruction because it expects technology to solve its moral problems: "The Krell forgot one danger, their own subconscious desire for lust and destruction. . . . After a million of years of shining sanity, they could hardly understand what power was destroying them." Here Hollywood, as if terrified by its own subconscious desire to break the Production Code, takes a page from the America of John Adams and Alexis de Tocqueville. We are not going to end up like the Krell because we still honor "laws and religion." No amount of increased intelligence or technology can act as a substitute for morality. "Then it must be true," says Morbius when he realizes that he is the source of the monster outside the door. "I must be guilty." As the door turns white hot, Morbius cries, "Guilty! Guilty! My evil self is at that door, and I have no power to stop it."

Eventually, in a scene that would be remade over and over again, the commander and Morbius's daughter escape back into space and open the viewing port to see the planet detroyed in the explosion of the Krell reactor, a scene, which like the whole interlude on the forbidden planet, "reminds us that we are after all not God."

*Forbidden Planet* was a seminal Hollywood film. Its influence reaches down to the *Alien* series as well as to David Cronenberg, who named the school in *The Brood* the Krell School after the extinct race of superior beings in *Forbidden Planet*. "I hadn't realized the film had a similar premise to *Forbidden Planet* until I picked the name for the school," he said. "Then I made the connection: creatures from the unconscious, making the mental physical. That's what *The Brood* and *Forbidden Planet* are really about. I was really knocked out by that film as a kid."[28]

# 7

# The Body Snatchers

U NLIKE SENATOR JOSEPH MCCARTHY OF WISCONSIN, who claimed that the State Department had fallen under the sway of a foreign power, Representative Carroll Reece of Tennessee believed the source of subversion—both agreed that subversion was taking place—was closer to home, in the tax-exempt foundations created from the wealth of America's great industrial families. Technically known as the Special Committee to Investigate Tax-Exempt Foundations and Comparable Organizations, the "Reece Committee" was appointed by the Eighty-third Congress and instructed to make a study of the use of such resources for "un-American and subversive activities; for political purposes, propaganda, or attempts to influence legislation." Now all but forgotten, the Reece Committee hearings, not the McCarthy hearings, dominated the news and editorial comment of 1954. Citing the Ford family, which transferred roughly 90 percent of its Ford holdings to a foundation, thereby escaping estate taxes on its fortune, the Reece Committee concluded, in a way that sounded a lot like Miles Binnell in *Body Snatchers*, that it was "possible that, in fifty or a hundred years, a great part of America will be controlled by pension and profit-sharing trusts and *foundations* and a large part of the balance by insurance companies and labor unions. What eventual repercussions may come from such development, one can only guess. It may be that we will in this manner reach some form of society similar to socialism, *without consciously intending it.*"[1]

In its ability to put both its assets and its social agenda beyond the reach of the government, the Ford family was no different from the Rockefellers or the Carnegies or a whole host of less wealthy and less well known families. In a column written on December 21, 1954, John O'Donnell of the *New York Daily News* claimed that the Reece Committee had the "almost impossible task" of telling "the taxpayers that the incredible was, in fact, the truth." "The incredible fact," he continued "was that the huge fortunes piled up by such industrial giants as John D. Rockefeller, Andrew Carnegie, and Henry Ford were today being used to destroy or discredit the free-enterprise system which gave them birth."[2]

In this, Congressman Reece was again more than a little like Miles Binnell, running up and down the crowded highway attempting to tell the world that the country had been taken over by alien invaders—who, of course, looked just like the pillars of capitalist society, and who were using their wealth to subvert the country's democratic institutions. In *Body Snatchers*, when Miles Binnell escapes Santa Mira, one of the citizens says, "Let him go. No one will believe him." The same could have been said of Reece, given the reaction of a skeptical media. Reece's claim that "these institutions may exert political influence, support subversion, or exhibit tendencies conflicting with our national traditions . . . free from any formal responsibility for their policies and actions and growing in number and wealth" and that this state of affairs "deserves the fullest attention of all who are concerned for the future of our Republic" was greeted for the most part by derisive cartoons portraying witch hunts in the nation's editorial pages.[3] The same people who did not like Senator McCarthy did not like Congressman Reece, and the fourth estate seemed bent on tarring the latter with the same brush used on the former.

Reece also claimed that the foundations controlled large segments of academic life and certain segments—the social sciences come in for particular criticism—to the point of "thought control." The vocabulary of science fiction as used in *Invasion of the Body Snatchers* is never far from René Wormser's account of the Reece Committee's hearings:

*The emergence of this special class in our society, endowed with immense powers of thought control, is a factor which must be taken into account in judging the merits of contemporary foundation operations. The concentration of power, or interlock, which has developed in foundation-supported social-science research and social-science education is largely the result of a capture of the integrated organizations by likeminded men. The plain, simple fact is that the so-called "liberal" movement in the United States has captured most of the major foundations and has done so chiefly through the professional administrator class, which has not hesitated to use these great public trust funds to political ends and with bias.*[4]

The Reece Committee and Miles Binnell shared certain convictions, the most striking of which is the belief, articulated in another context by Freud's nephew, Edward Bernays, that what calls itself a democracy has in reality been replaced by a new form of government, one run by "invisible governors" of the sort Bernays praised in his book *Propaganda*. If anything can be learned from Wormser's account of the Reece Committee, it is that many of the foundations' "professional administrator class" had become familiar with the terms Bernays used in his book and that an Americanized reading of the Illuminist tradition was proving so successful that the Eighty-third Congress felt compelled to investigate it.

Miles Binnell symbolized an entire nation that seemed to sense that no matter how similar American life looked on the surface, it was being changed in some fundamental way by invisible powers, whose goals were fundamentally alien. This alien conspiracy was composed primarily of professors in the social sciences like *Body Snatcher*'s Budlong, but its roots—long roots—were with the Enlightenment tradition of science and social revolution proposed long ago in Shelley's reading of Weishaupt and the Illuminati. In fact, the essence of Illuminism had become not only the essence of the new fields of advertising and human relations, it had become the *modus operandi* of the foundations as well, who took as their first task the pod-like conquest of academe by the painless method of dispensing money. In Wormser's words:

Pressure starts at the very bottom of the academic ladder. A foundation grant may enable a beginner to attain the precious doctorate which is the first rung. To secure such assistance, is it not likely that he will conform to what he may believe would please those who give him their financial grace? Then he becomes a teacher, at a salary sometimes below that of an ordinary laborer. Without supplemental help through a foundation grant, he can support his family only in poverty; he cannot set aside the time or the money necessary to enable him to do such study, research, and writing as may advance him in his career. Is he, then, likely to run counter to what may be wanted by a foundation considering him for a grant? This teacher finds, as he progresses in his career, that he has few sources from which to increase his income other than the foundations; without such accessory income, he cannot achieve those extracurricular but academic distinctions which give him prestige and advance him in the education hierarchy. These distinctions come often from research and writing. Great, dispensing intermediary organizations control learned journals and university presses; they hold the key to academic publications and form an effective instrument of patronage.[5]

The process described here is essentially the same as the cultural revolution Barruel described when he explained how the texts of the *philosophes* were promoted throughout France in the period preceding the Revolution and the procedure whereby those teachers who promoted Enlightenment in French schools were rewarded.

The Reece Committee was not as concerned with defending capitalism as it was "with the control of thought practiced by the dispensers of financial support."[6] The times in this regard collaborated with conservative myopia in failing to define the problem effectively. Since Moscow was seen as the *radix malorum*, the point of the committee often seemed to be to convince the public that Rockefeller was a communist. This of course was not the intent of the people on the committee, but its deliberations lent themselves to parody of this sort in the hands of a hostile press. Why would the Rockefellers want to promote socialism? The question was unanswerable on its own terms, but the terms proposed were not nuanced enough to capture the magnitude of the threat. Largely missing from the discussion was the idea of the Enlightenment, the role that science played in the Enlightenment's project of subverting morals, and the Illuminist vehicle to accomplish that subversion. As a result of this lack of nomenclature, plus a fairly obvious attempt at sabotage put on by Congressman Wayne Hays of Ohio, the committee was never able to articulate its concerns to the American public, so fixated on the threat of communist subversion.

Communism was "scientific" socialism and, as such, a tentacle of the Enlightenment. In the aftermath of World War ii, with the communist takeover of Eastern Europe and China still fresh in everyone's mind, the part was mistaken for the whole, and most American conservatives failed to see that the Enlightenment not only was, but had been the issue and the driving force behind revolution for the past two hundred years. Still, the Reece Committee was remarkably prescient and perceptive in understanding the peculiarly American turn that the Enlightenment would take under liberalism. At one point, the committee states: "In the public mind, the term 'subversion' is generally confined to Moscow-directed communist activity, or that of domestic communist allies in an international conspiracy." The committee goes on to assert that "socialist ideas can be legally promoted in the United States, that prominent figures have openly adopted them in the disguise of 'reform,' does not make them any less 'subversive.'"[7]

The Reece Committee hearings, as a result, go back and forth. At one point the chairman suggests that "we are now in the Third American Revolution, none the less serious because it is bloodless. This new revolution is a reform movement gone wrong. It has become an attempt to institute the paternal state in which individual liberty is to be subordinated and forgotten in a misapplication of the theory of the greatest good for the greatest number." But at another point the committee indicates that the Committee on Un-American Activities "produced evidence which supported its conclusion that there had been a Moscow-directed, specific plot to penetrate the American foundations and to use their funds for Communist propaganda and Communist influence upon our society. There was also evidence that this plot had succeeded in some measure."[8]

In the long run, it was the American version of the Enlightenment that was more subversive of American institutions than any foreign-based conspiracy, and people like Alfred Kinsey were more successful in subverting American mores than Alger Hiss or anyone else taking orders from Moscow. The distinction between a politically-minded manipulator and a true scholar is trenchant enough; but one wonders if the average citizen in 1954 was any different from the average resident of Santa Mira in being oblivious to the threat that politicized professors posed to the existence of the republic: "The politically minded manipulator often is rewarded with eminent status, whether he is a true scholar or not. The symbol of academic prestige is not necessarily an evidence of learning or of sound social judgment. Once an academician is selected to act as an 'expert,' he becomes one in the public eye because he has been so chosen. He may have succeeded in coming into office chiefly because he had developed good 'public relations.' If that was the case, he is likely to support whatever fads and foibles enabled him to succeed, rather than the thought of truly creative minds."[9]

The references to "experts" and "scientism" throughout make it clear that the whole Enlightenment tradition is being indicted, even if not by name: "These 'experts' have almost invariably followed the current fashion which grew up among teachers and political scientists under a barrage of communist and socialist propaganda and under the impact made by the depression of 1930. This fashion is one of confidence in the power of man to create heaven on earth by manipulating the structure of government." Even if it did not overcome the cultural barriers to an effective use of intellectual history, the Reece Committee did perform a valuable service. It gave voice to a number of conservative professors who tried to frame the issue as best they could.

The committee called on Dr. Ralph Cooper Hutchinson, president of Lafayette College, who attempted to explain "scientific humanism" by clarifying its four main tenets and the "particular dangers" which they entailed for the republic. One is that "all is natural and all truth is subject to discovery and determination through science." "As a consequence," he said, "there is no higher law, no law written in the heart, no law on the tables of stones, no law revealed in the sublimities of nature, no law in the inner conscience, no law of God." He described the second danger "as the belief, following the lead of Bacon, Lenin, Hogben and Bernal," that "there are no values save material and scientific realities." Since, third, "social progress is the only value" to scientific humanism, said Dr. Hutchinson in describing its fourth danger, "the end justifies the means," means which may be coercive and ignore the rights of the individual: "Inflamed by the fad for social progress and reform, we have given up the teaching of social idealism and have embarked on what we call 'liberal movements.' We are achieving social progress by legislation. Instead of persuading men, we command them. In our moral judgments we have gone over into the enemies' territory because while not denying God it is becoming very common to deny any higher law. We have substituted an opportunistic and relative ethic for the absolute. We are becoming a compromising, relativistic, uncertain people recognizing no absolute right or wrong, no higher law."[10]

Professor Hobbs of the University of Pennsylvania, in his turn, "gave example after example of such research which offered a direct danger to our society. What goes under the name of 'social science' today is often quackery. It is what Professor Hobbs called 'scientism.'" It involved, among other things, the "comptometer compulsion," the "fact-finding mania" of these foundation-supported "social scientists" and induced them to accept the principle of moral relativity—that moral laws are only relative: "the facts" speak for themselves and must dictate moral law; whatever "the facts" disclose is right: "Political control is thus to be left in the hands of the 'elite,' the 'social engineers.' What the people want is not necessarily good for them; they are not competent to decide. The *Führers* must decide it for them, so that we can have a scientifically based and intelligent society."[11]

．　．　．　．　．

The substitution of "science" for morals had been a staple of the Enlightenment since the time of La Mettrie, but it was new to the United States. Perhaps the most salient example was the Rockefeller-funded Kinsey reports, which were criticized by the Reece Committee:

An example of the sometimes explosive nature of foundation giving is the support by foundations of the late Dr. Kinsey in what
he called sex research. The Rockefeller Foundations supported
the National Research Council's Committee for Research in
problems of sex, with a total of $1,755,000 from 1931 to 1954. Of
this sum, the activities conducted by Dr. Kinsey received some
$414,000 from 1941 to 1949, as reported by the Rockefeller Foun-
dation to the Reece Committee. This amount is microscopic
compared with the total of $6,000,000,000 annually spent on
philanthropy in the United States. But the impact of this comparatively small sum on one subject was quite out of proportion
to the relative size of the two figures. One may approve or dis-
approve of Dr. Kinsey's efforts, and judge variously their impact
upon our sex mores. But the Kinsey incident does show that
comparatively small donations may have big repercussions in the
realm of ideas.[12]

If any villain emerged over the course of the Reece Committee's
deliberations it was the "social engineers," almost all of whom had been
subsidized by the foundations. Kinsey, in this regard, was just the worst
of a bad lot, all of whom shared a worldview based on the subversion
of the moral order in the name of "scientific" data. Reece continues:
"Thus, if Dr. Kinsey concludes that girls would be happier in the long
run if their marriages were preceded by considerable, and even unusual,
sex experience, then, say these 'social engineers,' the moral and legal
concepts which proscribe it should be abandoned."[13]
Wormser is struck by the supine behavior of the press in dealing
with the Kinsey reports. He does not mention it, but it was widely
known that every journalist who wrote an article on these reports using
Kinsey material had to have his article vetted by the Kinsey Institute,
ostensibly to assure accuracy. What followed was the effect predicted
by Bernays and others who followed in his footsteps. The impression
was given that public opinion favored certain changes to our legal
system, when in fact the media of public relations were being consciously manipulated by those who were interested in the change. The
public was left to suspect, in the manner of Miles Binnell, that the
pod creatures were taking over: "Perhaps the best illustration of this

[manipulation] is the remarkable number of writings which appeared after the publication of the reports on the Rockefeller Foundation-supported Kinsey studies. With the assumedly 'scientific' character of Dr. Kinsey's work behind us, we had such things offered to the public as this by one Anne G. Freegood, in the September 1953 issue of *Harper's*: 'The desert in this case is our current code of laws governing sexual activities and the background of Puritan tradition regarding sex under which this country still to some extent operates.'"[14]

Those who disagreed were cast in the role of Miles Binnell on the highway out of Santa Mira. In spite of the ridicule they received in the progressive press, many professors could and did come forward, and many of them reserved their strongest condemnations for the Kinsey reports. Professor Hobbs, for example, said, "Despite the patent limitations of the study and its persistent bias, its conclusions regarding sexual behavior were widely believed. They were present to college classes; medical doctors cited them in lectures; psychiatrists applauded them; a radio program indicated that the findings were serving as a basis for revision of moral codes relating to sex; and an editorial in a college student newspaper admonished the college administration to make provision for sexual outlets for the students in accordance with the 'scientific realities' as established by the book."[15]

Hobbs also pointed out that when it came to sexual morality, Kinsey was hardly a dispassionate observer, taking every opportunity to ridicule "socially approved patterns of sexual behavior," by calling them "rationalizations," while at the same time referring to socially condemned forms of sexual behavior as "normal" or "normal in the human animal." The result of "such pseudo-scientific presentations" could only be detrimental to "public morality." Because of his emphasis on statistics (mistakenly used, according to the American Statistical Association), Kinsey gave the impression that since "the findings are scientific in the same sense as the findings in physical science, then the issue becomes not a matter of whether he as a person is correct or incorrect, but of the impression which is given to the public, which can be quite unfortunate."[16]

The whole question of science in this regard gets subsumed into the "science" of public relations. What Kinsey said about sex may not be true, but it becomes "true" when enough people are mobilized by the management of information into changing laws that are now seen as "unscientific and outdated." Wormser notes that "special responsibility" of the Rockefeller Foundation for having financed the Kinsey "best sellers" comes sharply to roost in an article in *Harper's* in which Albert Deutsch states that what Kinsey said was true because the Rockefellers supported him: "So startling are its revelations, so contrary to what civilized man has been taught for generations, that *they would be unbelievable but for the impressive weight of the scientific agencies backing the survey.*"[17]

The notion of value by statistics was also criticized by the Reece Committee:

> Should concepts of value (legal, religious, ethical ideas) be abandoned merely because any number of men find them oppressive and neglect to live up to them? Are we justified in advocating a change in the criminal law because certain types of crimes are practiced widely? Shall we abrogate punishment for speeding, for theft, for adultery, for fraudulent voting, for income-tax evasion, if we find that such illegalities are practiced by a majority? By twenty percent of our people? By eighty percent? What percentage of our population must express itself, either by response to interviews or by action, in favor of an illegality to convince a social scientist that the law proscribing it should be abrogated?"[18]

There was no answer to the Reece critique, because even at this early stage the strategy of the revolutionaries was to control the flow of information, not to rebut arguments. The common denominator of the social sciences that the committee found it difficult to name was moral subversion: "*It seems to this Committee that there is a strong tendency on the part of many of the social scientists whose research is favored by the major foundations toward the concept that there are no absolutes, that everything is indeterminate, that no standards of conduct, morals, ethics and government are to be deemed inviolate, that everything, including basic moral law, is subject to change, and that it is the part of the social scien-*

*tists to take no principle for granted as a premise in social or juridical rea-*
*soning, however fundamental it may heretofore have been deemed to be*
*under our Judeo-Christian moral system."*[19]

If moral subversion was the goal of the Enlightenment—in other
words, the substitution of scientific fact for morals—the means to that
end was propaganda in the sense defined by Edward Bernays. The
committee cited the testimony of Stewart Chase, who explained how
foundation-supported and directed social science research was to function. The "scientific method," Chase claimed, echoing William
Godwin and countless other thinkers of the same stripe, can be "applied to the behavior of men as well as to the behavior of electrons."
Once the nature of man is laid bare by the instruments of science, man
can be scientifically managed as well, according to "the official line of
the foundation complex . . . through 'cultural determinism,' via a mold-
ing of our minds by propaganda." In short, the Reece Committee
stumbled upon the implementation of the Illuminist dream of controlling man by controlling his passions, a project that was carried out
over the next twenty years, as if the committee had never issued its
warnings.

The Reece Committee did a remarkable job of bringing out ideas
that were both difficult for the average man to understand and extremely damaging to the plans of the elites: *"What does the term 'sub-*
*version' mean? In contemporary usage and practice, it does not refer to*
*outright revolution, but to a promotion of tendencies which lead, in their*
*inevitable consequences, to the destruction of principles through perversion*
*or alienation. Subversion, in modern society, is not a sudden, cataclysmic*
*explosion, but a gradual undermining, a persistent chipping away at foun-*
*dations upon which beliefs rest."*[20]

One reason for the failure of the Reece Committee, aside from
the magnitude of the educative task they took upon themselves, was
that it was sabotaged by people sympathetic to the cause of "scientism"
and the foundations. Wormser describes in detail the role Congressman Wayne Hays of Ohio played in disrupting the deliberations of
the committee. In particular he recounts Hays defense of the Kinsey
reports:

Several lines of inquiry enraged Mr. Hays particularly. One, which disclosed his reluctance to permit freedom of inquiry, was a proposed study of the Kinsey reports. It was undoubtedly reported to him by Miss Lonergan that Dr. Ettinger had dug up some significant material about foundation support of the Kinsey projects. This brought Mr. Hays to a steaming rage, and he asked to see our entire Kinsey file. . . . Our appropriation for 1954 had, at the time, not yet been approved, and Mr. Hays stated emphatically to Mr. Dodd that *he would oppose any further appropriation to our Committee unless the Kinsey investigation were dropped.* His unreasoning opposition to any study of these projects was so great that he threatened to fight against the appropriation on the floor of the House. . . . The Kinsey reports did, in the course of the open hearings, become part of the Committee evidence through the testimony of Professor Hobbs, who used them as apt examples of 'scientism,' but the valuable material in our Kinsey file never saw the light of day."[21]

Hays's disruptive behavior was never portrayed as such because, according to Wormser, "On some papers, notably the *New York Times,* the *New York Herald Tribune,* and the *Washington Post-Times,* the editors were apparently determined, whatever might transpire at the hearings, to persuade the public that the Committee majority members were persecutors and that Mr. Hays was a knight in shining armor, protecting the virtue of the immaculate foundations. I do not remember one instance in which any of the three newspapers I have named commented critically on Mr. Hays's amazing behavior."[22]

Ultimately the failure of the Reece Committee to get its message to the public was, paradoxically, proof of the truth of its warnings about foundation influence and the cooperation of the instruments of culture in promoting Enlightenment values. One notable consequence of the hearings was the termination of Rockefeller's support for Kinsey, an action which so outraged Kinsey that he threatened to make his sex histories public, perhaps taking a page from Magnus Hirschfeld, and was only prevented from doing so by his sudden death. But Kinsey had outlived his usefulness by then. He had been picked up by the Rockefeller Foundation in 1941, ten years after becoming involved in funding studies in sexual physiology and behavior. After Kinsey had published his reports the damage to American mores was done. The 10-percent figure for homosexuality became enshrined in the public consciousness. Kinsey was a creature of the foundations, and as if in tacit admission of this fact, when the foundations pulled the plug, he died. The Reece Committee disbanded, largely as a result of Congressman Hays's outrageous behavior, leaving behind hardly a trace in the historical memory other than a prophetic warning about the Rockefellers as venture capitalists for Enlightenment ideas.

· · · · ·

The crucial issue at the dawn of the 1960s was nudity on the screen. Hollywood was feeling financially threatened by television on the one hand, which was stealing its family audience, and the new skin magazines like *Playboy*, on the other, which were founded in the wake of the Kinsey reports and were testing the borders of pornography.

After a number of unsuccessful attempts with vehicles like Billy Wilder's *Kiss Me, Stupid*, released in 1964, Hollywood finally succeeded in breaking the code in 1965 with the release of the Eli Landau film *The Pawnbroker*. During the course of the film a woman playing a black prostitute opened her blouse and exposed her breasts to the camera, breaking, as a result, section seven, subsection two, of the Motion Picture Production Code and one of Hollywood's last taboos.

The Legion of Decency, an important Irish Catholic response to the revolution, saw *The Pawnbroker* not as the harbinger of serious cinematic art but as something that the Legion's Monsignor Thomas Little said would "open the flood gates to a host of unscrupulous operators to make a quick buck." The next seven years of cinema were to prove Monsignor Little and the Legion right, as a few bared breasts eventually became pervasive on-screen nudity, culminating in 1973 with the release of *Deep Throat* and *The Devil in Miss Jones*, two porno epics that were among the ten top-grossing films for that year.

The summer of 1965 was significant for other reasons as well. In the spring of that year, the twelve-year campaign of John D. Rockefeller III to legalize contraception achieved its first major success with *Griswold v. Connecticut*, the Supreme Court decision striking down the Connecticut law banning the sale of contraceptives. After abandoning Kinsey, the Rockefellers put their money into developing a new contraceptive. They ended up with two, the Pill and the IUD, and with that in their technological arsenal, they set about using the techniques of Edward Bernays, now mobilized by Bernard Berelson as head of the Population Council, to launch a public relations campaign promoting the use of the contraceptive. It was an attack of the sort the Reece Committee had warned against, one in the classic mode of the Illuminist tradition. It used all of the media of communication to convince the public that overpopulation threatened the survival of the entire human race, and then used the ensuing hysteria to get the laws of the United States changed. Once the laws prohibiting the sale of contraceptives were declared unconstitutional, the public relations machinery focused on the hearings of Senator Ernest Gruening of Alaska, who spent the summer of 1965 predicting that overpopulation would cause worldwide starvation, and proposing that the United States government fund contraceptives to avert the impending catastrophe.

After Lyndon Johnson's landslide victory, an undersecretary of transportation mulled over the passage of the landmark Civil Rights Act of 1964. Segregation had been made illegal, but the blacks had still to achieve economic parity with their white fellow citizens. As the result of his research, Undersecretary Daniel Patrick Moynihan noticed a correlation between economic well-being and family well-being. To be specific, he noticed a connection between poverty and illegitimacy. The source of the economic weakness in the black community was the weakness in the black family, which at the time manifested what Undersecretary Moynihan described as an epidemic of illegitimacy. By that he meant that 21 percent of all black children were born out of wedlock.

Moynihan immediately embarked on a program to strengthen the black family. He passed what came to be known as the Moynihan Report on to Bill Moyers, President Johnson's press secretary, who in turn passed it on to Lyndon Johnson, who was impressed with what he saw. So impressed, in fact, that he decided to make the Moynihan

Report the cornerstone of the Great Society's race program. In June of 1965, President Johnson delivered a speech at Howard University outlining the Moynihan Report to the leadership of the civil rights movement, including Martin Luther King. Everyone was unanimous in approving the new program of action.

But then something happened. Over the summer of 1965, the Left turned on the Moynihan Report, and then the civil rights establishment did too, and the Johnson administration followed suit. As a result, within the space of a year, from being the cornerstone of the Johnson administration's race policy Moynihan's report passed into oblivion. Eventually the White House symposium he proposed on the black family took place, but without him. The Enlightenment regime, a bipartisan adventure including both liberals and "conservatives" of a eugenic stripe, felt that the contraceptive was a better solution to the welfare problem than strengthening the black family. Strengthening the family was the antithesis of heteronomous, external control.

During the summer of 1965 a lawyer from Harrisburg, Pennsylvania, watched in disbelief as this scenario of cultural revolutions began to unroll before his eyes. William Bentley Ball, chief counsel for the Pennsylvania Catholic Conference, waited week after week for the Gruening hearings to give some indication that there was more than one point of view on overpopulation. "Where was the Catholic Church?", Ball kept wondering both to himself and to Archbishop John Krol of Philadelphia. To be more specific, why had the bishops' own organization in Washington not spoken against the Gruening hearings? What Ball did not know at the time was that the same forces that had stacked the deck in the Gruening hearings were also busy undermining the Church's opposition to contraception.

From early 1963 to just around the time of the *Griswold* decision, John D. Rockefeller III's Population Council had been funding a series of secret conferences at the University of Notre Dame, the purpose of which was to give the impression that the Church's teaching on contraception was no longer intellectually plausible. Rockefeller even took the extraordinary step of asking the Reverend Theodore M. Hesburgh, csc, to arrange an audience with Pope Paul VI, during which

Rockefeller volunteered to write the pope's birth-control encyclical, the one that eventually came to be known as *Humanae Vitae*. The pope did not accept Rockefeller's offer, but the U.S. government did, and the government was in the contraceptive business by the fall of 1965.

The control of the human person that "population control" allows is of course far more intimate and, therefore, far more complete than any previous form of political domination. Michael Schooyans makes the point that even "Marx' proletariat still had their children as their only riches. . . . On the other hand, the contemporary problem forces the individual into the most precarious situation, since it deprives him of all control over *his own concrete future*, over a real future for his offspring: a kind of *alienation* heretofore unknown."[23]

The result of "birth control" is not only more radical that the slavery of classical antiquity, but the means to that end are different as well. Instead of forcing people to act for the ends of those in power, the "invisible rulers" now induce the ruled to do so by getting them to act according to the rulers' unspoken sexual guidelines, because in controlling the agency responsible for the transmission of life, the controllers control human life at its source and most crucial point:

> This kind of domination is at once more cunning, more pernicious and more fatal in its effects. It is not at all new, but it has grown in an unprecedented way because of two decisive factors. On the one hand, it has benefitted from the use of the most sophisticated techniques of propaganda and indoctrination. On the other hand, its effectiveness is assured by the media's guarantee of publicity. . . . For contemporary totalitarianism the question is no longer one of exercising physical coercion; henceforth it is a matter of destroying the Ego in what is most profoundly personal in me. This is why contemporary totalitarianism has intellectual life as its target. It pummels the masses, but the intellectuals it reeducates by filtering, directing and dealing in information. It inculcates a portable ideology, for ideology can encroach upon intelligence and disarm its critical ability, imprisoning it in a "gulag of the spirit." Bit by bit, intellectuals are ensnared by manipulators of knowledge who are in the pay of the party, the race, the army, the powerful. Science is fostered to the

degree that it delivers new technologies that can be integrated into a global strategy for domination.[24]

As always, the instrument of control is passion: "Man, under the guise of being liberated and excited by the possibility of maximizing individual pleasure, disregards the stakes and consequences of sexuality." By taking control of pleasure at its source in sexuality, the neo-Illuminists take control of human life and dominate human conscience, manipulating it through guilt to defend the actions that enslaved it in the first place. Liberal politics becomes first the incitation to sexual vice, then the colonization of the procreative powers that are indissolubly associated with sexuality, and finally the political mobilization of the consequent guilt in an all-encompassing system that gives new meaning to the term totalitarian. Schooyans is one of the few who sees the full ramifications of this biocratic revolution: "We are at the dawn of a total war beyond the limits of anything we have known, and the horizon is already aflame with it. The present war is truly total in the sense that, by means of power over life, it aims at control over human beings in what is most inalienable; their existence, there personal capacity for making judgments, and decisions, and their responsibility before their conscience. The present war simultaneously involves each of these aspects as the stakes, the means and the goal."[25]

In an event that was as little heeded at the time as the warnings in *Forbidden Planet*, syphilis made a comeback after being almost completely eradicated through penicillin and epidemiological programs in the mid-1950s. In both the United States and France, the years 1964–65 brought an end to the post–World War II optimism as syphilitic infection, in spite of penicillin, began its climb to current rates, creating on the way more resistant strains of the bacillus. "The upsurge peaked in 1964 and 1965," according to Quetel, "but thereafter fell only slowly and partially, and to the present day there has only been a slight diminution to an average of around 4,000 cases per year (8 per 100,000)." The monster was still there, but no one was taking it seriously anymore.

# 8

## *Hollywood and Death*

JOHN CARPENTER, who reinvigorated the horror genre in the late 1970s with *Halloween*, called Alfred Hitchcock's *Psycho* the first slasher film. In this respect, *Psycho* (1960) was both a premonition and a farewell. The film was in many ways the sign that the warning of *Forbidden Planet* had gone unheeded and that Hollywood was determined to travel the road to sexually explicit films no matter what the cost. *Psycho* was probably the most influential horror film ever made. What no one seemed to notice at the time is that it took sexual liberation as its starting point, and then in the inchoate manner typical of the genre, tried to explain how sexual liberation led, first through sin, and then through crime, to death.

The opening scene takes place in a sleazy hotel room with the blinds drawn where a young couple, taking an extended lunch break that involves sexual relations, talk in desultory fashion after the consummation of the act about the principal sexual issue of the time, divorce and its consequences. They speak in particular about alimony payments, which the man cannot seem to afford and which, at least according to his rationalization, seems to prevent the couple from getting married. The sin leads to the crime—the woman steals forty thousand dollars from her employer's safe—which leads to flight, which leads to the Bates Motel and to death.

Donald Spoto tries to psychologize Hitchcock by attempting to trace the macabre in his films to Hitchcock's Catholic childhood. "Ours was a Catholic family," he quotes Hitchcock as saying later in life, "and in England you see, this is in itself an eccentricity. I had a strict religious upbringing. . . . I don't think I can be labeled a Catholic artist, but it may be that one's early upbringing influences a man's life and guides his instinct. . . . I am definitely not anti-religious; perhaps, I'm sometimes neglectful."[1]

Spoto also attempts to trace the macabre in Hitchcock's films to his unrequited love of his assistant, Joan Harrison, and the subsequent sublimation of that lust into gluttony. (At his peak weight, the five feet, eight inch Hitchcock tipped the scales at a life-threatening 365 pounds.) But the very fact that he sublimated his desires rather than acting on them gives some indication that he still had a modicum of control over them, which distinguished him from the culture at large at the time. In all, Hitchcock seems a singularly poor example of the man who projected his guilt into his films, notwithstanding Spoto's claim that "guilt of course is the predominant theme of Hitchcock's films."[2] Guilt may be their predominant theme, but to say that it is Hitchcock's guilt is far from obvious.

*Lifeboat* and *Psycho* have in common a deeply rooted sense of what was going on at the time, a sense that transcends personal preoccupation. Hitchcock's view of World War II was suffused by his sense of himself in a safe place far away from England, but that did not prevent him from portraying the conflict on a deeper level as a conflict between two fundamentally different views, one respectful of the moral order, one contemptuous of it.

Bosley Crowther, who would later use his position as film critic for the *New York Times* to campaign to overthrow the Production Code, now used it as a mouthpiece for chauvinism: "Unless we had seen it with our own eyes we would never in the world have believed that a film could have been made which sold out our democratic ideals and elevated the Nazi superman. Mr. Hitchcock and Mr. Steinbeck failed to grasp just what they had wrought. They certainly had no intention of elevating the superman ideal. . . . But we could have a sneaking suspicion that the Nazis with some cutting here and there, could turn *Lifeboat* into a whiplash against the 'decadent democracies.' And it is questionable whether such a picture, with such a theme, is judicious at this time."[3]

Hitchcock's *Psycho* was just as much in tune with the times as *Lifeboat* had been. We get the sense listening to the young nurse in *Lifeboat* talk about her affair with the doctor in England that adultery has something to do with the war and the carnage that had become so common. In *Psycho*, the same moral dynamic is portrayed from the other end of the psychic cultural spectrum—in other words, after the culture ignored the warnings given in *Lifeboat* about the moral law and the sanctity of human life, as a series of irrational violent actions that proceed mysteriously from sexual premises, with a theft as the bridge between the two. *The Birds*, Hitchcock's follow-up to *Psycho*, covers the same ground in an even more elliptical manner. As in *Forbidden Planet*, sexual intrigue disrupts the tranquil order of nature, which retaliates with birds.

. . . . .

By the 1970s, popular pornography and its necessary terminus in violence and injury had arrived. Linda Boreman had to learn this trajectory the hard way when she arrived in New York in December of 1972 to star in a series of eight-millimeter pornographic films with a holiday ambiance. "They were shot with Christmas trees and Christmas gifts, and there was one scene where we carried Christmas candles. All very sentimental," she wrote later. Boreman, later known as Linda Lovelace, had fallen under the spell of a pimp by the name of Chuck Traynor, who, as part of the regimen to keep her under his control, would subject her to various sessions of hypnotism, one of which allowed her to suppress her gag reflex and hence to perform the sexual equivalent of sword-swallowing on the clients Traynor procured for her. This soon caught the attention of a pornographic filmmaker by the name of Gerry Damiano, who got the idea of making a feature-length film around it, which he planned to call *Deep Throat*. The film's producer was a mafioso by the name of Lou Peraino, or Lou Perry, who initially had a falling out with Damiano over the star's physical endowments. Peraino wanted a star with larger breasts, but Damiano insisted on keeping Lovelace, first of all, because of her abilities, but also because she radiated a sense of innocence (this was America, remember!) while performing perverse sexual acts. "The most amazing thing about Linda," Damiano said to Traynor, "the truly amazing thing, is she still looks sweet and innocent. I don't know how come, but that's one thing I can't buy, sweet innocence."[4]

The combination of innocence and perversity was just what audiences wanted to see. During the second half of 1973, seeing *Deep Throat* became the secular equivalent of a religious pilgrimage for New York City's sexually enlightened, and it spawned, in the words of the *New York Times*, "a kind of porno chic." From its opening on June 12, 1973, to its being declared obscene in early 1974, *Deep Throat* drew an average of five thousand people weekly to the New Mature World Theater on West 49th Street. No news account of the film was complete without descriptions of the respectability of the film's patrons. The *New York Times*, which, along with *Screw* magazine, became one of the film's principal apologists, noted approvingly that the audience included "businessmen, women alone and dating couples, few of whom it might be presumed, would previously have gone to a film of sexual intercourse, fellatio, and cunnilingus." To show that they were hardly innocent bystanders in the sexual revolution, the *Times* noted that "members of the *New York Times* news staff went *en masse* during a recent lunch hour, to be followed a few days later by a group from the Book Review." If that did not assure that pornography had achieved a cachet of respectability, a procession of movie stars attended as well, "people like Johnny Carson, Mike Nichols, Sandy Dennis, Ben Gazzara and Jack Nicholson. . . . Some French UN diplomats went and insisted on paying with traveler's checks. . . . Members of the in-crowd from Elaine's [restaurant] announced that they were going for the second time."[5]

It must have come as something of a surprise to the in-crowd when, after six very profitable months, the film's distributor and the management of the New Mature World were hauled into court on an obscenity charge on December 18. The trial was accompanied by enormous amounts of publicity in which the cultural brokers in New York

City fell over themselves announcing that the sixty-two-minute film, which contained fifteen sex acts, including seven of fellatio and four of cunnilingus, was both humorous and trivial. The sexual revolution had arrived.

The *Times*'s coverage of the obscenity trial under Judge Joel Tyler was consistent with its coverage of the film itself. The judge was portrayed as a prudish crank. The defense attorneys brought forward a series of "scientific" experts who, in the mode of Magnus Hirschfeld and Alfred Kinsey, testified that the suppression of Linda Lovelace's gag reflex constituted normal sexual activity and a benefit to the republic. Professor Arthur Knight, film critic for *Saturday Review* and professor of film at the University of Southern California, one of the breeding grounds for the new wave of directors that would take over Hollywood at the end of the decade, claimed that *Deep Throat* had "redeeming social value because it might encourage people to expand their sexual horizons."[6] Because it was done in a "more professional" manner and because it was "more cleverly and amusingly written," it was "not a sleazy film by any means." Dr. Edward J. Hornick, a New York psychiatrist, claimed that the sex acts in *Deep Throat*, including a scene involving simultaneous intercourse among two men and a woman, were "well within the bounds of normal behavior." Beyond that, and here the psychiatrist probably came closer to the truth than most of the other experts defending the film, Hornick claimed that viewing the film would "lighten the load of guilt and shame often associated with sex." When asked by the assistant district attorney if viewing the film might "stimulate longing for sexual activity," Hornick responded, "I would hope so."[7] John Money, then a professor at Johns Hopkins, but formerly a collaborator on the Kinsey reports, testified that "people would be less likely to get divorces if they included *Deep Throat* in their sex education." The film was beneficial because, according to Money, "it puts an egg beater in people's brains." *Deep Throat* had redeeming social value, said Money, because "seeing explicit acts of fellatio, cunnilingus and other sexual intercourse in them would help remove inhibitions and mental blocks" and as a result "produce a saner attitude toward sex and firmer marriages."[8]

This is not to say that all the experts who testified favored the film. Ernest van den Haag, professor of social philosophy at New York University, found the film "obscene" and "without redeeming social value whatsoever": "Once you regard a person as merely a means to your pleasure," he continued, "then you will be ready to commit any act for your pleasure or displeasure—putting another person in a concentration camp or exploiting his teeth and hair."[9]

On March 7, 1974, Judge Tyler handed down his ruling: he declared *Deep Throat* obscene and imposed a fine of two million dollars. Despite the chic of porn, the testimony of the experts, and the biased reporting of the *Times*, Judge Tyler concluded that "this is one throat that deserves to be cut. I readily perform the operation in finding the defendant guilty as charged."[10] The following day the Marquee at the New Mature World read "Judge Cuts Throat. World Mourns."

Part of the difficulty that almost all of the pundits commenting on the case experienced was the inability to see anything wrong with the behavior exhibited in the film. Beyond that, it was clear that most of them were already familiar with pornographic films and hence somewhat jaded. Vincent Canby seemed perplexed both by the film's success and the notion that there might be something wrong with the culture that so avidly celebrated this sort of thing. He wrote: "*Deep Throat* has become the most financially successful hard core pornographic film ever to play New York. . . . For reasons that still baffle me, *Deep Throat* became the one porno film in New York chic to see and to be seen at, even before the court case, even before Earl Wilson wrote about it. When I went to see it last summer, mostly because of the Goldstein review [in *Screw*], I was so convinced of its junkiness that I didn't bother writing about it."[11]

The subsequent success of the film did not lessen Canby's bafflement. In the end, he fell back on the stock evaluation of an Enlightenment thinker: the substitution of technique for morals. "At the risk of sounding like the usual bored critic," Canby concluded, "I must say *Deep Throat* is much less erotic than technically amazing. How does she do it? The film has less to do with the manifold pleasures of sex than with physical engineering."[12]

Nora Ephron was more indignant but almost as much at a loss as Vincent Canby. She could not "help thinking that pornography that has this sort of impact must have some significance," but could not explain what the significance is. The reason for this is fairly simple: she, Canby, and the other critics see sexuality through the same mechanistic, Enlightenment lens the pornographers do; hence they have nothing to say. What is there to say? It is just people doing what comes naturally, captured on 35-mm film. Ephron claimed to be a connoisseur of stag films, as if to establish her credentials as a critic of the genre without noticing that the attitude toward sex that allowed her to partake of those films may blind her to deeper realities. Ephron found *Deep Throat* "one of the most unpleasant, disturbing films I have ever seen—it is not just anti-female but anti-sexual as well." But then, in the course of a phone conversation with Ms. Lovelace, she was shaken by the star's nonchalance.[13]

"I totally enjoyed myself making the movie, and all of a sudden I'm what they call a superstar," Lovelace told Ephron, leaving Ephron with the self-image as "a hung-up, uptight, middle class inhibited possibly puritanical feminist who lost her sense of humor at a skin flick." Lovelace's relationship with the pimp Chuck Traynor was hardly nonchalant. Ephron had no way of knowing this at the time, but she also had no way of suspecting that deeper, more sinister realities might be at play behind the porno-star exterior. "Everything that has happened to Linda Lovelace since" the making of *Deep Throat* had been, according to Ephron, "a kind of a goof."[14] Whether Ephron would have felt the same knowing of the beatings that were needed to coerce Lovelace into the activity she displayed in the films is something we do not know. By the time the word got out, the cultural Left was pretending it could not hear.

Of all the pundits who tried to make sense of the porno chic phenomenon, the most perceptive was William S. Pechter writing in *Commentary*. The chief reason that porno had become chic, according to Pechter, was that the culture wanted pornography, "but we don't want to admit to wanting it, and so we want it cloaked in art or in some other socially respectable disguise; fun and 'keeping up' will do, as witness the cultural legitimization of *Deep Throat*." The culture wanted to believe that perversity is funny. This reflected, more than anything else, a sense of ill ease because taboos had been violated. Pechter was perceptive enough to see that Lovelace's running nose and tearing eyes indicated that she was not enjoying herself as much as everyone assumed in acting out the sadistic male fantasy which is the film's major premise. But every other misgiving, even from the most perceptive pundits, was more or less a cultural premonition. In spite of the "lightly comic tone" the film affected, Pechter detected a premonition of death in that the "two totemic images of the contemporary cinema are those twin orifices of birth and death: the vagina and the bullet hole."[15]

The connection between the vagina and the bullet hole as cinematic icons became less tentative as the decade progressed. For those with the eyes to see, it could be seen in any number of the decade's cultural phenomena. To begin with, historians of the cinema noticed, without much of an explanation, that "porno chic" rose and fell during the decade, and that the horror genre was firmly in born-again fashion by 1980. Then there was feminism, whose authors rarely understood their own texts, but whose texts provided innumerable case histories of the women who adopted left-wing morals only to discover ten years later just how dangerous that had become because of the increasingly violent nature the trajectory of pornography had taken.

Then, too, there were the peculiar circumstances surrounding those connected with the major pornographic productions of the 1970s. After grossing 3.2 million dollars on a twenty-five thousand dollar investment in *Deep Throat*, producers Lou Perry and Phil Parisi announced in a large ad on the pages of *Variety* their intention to shoot *Deep Throat II* in New York. "We're going to make lightning strike twice," the ad claimed. "If you like 'Throat,' you'll love Throat II." The sequel promised a repeat performance from Linda Lovelace, who was promised one thousand dollars a day "plus expenses for her and her manager, plus a percentage of the future box office receipts."[16]

The sequel never got made. Instead, in a turn of events that substantiated in uncanny fashion the cultural trajectory of the 1970s, Lou Perry founded a production company with the profits from *Deep Throat* and as his first new venture bought the rights to the *Texas Chainsaw*

*Massacre*, which in equally uncanny fashion became every bit the cult film of 1975 that *Deep Throat* was in 1973. The 1970s premier skin flick had given birth to that decade's premier horror film.

Shortly after dawn on July 15, 1973, when *Deep Throat* was packing them in to the New Mature World, "a bunch of Austin [Texas] hippies" gathered on Quick Hill Road, outside the town of Round Rock, to do a sixteen millimeter film based loosely on the story of Ed Gein, a Wisconsin handyman who had been arrested for murder twenty years before. When the police arrived to arrest Gein they found lampshades made from human skin and human organs cooking away in pots on the stove. It was not the first time Gein had inspired a film: Hitchcock's *Psycho* was based on the same events.[17]

One year after the *Texas Chainsaw Massacre* was made in the blazing Texas heat, with the young actors covered in animal blood, Peraino agreed to pay the film's backers two hundred thousand dollars up front for the rights plus a percentage of the profits. But soon, embroiled in a series of obscenity trials, Perry quietly liquidated his Bryanston films and disappeared back into the underworld, but not before *Massacre* had become even more spectacularly successful at the box office than *Deep Throat*, grossing roughly ten times as much worldwide.

Tobe Hooper, the film's young director, went on to become a bona fide Hollywood director, eventually collaborating with Stephen Spielberg, one of *Massacre*'s early admirers. *Massacre* evidently touched a chord with younger audiences, although not one that the actors thought needed to be touched. Actor Bill Vail, who went from being hung on meat hooks to being stored in the deep freeze in *Massacre*, attended a showing of the film in New York at Times Square not far from where the Perry production of *Deep Throat* had been a hit. Vail recalls that the audience "of mostly street kids" were, in his words, "totally into what was happening on the screen, eating it up with a spoon, shouting 'Get her, cut that bitch.'" Vail, according to his own testimony, left the theater stunned.[18]

Eventually, Lovelace escaped from Traynor's clutches, and after refusing to do any more pornographic films for Hollywood, was blacklisted by the industry. She eventually married her high-school sweetheart and settled down to the life of an honest, if penurious, house-wife from New Jersey.

In 1980, Linda (Lovelace) Boreman's memoir of her time in bond-age to the white slave trade came out, and the premonition of horror evoked by porno films like *Deep Throat* was substantiated. But Linda Lovelace found that it was easier to get lies into print as the star of *Deep Throat* than it was to tell the truth as the co-author of *Ordeal*, her memoir. "I live for sex," Lovelace had said in her first foray into the publishing world, *Inside Linda Lovelace*, "and will never get enough of it, and will continue to try every day to tune my mechanism to finer and finer perfection."[19] The author of those words was, by his own admission, Chuck Traynor, but the tradition behind them was pure Enlightenment. Linda Lovelace, the female robot, was the culmina-tion of the intellectual trajectory set in motion by books like La Mettrie's *Man a Machine* and Sade's *Justine*.

The same imagery continues throughout *Ordeal*. Describing her first encounter as a prostitute, with five men, she writes: "They were playing musical chairs with parts of my body. I had the feeling that this was no more exciting for them than it was for me; they were ro-bots with a robot." When told to act out a lesbian scene in an 8-mm porno film, Lovelace writes, "I thought of myself as a metal robot, no human feelings at all, and that worked for a while. I was feeling noth-ing. A skinny naked girl was kissing me on the mouth, and I felt nothing at all. She tried to put her tongue in my mouth, but she learned that you can't pry open a robot's lips." The longer Lovelace continued in prostitution, the less she was able to experience things "that made me feel good or bad. I felt as though my self had been taken away from me. I was not a person anymore. I was a robot, a vegetable, a wind-up toy, a f——— and s———ing doll. I had become someone else's thing. If it didn't do . . . whatever—I got beaten. So I simply did it. Whatever."[20]

When she tried to tell the real story of what it was like to be a sex machine, the fourth estate folded up its collective notepad and walked away. By repudiating the Enlightenment's dream of unlim-ited mechanical sex, Linda Lovelace had become the female version of Miles Binnell, cast in that role by the very people who had promoted her so avidly to superstar status a few years earlier. By the time Linda Lovelace was willing to tell her story, the increasingly and surprisingly violent fallout of the sexual revolution ensured that many other women would tell theirs as well. One of the particularly cathartic moments in this regard was provided by the Meese Commission on Pornography.

·  ·  ·  ·  ·

At the Minnesota hearings, Boreman testified that "during the filming of *Deep Throat*, actually after the first day, I suffered a brutal beating in my room for smiling on the set." Lovelace was disappointed by the film crew's lack of response: "I figure out of twenty people, there might be one human being that would do something to help me" as she was being beaten and screaming for help, but "nobody, not one person came to help me." Thirteen years later, she felt justified in extrapolating from that one incident to the behavior of the culture at large; she felt "very hurt and very disappointed in my society and my country," for allowing her to be raped and beaten for the sexual titillation of moviegoers across the country. That the film was still in circulation and that one day one of her three children might see it only intensified the sense of violation and betrayal that the culture allowed. "Virtually every time someone watches that film, they are watching me being raped," she said.[21]

At that point in the hearings, Lovelace was interrupted by Andrea Dworkin, who documented the rise of rape of the throat and subsequent injury in the wake of the film's distribution by reading a letter from a counselor at a New York crisis center for women. "I was staying at this guy's house," Miss D. testified, "and he tried to make me have oral sex with him. He said he'd seen far out stuff in movies, and that it would be fun to mentally and physically torture a woman."[22] Dworkin made the connection between this sort of "throat rape" trauma and the release of *Deep Throat*, in particular citing women who "show up in emergency rooms because men believe they can penetrate, deep-thrust to the bottom of a women's throat."[23]

But *Deep Throat* was only the most famous of a whole flood of pornographic films, all of which advocated some form of sexual torture. Wanda Richardson, a worker at the Harriet Tubman Women's Shelter, described the

> many, many examples of women coming to the shelter who have cases of combined sexual and physical assault where the violence and the sex is intertwined, but you can't tell the difference, it's so closely intertwined. They are a target not only for violence but also seen as sexually appealing. And a lot of times this is acted out at home where men will beat a woman and find that very sexually arousing. Many of the women come and say that immediately after he has done this to me, how could he expect me to not be upset like nothing has happened and to them nothing has happened. To the woman it has been a degrading experience, and to the man it has been sexually exciting.[24]

The women's movement was gradually turning into the sexual revolution's trauma ward. Much of the feminists' ire against patriarchy turns out, upon closer inspection, to be the inchoate rage they felt at being sexual guinea pigs in the hands of the sexual revolutionaries.

Diana West's *Rape in Marriage* and the subsequent campaign to change the country's laws to allow prosecution of husbands (culminating in the famous *Rideout* case, among others) serve as an index of the moral illiteracy of the feminist Left and its unfortunate penchant to blame the victim, in this case making matrimony the cause of the ills that grew out of the *abandonment* of matrimony. The anger of one of the "typical" women in West's book (all of whom lived in Berkeley, California, when surveyed) is instructive. She had just been sodomized by her boyfriend and was now a willing conscript fighting against "rape in marriage." The same sort of moral obtuseness often found its way into the Meese Committee testimony, which was informed that "battering happens behind the lace curtain of the sacred home."

Lace curtain or not, what become clear from the testimony is that once sexuality is "liberated" from matrimony and the moral order, it becomes an increasingly dangerous proposition. It became normative for the female companions of the liberated, who got their blueprints for sexual exploration from what they saw in the x-rated bookstores. One woman was "taken repeatedly by her boyfriend to the Rialto Theater and made to watch x-rated movies" and then taken home to act out what they saw. Since the movies were extremely violent, the woman eventually "ended up in the hospital," and after that in a shelter for battered women. Another woman was "imprisoned in the house by her husband," forced to watch pornographic video cassettes while tied to a chair, and then forced to act out what they were seeing on the screen. She too ended up severely injured and eventually in a shelter for women.

As of 1986, the consensus emerging among those running shelters for abused women was that sexual license was an all or nothing proposition. Sexual violence was "a continuum," a "monster," a living being with a will and agenda of its own, which could be kept at bay with effort and could not be unchained without violence. It was not a stable set of poses, or a force, like electricity, that could be turned up or down at will. It was like an addiction in which the dosage had to be increased to attain the same pleasure. Cheryl Champion, who worked in the field of sexual abuse from 1971 to 1983, noticed that "over the last 12 years pornography has become more and more violent, that the themes in it have become more and more explicit. It is, in a sense, as if we can't get enough of it, and so once you have seen one murder, not so explicitly, you need to have more and more portrayed realistically. You will find that people become saturated and those juveniles you see starting out with low levels of magazines that simply portray nudity, quickly move on to those in which instructions on how to rape and murder . . . are published." She is backed by psychologist Floyd Winecoff who says that instead of providing a release of tension, pornography "becomes a source of addiction," like alcohol: "There is temporary relief, but it is mood altering. And it is reinforcing, i.e., you want more because you got relief. It is this reinforcing characteristic that leads men to want the experience which they have in photographic fantasy to happen in real life."[25]

As a result, an endless search ensues to make the docile fantasy woman available in real life. When the actual woman objects because of physical pain or her repugnance at degradation, violence occurs because the "man who is already addicted to the feeling of needing to have sex, and the fantasy of being in control, becomes desperate in his behavior when confronted by a women who doesn't want what's being given out." As Michael Laslett writes, "I have been raised in a pornographic society. Pornographic images of women have surrounded and bombarded me throughout my life. Images which depict women primarily as sexual objects are available to me at any time, as sexually submissive, as meaning, yes even when they say no, as always wanting sex, and as finding abuse sexually enjoyable. . . . I am the result of a systematic socialization process which trains all men to oppress women, because it is in the interests of men as the economic, political, sexual and cultural rulers of this society to keep women down. Pornography is a crucial tool in the maintenance of male power."[26]

Nora Ephron can plausibly plead ignorance as her defense of the article she did on *Deep Throat* in *Esquire* in 1973. But the same can hardly be said of Betty Friedan and the other apologists for pornography who participated in a media event on January 16, 1986, that was eventually released as a pamphlet entitled *The Meese Commission Exposed: Proceedings of a National Coalition Against Censorship*. In attendance, in addition to Friedan, were Colleen Dewhurst, who eventually became head of the National Endowment for the Arts, Harriet Pilpel of the ACLU, who made a career of defending Alfred Kinsey long after the man was in his grave, and author Kurt Vonnegut.

Friedan, who has made a career out of portraying herself as sensitive to the needs of women, not only ignored the testimony of women like Linda Boreman who were tortured for the nation's sexual titillation, but actually indicted them for treason to their sex for collaborating with the Reagan administration. Ignoring the testimony of women who almost died as a result of pornography-inspired sexual experimentation, Friedan outdid even herself in claiming that "suppressing pornography is extremely dangerous to women." Not that Friedan likes pornography—"I find a lot of it . . . very boring, but I recognize the right of others who choose to be titillated in that way"— even as the trajectory of pornography by this time had made it clear, if the torture and death of women were necessary to gratify that wish.[27]

At this point, the Enlightenment had completed its odyssey from sex to horror. In the end, there is little difference between the feminist Friedan and the misogynist Marquis de Sade. Both agree that women are expendable accessories in the gratification of illicit passion; both agree that the human life of the weak is not as important as the gratification of the passions of the strong; both agree that the freedom of the powerful can require the torture and even murder of helpless women. In this regard, sexual slavery is one of the logical sequels of the legalization of abortion, which Ms. Friedan also defended. The only irony is that Friedan claims to be supporting women while espousing essentially Sadean views. It is a tribute to the Illuminist view of cultural determinism. Saying that feminism supported the torture of women makes Orwell's claim that "black is white" seem modest by comparison. Feminism, as Friedan's testimony makes clear, was from the start the women's auxiliary of sexual liberation. It demanded jobs and affirmative action, but essentially ratified the Left's demolition of the moral order, no matter what that meant in terms of women's suffering and death.

If hubris was involved, it was the hubris of the "invisible government," which felt that if the public swallowed the unnatural behavior that had been offered them by the mid-1980s, that same public in the hands of the Illuminist media elites and their spokesmen would swallow anything. "You know," Friedan continued, "some pornography certainly does degrade woman. It also degrades men and it degrades sex. The pornography that pushes violence is particularly deplorable. But the forces that want to suppress pornography are not in favor of suppressing guns." The non sequitur notwithstanding, what the Meese Commission and the unfortunate women who testified before it had learned was that pornography is an inherently unstable trajectory that begins with illicit sex and invariably ends in torture and death. Friedan said in her statement that "the ultimate obscenity in America is murderous violence" without the slightest indication that the evidence about the source of murderous violence in the libido emancipated from morals was all a matter of public record.[28] One escapee from sexual slavery told the Meese commission, "The pimp made pornography of all of us. He also made tape recordings of us having sex with him and recordings of our screams and pleading when he gave us brutal beatings. It was not unusual for him to threaten us with death. He would later use these recordings to humiliate us by playing them for his friends in our presence, for his own sexual arousal and to terrorize us and other women he brought home."[29]

The deliberate suppression of the truth about "liberated" sexuality by media elites, the invisible government mentioned by Bernays, is the main reason horror films became popular in the late 1970s, after an absence of more than a decade from the collective cultural consciousness. Horror was the only genre that told the truth about the sexual lives people were living in the gory aftermath of the sexual revolution. Robin Wood and others choose to see some Reagan administration–inspired conspiracy behind the decline of porno chic and the rise of horror in the 1970s, but the real explanation is at once simpler and more complex. Sex disconnected from the moral order is horrifying. The culture had to learn that lesson the hard way, and Hollywood was only ratifying in its way what the culture had learned in the bedroom and was choosing at the box office as catharsis. "Even those who set themselves up against you," wrote St. Augustine, "do but copy you in a perverse way."

. . . . .

During the late 1970s, Hollywood was simply portraying Nemesis as the monster who returns to restore moral equilibrium, because the people who had been damaged by sexual liberation had an unfilled psychic need to have their situation described and were willing to pay handsomely those who could describe it. By 1980 the light-hearted tone of *Deep Throat* no longer made sense as an adequate description of the real consequences of sexual revolution, but *Alien*, which also portrayed oral sex, did. The box office became Hollywood's vehicle back to reality.

But the vehicle is not the destination, a confusion Michael Medved suffers in his *Hollywood vs. America*, where he criticizes the film industry for being "hopelessly out of touch with the public they are trying to reach." According to Medved, the film industry does not "understand the values of the average American family, or the special concerns of the typical parents who worry about unwholesome influences on their kids."[30]   Medved goes on to cite one big budget debacle after another, from *The Last Temptation of Christ* to *Naked Lunch*, as an indication that Hollywood is willing to put ideology over profits in its campaign to force its perverse view of humanity down the throats of the American public.

The argument is effective if not pushed too far.  To begin with, the whole idea of a culture war makes sense only if the instruments of culture can influence behavior, and if that is the case, then we can hardly speak of the American public as untouched by the corruption coming out of Hollywood.  The reason Hollywood has so much power is that so many people pay to see the corrupting films that Hollywood wants to sell.

But another point about Hollywood's intentions needs to be made as well.  No one will deny that the industry has a fairly coherent set of values, all of which are contrary to the moral wisdom of the West. Medved quotes the Lichter-Rothman survey of Hollywood attitudes that corroborated what the country had suspected all along: the industry is dominated by sexual revolutionaries.  To give just one example, only 16 percent of those surveyed agreed with the statement "adultery is wrong."  Fifty-one percent, on the other hand, refused to condemn marital infidelity "in even the mildest terms."[31]  Even granting all this, horror presents an anomalous situation, for as Medved himself conceded in a recent conversation, the message of horror contradicts the message of sexual liberation in such a radical way that it seems to cast the whole notion intentionally into doubt when it comes to film.  ("Yes," Medved said when I brought up the horror genre in light of his thesis, "they all get killed while having sex.")

Human beings find sexuality endlessly stimulating.  Prostitution is just one indication that men are willing to pay to have these desires gratified outside the moral order.  Hollywood broke the Production Code because it recognized that it could make a lot of money by exploiting these desires.  But why wasn't the history of film from then on just one more technically refined pornographic extravaganza after another?  Why did *Film Comment* in its retrospective of the 1970s take note of the rise and fall of porno chic? Why, given the Enlightenment's view of human sexuality, would porn ever become passé, as it did in the 1970s? After winning the cultural war, the pornographers were defeated by something that was completely outside their psychic equation. And instead of turning out bigger and better sex pictures, the decade ended by portraying monsters. How did this happen?

To answer this question we have to explain the not-so-simple relationship between intention and reality. If the horror tradition does anything, it calls into question the relationship between what you want and what you get.

One of the axioms of contemporary American culture is the sovereignty of human desire. Human intention is nothing more than the executive branch of human desire, and now that human intention has at its disposal the power of science and technology, human desire has hegemony over reality. That was, of course, the dream of the Enlightenment, and in a way it has come true. But does desire (and therefore intention) really rule over reality? The horror tradition seems to indicate otherwise. In fact the monster is in many ways nothing more than the being that contradicts our intentions. The one area, indicated above, where there seems to be all but universal consensus that desire has hegemony over reality is in the realm of sexuality, but ironically—or perhaps not so ironically—it is precisely this area that is so thickly inhabited with monsters. There must, therefore, be some sort of connection here, something that contravenes the conventional wisdom when it comes to the tricky relationship between intention and result.

The key lies in understanding the Enlightenment's idea of the universe as a machine, which is to say, something that operates according to its own endogenous laws. This machine originally had a creator of sorts, the *Deus absconditus* of the philosophes, but even that pale approximation of God was attenuated to the point of nonexistence when Darwin proposed evolution as the fulfillment of the Enlightenment dream: creation without a creator. Once that truncation of the universe had been accomplished, only one set of intentions was left in the universe, namely, man's. If anything was intended, then man alone could do the intending. That, combined with the ever-increasing power of technology, led to the illusion that intention now somehow had hegemony over being, which was in turn seen as nothing but an empty vehicle that could be imbued with whatever meaning man thought appropriate.

Nowhere was this more the case than in human sexuality, which was seen by the social engineers as one more river to be channeled as the engineers saw fit. Social engineering invariably took sexuality as its prime challenge, since sexual liberation was the engine that drove the Enlightenment, and in many ways was the prime criterion of whether it was working. Since the only people who took up the challenge of reengineering sexuality were those who felt it had no inherent meaning anyway, the only barriers were the classic villains of Enlightenment mythology, religion (read *superstition*) and morals, its sickly offspring. Since both religion and morals were the offspring of social conditioning, all that was needed was to change the conditioning to bring about a new morality; all the other projects in between were obstacles that the social sciences could smooth away.

But suppose nature had a sense of purpose written into its very being? Suppose, *pace* Darwin, it was, in fact, creation, that is, the orderly reasonable work of a Creator. Darwin simply avoided the issue, and those who were avid to escape the eternal responsibilities consequent to existence as a rational being in a created universe were hardly going to bring them up either. So the notion of nature as tabula rasa waiting for man's intention became, in effect, the unofficial ideology of the West, both capitalist and socialist.

Sexuality was thus seen as just one more "natural" phenomenon, one more mechanism that needed to be explained according to physical laws, which, once complete, would dispense with any connection sex might have to either morals or procreation. But every organ in every animal has a very definite function, an all or nothing propositions for the animal concerned. There is no such thing as half an eye, for example. An eye either sees, in which case it confers an advantage in the struggle for existence which might be fostered by natural selection, or it does not, in which case it does not confer any advantage and, therefore, cannot be selected, naturally or otherwise. Like seeing, sex has a purpose, and its purpose is reproduction. This is not its only purpose, but just as the eye may have other purposes, such as being an attractive ornament for a pretty face, all of its purposes revolve around the purpose which is essential to its being.

Janet Smith makes the counter-Enlightenment point about sexuality in her book on contraception, *Humanae Vitae: A Generation Later*:

> Sexual organs are naturally ordered to procreation and nothing can render them not ordered to procreation. This ordination, whether capable of being actualized or not, is inherent. This is equivalent to saying that eyes that are being used to see, eyes that are closed, and blind eyes are still ordered to seeing; eyes blind at birth and eyes blinded by some deliberate act are still ordered to seeing. "Being ordered to seeing" means that the eye, even the eye that cannot perform its function, has a natural function and specific work. Only eyes can be "given" or restored to the power of seeing because only eyes do that kind of work; ears and noses do not. The same is true of sexual organs; sexual organs, whether fertile or infertile, temporarily or permanently, by the choice of the individual or not, are ordered to procreation. They are organs of the reproductive kind; thus, they are often called reproductive organs; the word genitals has Latin roots with the word birth.[32]

At the core of sexual liberation, the Enlightenment's driving force, was essentially the suppression of the generative function of human sexuality in the interest of some other goal, a human goal, which was grafted onto it and became sexuality's main meaning. Because every sexual act is in its essence a procreative act (although not all sexual acts lead to conception), provision must be made for the offspring that might eventuate from that act. This has become the major burden of mankind beyond the necessities of life. Once the necessities have been taken care of, the seemingly arbitrary nature of this connection looms large in the minds of those who are especially eager for sexual pleasure or who wish to transcend the human condition; hence the utopian community of sexual sharing proposed by Shelley and his circle and virtually every other revolutionary.

The most obvious solution to this problem came with the invention of the oral contraceptive in the 1960s. That invention, along with penicillin to control syphilis, was the technological sine qua non of the most recent phase of sexual liberation. But thwarting reproduction in no way changes the nature of the sexual act, no more than rendering a man blind changes the nature of seeing. The same is true of sexuality. In fact, the act of suppression may well do nothing more than fix the nature of the act in the mind of the suppressor in a more insistent way than would sex without the suppression.

The monster is essentially a reminder of the gap between intention and reality, a reminder of that suppression. In his essay on "the uncanny" (*Das Unheimliche*), Freud talks about the return of the repressed. Citing Schelling, Freud calls the uncanny, "everything that is supposed to remain a secret and hidden but which reveals itself." The uncanny moment is the "moment of unintended repetition," Freud continues, "which we would otherwise speak of only as 'coincidence.'"[33] The thing that causes terror is the something that has been repressed and returns. "Un" in the word "Unheimlich" or "uncanny" is the mark of repression.

Freud tries to psychologize the concept of conscience, but clearly the role of conscience is central here and, furthermore, the moral order is the vehicle of psychic representation. Thus sexual activity of the liberated sort, which attempts to repress the procreative nature of the sexual action, brings to mind the very thing it attempts to repress, namely, reproduction, every time it engages in it. Sexual liberation, that is, becomes a radically schizophrenic enterprise. Every time the man commits the sexual act he is confronted with the very thing he hoped to repress by acting outside the moral order. His intention only confounds itself by confronting an ineradicable "nature" in the very heart of the thing he hoped to engineer according to his desires. All monsters are, as Morbius discovered, ultimately monsters from the Id. What is true of the individual psyche is also true of its cultural reflection, and in turn, in its display in film.

As far as desire and intention go, what Hollywood wanted was clear. Over a period of two years, from 1965 to 1967, the movie moguls broke the power of the Production Code and arrogated to themselves the right to show nudity and soon thereafter sexual activity on the screen of first-run movies. What they got—and by extension what the nation that supported them got—was something that completely surpassed their intentions, but a something which nonetheless substantiated the moral law in a way they could not have foreseen and which they probably would still not admit. To recapitulate the past forty years of film history, which was in its way a recapitulation of the past two hundred and fifty years of the Enlightenment: they wanted sex but got horror instead.

9

*Alien and Contraception*

ELECTRICITY WAS THE PRIME FORCE for classical Enlightenment culture, and Frankenstein was its monster, the application of that force gone awry. Blood was the prime force for
the Darwinian modification of that culture; Dracula was its monster,
its ultimate embodiment. In the final phase of this trajectory, which
found its best expression in the film medium, *Alien*, following on the
heels of *Psycho* and *Deep Throat*, embodied the result of the culture's
conversion, prompted by the contraceptive, to sexual liberation.

The contraceptive was the technological breakthrough that would
make the Enlightenment dream of unlimited, untrammeled, and is-
sueless sex a reality. Unfortunately, the very act of repression involved
in the act of contraception reinstated the life that was suppressed in
the form of a monster that took its revenge. The procreative function
of sexuality was suppressed because the essence of sexual liberation is
the separation of life and love. The consequence is the death of both
life and love, each in its separate way, but the immediate consequence
of this repression was the return of the repressed.

The idea for *Alien* came from a scriptwriter by the name of Dan
O'Bannon, a friend of John Carpenter at the University of Southern
California film school, where they had collaborated on a film called
*Dark Star*, itself in part the inspiration for *Star Wars*. In 1975 O'Bannon

got a call from Alejandro Jodorowsky, whose psychedelic Western, *El Topo*, had become one of the certified cult films of the 1960s. Jodorowsky was in Paris filming *Dune*, and O'Bannon found the director "a genuine mystic, mesmerizing in a nearly supernatural way." So when Jodorowsky called O'Bannon and said, "I want you to direct the special effects on *Dune*. Sell everything you own, come to Paris. I come into your life like a hurricane," O'Bannon obeyed.[1]

Jodorowsky went out of O'Bannon's life in hurricane fashion as well. His mysticism did not extend to financial matters. The producers of the film went broke after having invested two million dollars, and O'Bannon went home, equally broke, and sublimated his anger and frustration by writing the script for *Alien*. "Instead of going out and murdering people," O'Bannon told *Film Comment* after *Alien* had become a film legend, "instead of suppressing anger, I write screen plays. The angrier I am, the better I write. Take *Alien*. I was mad that *Dune* had collapsed, I was living on Ron Shusett's couch. I didn't have two dimes to rub together. I had serious stomach problems. So I embodied all this physical and mental pain in the *Alien* monster."[2]

As O'Bannon told *Film Comment*, trying to explain the source of his horror imagery, "We children growing up, most of us felt safe: our parents would protect us, cops were our friends; we were largely oblivious to world unrest. Both because we are now adults and because the world has changed, that comforting obliviousness is gone. Somebody gets shot down the street. Banks cut off your money because of some twisted clerical error. Noises get on your nerves. Privacy is gone." O'Bannon grew up in St. Louis after World War II, and his sense that "the world has changed" corresponds roughly to our cultural revolution, as does his sense that a lack of privacy is at the root of the menace.[3]

What O'Bannon came up with in terms of special effects, however, was about as intimidating as the beach ball that represented the monster in *Dark Star*. Liking the story but not the physical appearance of the monster, O'Bannon remembered H. R. Giger from his illfated collaboration with Jodorowsky on *Dune*. According to O'Bannon, "I told Ridley [Scott, director of *Alien*], 'When you see this man's work it'll be so disturbing that you'll know that it—and he—is what you want.'"[4] Giger, born in 1940, is six years older than O'Bannon and grew up in a small town Switzerland, where he still resides. His father was a pharmacist. Giger was an only child whose early interest in guns was supplemented but not supplanted by an interest in sexual experimentation that took on a progressively darker tone as the sexual revolution matured into the death-oriented thing it was to become by the time *Alien* was made. Like O'Bannon, Giger seems to connect menace with lack of privacy. Giger ultimately got the *Alien* job because of a book he had published in 1975 called *Necronomicon*, which documents among other things his tumultuous and unhappy affair with a Swiss actress by the name of Li Tobler. O'Bannon felt that Giger's drawings best embodied the monster he had in mind, and Ridley Scott concurred, but the source of Giger's monster was his affair with Tobler. The monster was, in other words, a representation of sexual trauma.

On February 14, 1970, Giger had a dream remarkably similar to what happened to Steve Frehling in *Poltergeist II*. Giger dreamed he was lying on a bed and watching his girlfriend Li dance "in a yellow dress which sprayed sparks of yellow light across the room." Suddenly, in the middle of the dance, the room took on the characteristics of a living being:

> The walls pulsated in time with my heart-beat. The first sign of anxiety came when I suddenly had to piss and went to the lavatory. The edge of the wc bowl grew slowly toward my penis like a wide open vagina as if to castrate me. At first, the idea amused me, but suddenly the whole room began to grow narrower and narrower, the walls and pipes took on the aspect of loose skin with festering wounds, and small, repellent creatures glared out at me from the dark corners and cracks. I turned and hurried towards the exit, but the door was infinitely far away and very narrow and tall. The walls hemmed me in like two paunchy lumps of flesh. I leapt for the door, drew the bolt and rushed into the corridor, gasping for breath. Rid of the specter, I went into Li's room and lay down. Little B[oris Buehler, son of Li's friend] was also in the room and wanted to play with me. He began to trample on the bed beside me, kicking me. I was as helpless as a small child

and could not defend myself. Li finally rescued me from my diminutive tormentor, who had now turned into a little violet-green devil with an offensively mean and aggressive expression. Li took B to his mother who was hanging around in the kitchen. But the couple of kicks in the stomach had been enough. I felt sick. The air in the room was stifling. My only thought was to throw open the window and escape to the garden, for the room was at ground level. But at the last minute I noticed a woman looking at me strangely. The vomit already in my mouth, I turned round, rushed into the corridor and suddenly stopped dead—I was afraid to go into the narrow lavatory again. In the kitchen on the right I noticed E. with her son, both staring at me. The only sanctuary was the small bathroom and the rusty blue bath-tub with its flaking enamel. So I grabbed Li by the hand and dragged her into the bathroom, where I vomited into the bath-tub. The vomit spewed endlessly from my mouth in the form of a thick, grey, leathery worm turning into a kind of primeval slime, and once into the living intestines of a slaughtered pig. During this whole performance I had held Li firmly by the left wrist . She had been struggling to free the clogged waste pipe by pok-ing at it with a ballpoint pen. Finally she could no longer stand the repulsive, garlic-impregnated smell, and we both vomited together into the bathtub, hand in hand, while the gas water heater glared at us malevolently. Now I was afraid of being alone, and Li had to keep holding me by the hand, like a small child.

Eventually Giger and his girlfriend escape from the malevolent house, but once he gets outside everything seems just as threatening. His imagination turns "harmless passers-by . . . into crazed murderers. Ev-erything seemed hostile towards me—houses, cars, trees—only water could calm me down. A trench dug by the roadside threatened to swallow me up. Despite Li's assurances that it was not so, the pave-ment seemed to slant violently, so that I kept sliding sideways into the trench. I clung to Li with tear-filled eyes, for I seemed lost with-out her."[5]

Giger made it clear that he never wanted to marry Tobler, and beyond that, that he never wanted to have children. He claims that he never fathered a child by her, and never procured an abortion, but his art is full of images of abortion and dead babies.  As a result we are faced with two options: either Giger is not telling the truth when he says that he never aborted any of his children, or the fear and hatred of children, the prevention of children by contraception, is so morally significant that it embeds itself onto his consciousness every bit as indelibly as an abortion would.  There is some evidence for the latter interpretation in Giger's other paintings.  In a painting entitled *Noracyclin* (contraceptive pills) done in 1965, the round pill dispenser becomes the magazine for a revolver, the name of the contraceptive written on the barrel of the gun.  Giger's imagery substantiates in a perverse way the teaching of the Fathers of the Church, who were all but unanimous in viewing contraception as a form of homicide.

In 1974 Giger painted *The Spell II*, something he refers to as a "ritual picture," in which a figure resembling Li presides over a mechanical altar.  In between her spread legs, a dead baby's head drops into a pan in a clear reference to abortion, perhaps in a ritual setting as described, among others, by J. K. Huysman in his satanic novel *Là-Bas*.  On either side of the Li figure, on top of the altar where the candles are placed for a Catholic Mass, there are six condoms surmounted by the heads of dead babies, an indication that prolephobia, the hatred of children, is the main issue here.  Contraception or abortion are merely means that should not be confused with the end.

In a portrait of Tobler that Giger painted in 1967, she is portrayed as having an abdomen devoid of organs and a growth on the back of her skull.  The reference to prolephobia and its psychic consequences is obvious.  The womb was scraped clean, but the fetus instead of disappearing simply changed its place of residence.  Once it was prevented from growing in her womb, it started growing in her mind, a troubled conscience that could not be repressed.  All of the images are monstrous bio-mechanoids, to use Giger's term, and representations of the logical outcome of La Mettrie's assertion that man is a machine.

Giger's dream suddenly takes on meaning in light of his attitude toward children.  Living with Li's girlfriend Eveline Buehler means living with Eveline's child, Boris, who becomes in Giger's words, a "diminutive tormentor," who kicks Giger in the stomach, the place closest to the womb, and brings on nausea, and then vomiting.  The vomiting is an instance of what Freud would have called "the return of the repressed." Seeing little Boris reminds Giger of the actions he has taken to thwart childbearing. The discomfort is so acute that vomiting up the repressed guilt is the only action that brings relief.

But the relief is only temporary. If Giger can repress his own progeny so ruthlessly, then he can no longer count on moral restraint on the part of those who might threaten him. The result is terror. Sexual liberation, once again, has led to horror. What before might have been perceived as "harmless passers-by" have been transformed by "my brain . . . into crazed murderers." His only hope is Li, but that hope is conditional. If through her he could welcome children, the world might lose its threatening aspect. But like so many, Giger cannot make up his mind. He wants to be able to repress children with impunity, but he does not want Little Boris's kicks to remind him that his actions have made the world a dangerous place.

The dominant culture has attempted to disconnect sexual activity from offspring; it has attempted to repress the procreative by any means necessary, including murder, but the moral order will not allow itself to be repressed. Vomiting in Giger's dream and in films like *Poltergeist II* is the unmistakable sign that the intrinsically procreative nature of the sexual act, in its turn, will not allow itself to be repressed. Both suburbia and bohemia are haunted by prolephobia. All the Frehling family of *Poltergeist II* wants is to be left alone to live a normal suburban life. But their house is haunted and their lives are full of horror, the indication that they have forgotten the connection between good and evil. Life becomes a series of inexplicable events.

Prolephobia is the Rosetta Stone that explains the culture that embraces the contraceptive as its vehicle to freedom. The monsters that haunt both Steve Frehling's suburbia and H. R. Giger's bohemia are the souls of the rejected children. In films like *Poltergeist II*, in the work of H. R. Giger, in the utterances of Kate Michelman, and in the uneasiness of the culture and its increasingly frequent scenes of horror, the force that propels the corpses out of the ground is the uneasy conscience that can only find rest by confessing, that is, airing its wicked deeds. In Hollywood's terms, the need for confession is so urgent that it takes the form of vomiting up the monster, as in *Polter-*

*geist II*, or having the fetus-monster explode out of John Hurt's stomach, as in *Alien*.

What is true of individuals is true of cultures as well. *Alien* is about procreation: it is a treatise on the culture's neurotic reaction to the truth that procreation is a part of sex. Like Giger's art, which provides the visual imagery for the film, *Alien* is an expression of fear and hatred of children: the fetus is portrayed as a monster. Technology overcomes the problematic fact that children are inseparably linked with sexuality. It also overcomes the problem of venereal disease, the outcome of promiscuous sex. So the feminist, in order to bring about liberation from nature, must put all her eggs in the technological basket. Unfortunately, and this is the recurrent nightmare of *Alien*, technology fails to deliver on its promise. This is true for a number of reasons. Technology often fails; it does not prevent all pregnancies, nor does it cure or prevent all diseases. But it fails for a deeper reason because the problems created by the abandonment of the moral order are not amenable to technological solutions. *Forbidden Planet* gives the best explanation of this truth in the horror-science fiction genre, but *Alien* in its inchoate way comes close to making the same statement. The real monsters are "monsters from the Id." After two hundred years of unhappiness, the consensus on Enlightenment culture that emerges in the tropes of horror is that technology, as in the final scenes of *Forbidden Planet*, cannot stop "monsters from the Id." In the absence of moral restraint, the only way to destroy them is by destroying ourselves, which makes sense, in a way, since the monsters are simply externalizations of our immoral desires.

The trek of the astronauts through the vaginal opening of the derelict spaceship in *Alien* is in many ways analogous to the trajectory of pornography. As the violation becomes more overt, the situation becomes more dangerous. The Alien, in this respect, is quite simply the sexual drive emancipated from the moral order; the Alien is sex, as Ash, a member of the crew, says, "unclouded by conscience, remorse or delusions of morality."[6] The unique testimony of horror literature is that the liberation that everyone sees as a universal good turns out to inspire horror instead. The monster's arrival is the admission of what everyone knows, but what no one can admit.

This ambivalence becomes impossible to avoid in the two sequels to *Alien*. In *Aliens*, the second part of this saga, Ripley (Sigourney Weaver) returns to the planet she barely escaped in *Alien* to destroy the female monster, which by its uncontrolled fertility threatens the well-being of the universe. *Aliens* is a feminist fantasy. Like her feminist sisters, Ripley feels that in order to survive, indeed in order for the universe to survive, she must destroy female fertility. We have in the *Alien* trilogy the entire psychic trajectory of population control, which begins with the personal use of contraception and abortion as solutions to personal problems and then becomes generalized, through the guilty conscience, into a solution for global problems. According to feminism, fecundity is the enemy, and technology the cure. The ambivalence arrives with the realization that in neutering herself, the feminist negates what makes her unique as a female and a human being. As Ripley discovers in *Alien III*, in destroying her fertility she must destroy herself.

*Alien* is Nemesis, which according to William Godwin's book on Greek mythology is a "personification of the moral indignation felt at all derangements of the natural equilibrium of things." Nemesis, like the Alien, is a female with preternatural power, in other words, a goddess who "hates every transgression of the bound of moderation and restores the proper and normal order of things." Nemesis, the divinity of chastisement and vengeance, is also called Adrastia . . . meaning "she whom none can escape." It takes Ripley three films to find this out.

*Alien* and its sequels become, as a result, a feminist meditation on the technological means needed to destroy fertility and the psychic ambivalence that results from using those means. The end of *Alien* is an elaborate description of how Ripley got rid of the Alien that has an uncanny resemblance to abortion, abortion being the obvious technological solution to an unwanted intruder in the female body: "With the Alien nowhere in sight Ripley cautiously moves through the passageway into the shuttlecraft. The shuttlecraft door closes just as the first series of minor explosions begin to rock the Nostromo. Finally, the Narcissus is launched and pulls rapidly away from the mother ship. After watching the final destiny of her ship and crewmates, Ripley prepares for hypersleep and the long uncertain journey home. As part of these preparations she puts her cat in the freezerino."[7] Ripley then takes off her clothes, and as soon as she does so the Alien reappears. Here we have the truncated causality of the horror genre. As in *The Bacchae*, *The Blob*, *Blood Feast*, *Slumber Party Massacre*, and countless other examples, as soon as an attractive young woman removes any article of clothing a monster appears whose task is to kill the woman and destroy the city, or in this instance the spaceship.

More vulnerable than ever before, Ripley retreats into the cramped quarters of the equipment locker and watches incredulously as the Alien moves through the maze of machinery. The Alien confronts Ripley and, "in a macabre display of its power," bares its teeth.[8] In fact, what the Alien exhibits is its penis-like tongue with teeth on the end. In another reference to *Deep Throat*, the Alien flicks out his penis tongue next to her mouth. Once again the feminist fantasy-phobia intrudes.

"Cautiously and methodically Ripley continues to follow her plan, hoping against all hope that she will have enough time to carry it through." This plan entails having Ripley "push . . . buttons to release the hot gases she hopes will jolt the Alien from its lair and into a position to be blown from the ship."[9] After two unsuccessful tries, Ripley finds the right button and sends the creature reeling. Unfortunately she does not succeed in killing it and is forced to take more drastic measures, ones that unsurprisingly jeopardize her own life as well—as is often the case with abortion. The more the monster foils her technological efforts to destroy it, the more it becomes apparent that the creature is in some way a manifestation of herself. What thing is it that is closest to a woman's self and yet not that woman? We have two possibilities: as in *Forbidden Planet*, the woman's disordered desires or her guilty conscience, and, more directly related to the imagery of the film itself, an unborn child. In *Alien*, the two possibilities are fused into one monster. The two are related in real life as well. The inordinate desire that leads to sexual union outside marriage often results in an unwanted intruder in the body, an Alien being that causes fear and loathing. Women in this situation are prone to seek a technological solution to a moral problem, that is, abortion, which is precisely what happens in the film.

Ripley cannot get rid of the Alien, who remains in the spaceship and continues to stalk her. According to the film's screenplay, "the Alien is almost upon her when Ripley suddenly turns to her control panel ready to blow open the shuttlecraft's hatch. Ripley's hand slams hard on the activator button. . . . The hatch flies open, air whooshes from the craft as the ship quickly depressurizes, and the Alien is jettisoned into space."[10] The monster, in other words, is sucked out of the spaceship by the vacuum, just as the fetus is sucked from its mother's womb by a suction abortion machine.

In keeping with the nightmare quality of this film (technology is omnipresent and all-powerful, though it never really achieves what it is supposed to achieve), the Alien is not really aborted after all, but "remains suspended in space by the umbilical-like graplon rope." The "umbilical-like" rope indicates that the abortion was not successful after all, but probably not in any physical sense. We have most likely entered the realm of conscience, and the "return of the repressed" represents the guilt that resides in the conscience of the mother after the abortion has been successfully completed. In the nightmare world of *Alien*, the success of the abortion guarantees its failure, because in killing her child the mother implants it eternally into her guilt-ridden conscience. This explains the sickening sense of return, the return of the repressed, that permeates all three *Alien* films. At this point, the unfortunate Alien makes the mistake of attempting to reboard the craft through its exhaust engine. Ripley acts quickly; she fires up the space craft's engines, "And finally, almost in disbelief, Ripley watches as the last vestige of the Alien disappears into space."[11]

The relief, of course, is only temporary.

In *Aliens*, Ripley is asked to return to do battle against the hyperfertile female monster. It has laid "thousands of eggs," and has become a "hostile organism" that "has colonized the planet," outreproducing the human families that live there. Differential fertility is the recurrent fantasy of contraceptive societies. Their solution is to destroy the beings that threaten to outreproduce them. Ripley, in this

respect, makes it clear that she is not going to go back out there unless the mission is "To destroy not to study, right?"

Vasquez, the female marine in *Aliens,* struts through the film in
macho parody of a man and a marine. The male commander of the
mission is hopelessly inadequate and is promptly dismissed by Ripley
in a moment of crisis. The film has the feel of feminist propaganda
save that the women do not fare much better than the men. Vasquez
has to commit suicide in the arms of a man to escape the monster.
Ripley, as in the first film, is left to fight the monster alone, but with
the help of technology, dressed up in a "forklift" suit. The monster
has the uncanny ability to evade the most destructive forces known to
man, forces that are unleashed without qualms of conscience and include the nuclear destruction of the entire planet.

Just why the monster is indestructible becomes clear by the middle
of the film. The marines are equipped with motion detectors that allow
them to perceive the monster without actually seeing it. As the monsters approach, the marines weld the compartment door shut only to
have the monsters go over and under it through what look like heat-
ing ducts. The cinematic reference to the Krell of *Forbidden Planet* is
clear, which means that the monsters in the language of horror-science fiction films are monsters from the Id, which is why they defeat
technology so easily, why they invariably end up back on the spaceship with Ripley after the nuclear bombs have gone off, and why Ripley
can only kill the monster by killing herself, as she does in *Aliens III.*

None of this understanding of the connection between maternity
and femininity makes it into Barbara Creed's critique of *Alien,* which
lurches from one misapplied Freudian paradigm to another without
pursuing any one of them to a consistent conclusion. After establishing the spaceship as the "archaic mother," Creed goes on to describe
an Alien's popping out of an egg and attaching itself to Hurt's face as
"a representation of the primal scene," recalling Freud's reference to a
fantasy where the subject imagines travelling back inside the womb
to watch his parents having sexual intercourse, perhaps to watch himself being conceived.[12]

Creed informs us that "the notion of the fecund mother-as-abyss
. . . is central to *Alien*; it is the abyss, the cannibalizing black hole from

which and to which all life returns that is represented in the film as a source of deepest terror."[13]  As with all of the other Freudian paradigms she brings to bear on the text, the "fecund mother-as-abyss" confuses rather than clarifies the issue.  Is fecundity the source of terror or is the source of terror fecundity released from morality—in other words, sexuality emancipated from the moral law?  If the issue were merely fecundity, technology would be more consoling and more effective in eradicating the monsters.  Although contraception fails a certain percentage of the time, abortion works most of the time.  The fact that the monster inevitably returns after seemingly successful attempts to eradicate it indicates that the monster is not a physical entity.  It is something psychic, like the ineradicable pangs of bad conscience or something as relentless as the libido—or monsters from the Id, to use the terminology of *Forbidden Planet* that was appropriated in *Aliens*.

Creed relies consistently on Freudian jargon and concepts which simply do not apply.  Central to her understanding of horror is the "Freudian position that woman horrifies because she is castrated":

> The concept of the monstrous-feminine, as constructed within by a patriarchal and phallocentric ideology, is related intimately to the problem of sexual difference and castration.  If we accept Freud's interpretation that the "Medusa's head takes the place of a representation of the female genitals," we can see that the Medusan myth is mediated by a narrative about the difference of female sexuality as a difference which is grounded in monstrousness and which invokes castration anxiety in the male spectator. "The sight of the Medusa's head makes the spectator stiff with terror, turns him to stone". . . . In this respect, it could well be maintained that it is womens' sexuality, that which renders them desirable—but also threatening—to men, which constitutes the real problem that the horror cinema exists to explore, and which constitutes also and ultimately that which is really monstrous.[14]

Creed sees a connection between procreation and the monster in *Alien* but then gets sidetracked when she tries to understand the connection through Freudian paradigms.  Creed is correct in seeing the wrecked spaceship as a representation of the female body. The crew members enter that body-spaceship through a vaginal opening between what looks like two outspread legs. Once inside, Hurt lowers himself into what looks like the spaceship's equivalent of a uterus, a hollow slimy space full of eggs. At this point in her discussion, Creed changes Freudian horses. Now the source of horror is no longer the female as castrated male: when "woman is represented as monstrous it is always in relation to her mothering and reproductive functions." Creed then cites Julia Kristeva's conclusion in *Powers of Horror*: "Fear of the archaic mother turns out to be essentially fear of her generative power."[15]

Creed cannot seem to answer basic questions about fertility. Is it, for example, good or bad? Is motherhood good or bad? When it comes to the procreative powers of the female, feminists like Creed are hardly sympathetic, as their support of abortion shows. Feminist complicity in this violation of woman's procreative power can only lead to further neurotic avoidance of the issue that will not go away, and so in *Alien*, it leads to the creation of a monster, a nameless monster in the mode of Frankenstein, which both exhibits and denies the feminist's ambivalence about her procreative powers.

*Alien* is relentlessly feminist in its attack on fertility. By making the monster into a fertile female, *Alien* seems to be forcing the perceptive viewer to certain conclusions, conclusions consistent with feminism, but conclusions no feminist would care to admit. As a result, the hermeneutic machinery breaks down as she struggles to decide whether the primal mother is good or bad. Just what is the monster here? To answer that question the ambivalence toward being female needs to be resolved. Creed attempts an answer, but as before is hindered by the Freudian worldview: "The central characteristic of the archaic mother is her total dedication to the generative, procreative principle. She is the mother who conceives all by herself, the original parent, the godhead of all fertility and the origin of procreation. She is outside morality and the law. Ash, the Science Officer, who is also a cyborg, delivers a eulogy to the eponymous Alien of the film which could be a description of this mother: 'I admire its purity; a survivor unclouded by conscience, remorse or delusions of morality.'"[16]

As before, Creed stumbles across a crucial passage and then ignores it because it does not conform to the Freudian paradigm that purports to explain it. A more apt interpretive paradigm comes from Andrea Dworkin. At the hearings of the Meese Commission on pornography in 1983, Dworkin read into the record a "letter . . . from a New York crisis worker about the increased existence of rape of the throat, since the distribution of the movie *Deep Throat*."[17] In her book *Intercourse*, Dworkin developed the same theme further, talking about the throat becoming during the 1970s a substitute for the vagina and as a result "the harbinger of what has become a common practice of sexual assault now: throat rape, deep thrusting into the throat as if it were a female genital, a vagina, in the manner of the pornographic film *Deep Throat*."[18] *Alien* is, on this view, the sequel to *Deep Throat*. Both are about oral sex; only by 1979 oral sex is not fun anymore. *Alien* implies that it had become apparent that oral sex could kill you.

As Ash says, the most significant thing about the monster in *Alien* is that it exists without "a conscience, remorse, or delusions of morality." The monster in *Alien*, in other words, is sex disconnected from morals, now returned as a destructive force. Like the Alien, the moral order cannot be destroyed. It can be repressed, but as Ripley learns, the repressed always returns. What could have been embraced as a principle of order returns as a principle of destruction. What could have been embraced as a child was destroyed as a fetus, which now achieves immortality in the guilty conscience of the woman who destroyed it. Alien is a horror film in the classic mode. It is the antithesis of what the Marquis de Sade espoused in his pornographic tracts; it is the essence of what Mary Shelley warned against in Frankenstein, and it remains incomprehensible to those who attempt to understand horror while at the same time espousing the Enlightenment.

CONCLUSION

# *Misreading Horror*

HORROR IS A LOT LIKE THE WEATHER; it is both familiar and incomprehensible. Everyone talks about horror, but no one understands it; and no one understands it because to understand it would mean to violate the desire our culture holds most sacred, namely, the desire for sexual liberation. Horror, to state the matter succinctly, is the Counter-Enlightenment, a negative reaction to the Enlightenment. But it is invariably a more or less unconscious reaction; indeed, the very imagery of horror—the monster that has no name—shrouds horror from conscious explication. The creator of the fictions of horror is simply someone who takes the premises of the Enlightenment to their logical conclusion. But in doing so, these artists generally do not understand the full implications of the fictions they create. The creators of the fictions of horror—Mary Shelley is a good example—create them, more often than not, as a way of representing something which they cannot bring themselves to articulate. Monsters thus invariably involve repression, and repression invariably involves the return of the repressed in a disguised, more palatable form.

As long as Enlightenment values perdure, there will be a psychic demand, and hence a market, for horror. The appearance of the monster always coincides with the implementation of Enlightenment values, especially in the form of revolution. Monsters always appear after

258

revolutions as mute witness to reform gone wrong, to freedom run amok, and most particularly to love and procreation untimely ripped from the sacramental matrix of matrimony. The Enlightenment asserts that man is a machine; the arrival of the monster on the scene is an indication that large numbers of people have acted on that essentially sexual premise and are suffering the consequences.

*Frankenstein*, an enduring cultural myth, articulated, in its inchoate way, the English reaction to the French Revolution, as mediated through the extensive reading and bad experiences of Mary Shelley, an eighteen-year-old girl who was both the daughter and lover of left-wing revolutionaries. Murnau's *Nosferatu* articulated, in its inchoate way, Germany's reaction to the Russian Revolution of 1917 and the German revolution following its defeat of World War 1 and its cultural implementation in the Weimar Republic. James Whale resurrected the Frankenstein myth as an allegory for the rise of the Nazi eugenics program in Germany. The *Bride of Frankenstein* was his protest against Hitler's use of science to bring about the master race. *Alien*, the archetypal monster of the 1970s and 1980s, the successor to *Frankenstein* and *Dracula*, arrived on the scene as a direct consequence of a number of key events, specifically, the breaking of the Hollywood Production Code in 1965 and the arrival of pornography to first-run theaters in the 1970s. *Alien* was America's comment on *Deep Throat*, and *Roe v. Wade*, the Supreme Court decision legalizing abortion.

More recently, actor-producer Kenneth Branagh said that his remake of *Frankenstein* was a comment on the current craze for eugenics. Victor Frankenstein, according to Branagh, "is not a mad scientist but a dangerously sane one." The monster is a protest against "brilliant men of science" who want to "interfere in the matters of life and death":

> for example, should parents choose the sex of their child? We can all see these developments taking place. It's now an imaginable step, to prevent people from dying. There's a place in the script where Victor says, "Listen, if we can replace one part of a person—a heart or a lung—then soon we will be able to replace every part. And if we can do that, we can design a life, a being that won't grow old, that won't sicken, a being that will be more

intelligent than us, more civilized than us.". . . We hope audiences today may find parallels with Victor today in some amazing scientist who might be an inch way from curing AIDS or
cancer, and needs to make some difficult decisions.[1]

Branagh is insightful here, but, as with every critic of horror, he backs
away the minute he tries to explain horror. This phenomenon is so
common that it deserves an explanation, one that requires the Enlightenment as its major premise.

Only those outside something can see it for what it is. The critics cannot understand horror because they cannot understand the
Enlightenment, and they cannot understand the Enlightenment because they are inside it, espousing its goals. Those who aspire to explicate horror rather than merely represent horror in artistic form are,
therefore, in a bind because to be a critic in a culture like ours entails
a commitment to Enlightenment values. Nevertheless, because the
critic internalizes the imperatives of the Enlightenment, he cannot
explain them. These imperatives, for him, *are* the explanation.

So there are only misreadings of horror. Horror haunts the Enlightenment as its uncanny doppelganger. *Frankenstein* is the inchoate protest of someone who accepts the premises of the Enlightenment
but who recognizes that they do not work, and what is worse, cause
horrific suffering and death when implemented. So the culture is
locked in a curious dialectic. It keeps producing horror, because it
cannot understand horror, and that, in turn, is because it cannot understand the cause of horror.

The dilemma is distressing for the critic because it is his job to
explain things in a rational manner. With the unnameable monster,
the critic—unlike the ordinary moviegoer, who receives some catharsis from simply seeing a representation of a monster who symbolizes
his fears—follows a trajectory predictable by anyone familiar with the
genre: first the critic touches on the real issue (that is, sex), then he
backs away from it; then he chides the producer of horror fiction for
failing in the very act of succeeding. The critic, in other words, blames
the artist for the critic's own failure of nerve and vision.

David Hogan's book *Dark Romance* is a good example. As critiques of horror go, it is better than most and mercifully free from the Freudian jargon that is the occupational hazard of critics of horror films. The premise of Hogan's book, that there is a connection between sex and horror, is sharpened by his countercultural perception that "sexual behavior and its ultimate purpose, children, are quite clearly the antithesis of death. If one is to examine death, then, one must examine sex." Yet after this promising beginning, he lapses quickly into proposing as solutions the Enlightenment imagery that he should be explicating. He tells us: "As sexual machines, we have been beautifully designed. And yet, there are many among us whose sexual lives have not been beautifully realized. Why not? We share similar equipment and urges, but are very independent in our uses of them. A shared consciousness gives each of us a general idea of appropriate sexual conduct, but our free will may cause us to behave in ways that lead to conflict."[2]

Before long, Hogan has fallen into the trap of criticizing the author for producing horror stories that are faithful to the genre. "Once again," Hogan sniffs dismissively about one movie, "nature has punished untoward sexual conduct." The idea is clearly retrograde from the Enlightenment point of view—but that is precisely the point. To say that horror is retrograde is simply another way of saying that it is a critique of the Enlightenment. That anyone could be critical of sexual liberation, not the details of the genre, which are not particularly complex, is what baffles the critics time and time again. "Commercial cinema," Hogan informs us at another point, "has vilified and punished the independent spirit when that spirit should have been celebrated."[3]

The criticism bespeaks a fundamental misunderstanding of the genre. Horror depicts the confrontation between the liberation that Enlightenment culture has espoused for over two hundred years and the horrendous consequences that follow from it. The critic cannot see beyond his own Enlightenment blinders, however, and as a result chides the producers of horror fictions for the very contribution that makes the genre unique as a protest against Enlightenment values.

The best example of this blindness in *Dark Romance* is Hogan's misreading of *Blood Feast*, a 1960s gore film that was reputed to be the most advanced example of its kind.   Produced over a period of nine days in Miami in 1963 at a cost of fifty thousand dollars, *Blood Feast* borrows heavily from *Psycho* and manifests the cultural contradictions of the time.   Directed by a refugee from skin flicks, and starring a former Playboy Bunny, *Blood Feast* observes the pre-1965 Hollywood production code ban on nudity but outdoes itself, and any other film of the time, including *Psycho*, in its graphic, labored representation of blood and gore.   The two contradictory impulses are brought together in one scene where the police break into (in this film) the mad caterer's shrine to Ishtar (mistakenly identified as an Egyptian goddess).   The dead woman is shown covered with blood and gore and a strategically placed scarf to satisfy the still-influential production code people.   *Blood Feast*, according to Hogan, "signalled the official birth of the gore film ... and the beginning of open season on young actresses."   Hogan makes the statement ironically—almost light-heartedly—without understanding its deeper implications.[4]

*Blood Feast* is about cannibalism; it is over the top in blood and gore by any day's standards; it is obviously modeled on *Psycho*, which was itself based on a story about cannibalism, also the source for the *Texas Chainsaw Massacre*.   Although no one would claim that it reached the level of Hitchcock's art in *Psycho*, *Blood Feast* does apprehend *Pscyho*'s central moral point—the moral of all horror films—that sexual sin leads to death.   It is precisely the moral gist of *Blood Feast* that annoys Hogan as a defender of Enlightenment values.

Hogan ostensibly sets out to explain the connection between sex and horror, but by the time he is finished, he has shifted to the didactic mode, upbraiding the  film's director for not getting it right when it comes to sexual liberation.   Hogan tell us disapprovingly: "The women in *Blood Feast* are punished because they are pretty and sexual.   The girl who necks on the beach and the one who keeps a motel room have sealed their dooms.   Bad girls!   The villain, working from a surprisingly Puritan morality that informs virtually all subsequent gore films, metes out retribution and justice just as he metes out death."[5]

Hogan here sounds a note that recurs in almost every contemporary attempt to explicate horror. The critic starts by seeing a connection between sex and horror but quickly shifts from the descriptive to the prescriptive mode and condemns the horror filmmakers for their "surprisingly Puritan morality." As anyone who has seen a number of films in the horror-slasher genre could attest, there is nothing surprising about this morality at all. The message of slasher films is very simple: you screw, you die.

From Euripides' prototypical myth of horror, *The Bacchae*, to *The Blob*, the plot of every horror story is essentially the same. If you violate sexual morals, you will be punished by death, and the city will be destroyed: tampering with sexual morals is a threat to civilization. In horror films, there is only one set of sexual norms, those limiting sex to the married state. As soon as we see the young woman making out on the beach in *Blood Feast*, we know that it is only a matter of time before the Egyptian caterer appears with his machete to chop off the top of her head and make soup out of her brains. This is the standard horror plot, and yet contemporary critics invariably find this endorsement of the moral order "surprising" and "Puritanical."

All monster stories, beginning with *Frankenstein*, the first of the genre, are in effect protests against the Enlightenment's desacralization of man. The reward for turning man into a machine has always been sexual, but terror is its immediate consequence. If man is simply the locus of local motions with no transcendent purpose then he can do with his body what he wants. But if he can use other bodies in that fashion, then other bodies can use him. And so the transformation of man into a machine—that is, sexual liberation—is quickly followed by terror. Suddenly, sexual liberation is fraught with fear.

The Enlightenment explicators of horror never get this far. Their engines invariably stall when they reach the first obstacle to Enlightenment thought, the "surprisingly Puritan morality." Hogan tells us disapprovingly: "Gore filmmakers unfairly exploited the insecurities of their audience by offering a distressingly conservative, even vengeful morality in the guise of trendiness and free-spiritedness. Gore cinema is not liberating (though the kids who flocked to theaters may think otherwise), but suffocating, the work of cynical adults having a go at the vulnerability of children."[6]

Hogan gets horror exactly wrong, primarily because he gets morality, which he finds "distressingly conservative," exactly wrong. Morality can be seen by purveyors of the Enlightenment only as an arbitrary restraint of freedom. This is the verdict of the Marquis de Sade, who is so popular today, according to Roger Shattuck ("Rehabilitating a Monster," *New York Times Book Review*) because he took the premises of the Enlightenment to their logical conclusion. "These words, vice and virtue," Dolmance tells Eugenie in Sade's *Philosophy in the Bedroom*, "contain for us naught but local ideas. . . . All is relative to our manners and the climate we inhabit; what is a crime here is often a virtue several hundred leagues hence, and the virtues of another hemisphere might well reverse themselves into crimes in our own."[7]

At another point, Dolmance proposes Enlightenment science as the ultimate sexual permission slip. Anyone who disagrees is merely a collaborator in his own oppression. Morality is the antithesis of both nature and freedom, which is nothing more than conformity to nature's laws. Dolmance says: "As we gradually proceeded to our enlightenment, we came more and more to feel that, motion being inherent in matter, the prime mover existed only as an illusion, and that all that exists essentially having to be in motion, the motor was useless; we sensed that this chimerical divinity, prudently invented by the earliest legislators was in their hands simply one more means to enthrall us."[8]

The structure of the Marquis de Sade's novels is the structure of Enlightenment thought: libertinism interspersed with rationalization. In this respect, the Marquis de Sade's novels are a perverse tribute to man's moral nature. He cannot engage in immoral sexual activity without coming up with an elaborate justification. The more perverse the activity, the more elaborate the justification needed, and the Enlightenment, especially the notion of man as a machine, provided the prime philosophical rationalization of sexual license for Sade and for those who followed in his footsteps. As always, in the period between debauches, Dolmance instructs the unenlightened: "Since, however the torch of philosophy has dissipated all those impostures, since the celestial chimera has been tumbled in the dust, since better instructed

of physic's laws and secrets, we have evolved the principle of generation, and now that this material mechanism offers nothing more astonishing to the eye than the development of a germ of wheat, we have
been called back to Nature and away from human error." As Dolmance
concedes in the middle of one of his moral treatises: "Tis amazing how
this fine lad's superb ass does preoccupy my mind while I talk."[9]

The critics, insofar as they espouse sexual liberation, are in much
the same situation; hence, their inability to interpret horror. Hence,
too, Mary Shelley's ability to create a fiction that would continue to
subvert the Enlightenment for two hundred years. Mary Shelley was
first of all a female, which in the Marquis de Sade's anthropology
meant she was a victim whose life was in constant danger, a state that
clears the mind wonderfully of illusions generated by sexual desire.

But Hogan seems unable to question the hegemony of Sadean
desire over the bodies of eighteen-year-old girls. Since he accepts
Enlightenment morals by default, he seems incapable of understanding that, when it comes to protecting the vulnerable and childbearing, the moral order is not necessarily a bad thing. As the famous
story of the eighteen-year-old Mary Shelley makes clear, children are
most vulnerable precisely when they follow the sexual liberationist
creed of their elders.

Wes Craven's early film, *Last House on the Left* (1972), is a significant contribution to the horror genre in this regard and another point
of departure in discussing the connection between horror and Enlightenment morality. Like *The Texas Chainsaw Massacre*, *Last House on
the Left* is a film about the end of the hippie idyll. Just as *The Texas
Chainsaw Massacre* was about the last time you picked up a hitchhiker,
so *Last House* was about the last time you went to a rock concert, or
perhaps, the last rock concert your daughter ever attended. It is about
the implosion of Enlightenment values and the people who get hurt
and killed when that happens.

At the beginning of the film, the liberal professor sends his daughter off to a rock concert as part of her birthday present. (Dad gives
her a peace symbol as the other part before she leaves.) The concert
in question is being given by a group called Blood Lust ("Aren't they

the guys who dismantle live chickens in their act?" Dad asks. "I thought you were supposed to be the love generation.") The girls drink and talk about sex before arriving at the concert, only to be captured by a group of escaped convicts they meet while trying to buy drugs. The convicts proceed to torture and kill the professor's daughter, inadvertently ending up at the professor's house and spending the night in the dead girl's bedroom. In the course of the night, mom and dad discover that their guests have murdered their daughter, whereupon the mother bites off the penis of one murderer and the father cuts up the other with a chainsaw.

Hogan, unsurprisingly, fails to understand the message of *Last House*, the message of horror in general, namely, that children are vulnerable precisely because the authority figures in their lives espouse Enlightenment morals. The children of the 1960s who acted on these premises find, much as Mary Shelley did a century and a half earlier, that the same premises lead inexplicably to suffering and death. Hogan offers more Enlightenment platitudes. Horror films are "dangerous," he tells us, "because they offer a subliminal message, a warning that the penalties for tenderness, sexual curiosity, and gaiety are torture, mutilation and death. The films imply that we must prepare to become victims and resign ourselves to fates so horrible as to make meaningless the joys of our lives."[10]

Hogan gets it right in a way. Unfortunately, he misstates the situation because his view of sexual liberation is overly sanguine. "Tenderness, sexual curiosity, and gaiety" lead to "torture, mutilation, and death" only when they are pursued outside the moral order—which, like the monster, has no name. The victims in both *Blood Feast* and *Last House* are young and sexually desirable; they are also unwitting victims, kids who are playing with fire—sex, drugs, and rock and roll, in this instance—with the tacit approval of their parents. That things do not go as planned is the essence of the horror genre. But like the parents in *Last House on the Left*, who have to learn the hard way that liberation is dangerous, the Enlightenment critics cannot grasp that the values they espouse not only blind them to any understanding of horror, but caused it in the first place.

. . . . .

When it comes to framing a comprehensive theory of horror, no one exceeds the ambition of Robin Wood, nor does anyone fail as spectacularly. In the *American Nightmare* and *From Vietnam to Reagan*, Wood aspires to nothing less than "laying the foundations, stone by stone, for a theory of the American horror film."[11] Unfortunately, when he goes to the well, it is only to bring back buckets of the same old Enlightenment values—in this case, Freud and Marx—that cause critics like Barbara Creed so much trouble. The reason should be obvious enough. Both Freud and Marx are involved in suppressing morality by purporting to explain it as an epiphenomenon of some more basic—that is, sexual or economic—drive. As a result, both Freud and Marx, as well as their intellectual epigoni, participate in the same suppression of morals that create horror. A materialism that attempts to trace morals to more "basic" drives will only end up confounding the critics who use it as an interpretive tool.

Getting off on the same wrong foot as the two other misreaders of horror mentioned in this book, David Hogan and Barbara Creed, Wood tells us:

> The most significant development in film criticism and in progressive ideas generally . . . of the last few decades has clearly been the increasing confluence of Marx and Freud, or more precisely of the traditions of thought arising from them: the recognition that social revolution and sexual revolution are inseparably linked and necessary to each other. . . . It is psychoanalytic theory that has provided . . . the most effective means of examining the ways in which that [bourgeois] ideology is transmitted and perpetuated, centrally through the institutionalization of the patriarchal nuclear family. . . . it is here, through the medium of psychoanalytic theory, that Feminism and Gay Liberation join forces with Marxism in their progress toward a common aim, the overthrow of patriarchal capitalist ideology and the structures and institutions that sustain it and are sustained by it.[12]

This passage is typical of the sort of left-wing boilerplate that has been the *lingua franca* at universities in America during the last few decades. It sounds a bit dated and quaint in the aftermath of the fall of the Soviet Union, but it does underscore that Enlightenment ideology is consistent in the goals it proposes and the institutions it wants overthrown. But what is neither apparent nor consistent is Wood's use of this ideology as a way of interpreting horror films. Borrowing heavily from Freud, Wood, like Barbara Creed, comes up with a number of related explanations of horror. "The horror genre," he tells us at one point, "is the struggle for recognition of all that our civilization represses or oppresses." In addition, Wood tells us that "the general sexual content of the horror film has long been recognized, and the list of the monsters representing a generalized sexual threat would be interminable." Wood posits a general theory of horror based on the idea of repression. His "simple definition of horror films" is that "they are collective nightmares. The conditions under which a dream becomes a nightmare are that the repressed wish is, from the point of view of consciousness, so terrible that it must be repudiated as loathsome, and that it is so strong and powerful as to constitute a serious threat."[13]

To associate the monster in horror films with repression is correct, but Wood stumbles when he attempts to define what is being repressed. Throughout his critique, Wood shifts from the ideological, prescriptive mode to the empirical, descriptive mode without ever explaining—or, for that matter, understanding—how the two contradict each other. So, waxing empirical he tells us that "a simple and obvious basic formula for the horror film [is that] normality is threatened by the Monster." That sounds right, but then as soon as he attempts to explain what he means, Wood lapses back into the ideology that contradicts his observations: "I use 'normality' here," he continues, "in a strictly nonevaluative sense to mean simply 'conformity to the dominant social norms': one must firmly resist the common tendency to treat the word as if it were more or less synonymous with 'health.'"[14]

Wood is nothing if not firm in this regard; in fact, his critique becomes before long an attack on the notion that anything can be construed as both human and normal, lapsing once again into the ideological, prescriptive mode: "The definition of normality in horror films is in general boringly constant: the heterosexual monogamous couple, the family, and the social institutions (police, church, armed forces) that support and defend them." Given his view of "normality," Wood can only posit horror as the "fulfillment of our nightmare wish to smash the norms that oppress us and which our moral conditioning teaches us to revere."[15] So, according to Wood, horror means that "normality is threatened by a Monster," except for the fact that there is no such thing as normality, especially not when it comes to the family and sexual morality, which is explained away by a judicious application of Freud and Marx.

Beyond that, it turns out that there is no such thing as a monster either. Because if moral constraint of the sort proposed by the family, police, and armed forces is meaningless at best and a sinister form of social control at worst, then the monster who threatens normality is, according to Wood's theory, not a monster at all but rather a liberating force that sweeps away irrational taboos. The monster, in other words, is the Enlightenment hero. But that leaves us with many unanswered questions. For example, if this is the case, why should the characters in any film exhibit fear when the monster arrives on the scene? It would be a bit like the settlers in the wagon train cowering in fear when the cavalry arrived to save them. In other words, vacillating between his ideological and descriptive modes, Wood posits a thesis based on observation of actual horror movies and then strips the thesis of any meaning as soon as he attempts to explain it according to Enlightenment categories.

Central to this dilemma, and central to Wood's idea of horror, is the notion of repression of sexual urges. "The general sexual content of the horror film has long been recognized," Wood tells us, but then in the process of explaining it, he turns the chain of causality linking sex and horror in virtually every horror movie (woman takes off clothes; monster appears; monster kills woman; monster destroys city) upside down. According to Wood, the monster liberates us from a repressive social order by destroying "normality." Since he cannot really say that the gratification of all urges, no matter how perverse or destructive, is the goal of human life, Wood divides repression into two kinds: basic, which is good and which, not surprisingly, coincides with his own sexual proclivities; and surplus repression, which is bad because it contradicts these same proclivities: "Basic repression is universal, necessary and inescapable. It is what makes possible our development from an uncoordinated animal capable of little beyond screaming and convulsion into a human being; it is bound up with the ability to accept the postponement of gratification." Nevertheless, "surplus repression is specific to a particular culture and is the process whereby people are conditioned from earliest infancy to take on predetermined roles within that culture. In terms of our own culture, then, basic repression makes us distinctively human, capable of directing our own lives and co-existing with others; surplus repression makes us (if it works) into monogamous, heterosexual, bourgeois patriarchal capitalists."[16]

Surplus repression, according to Wood, means repressing homosexual tendencies. Wood, who happens to be a homosexual, now feels, citing Freud, "that our own civilization had reached a point where the burden of repression was becoming all-but-insupportable. . . . The struggle for liberation is not utopian, but a practical necessity." What then is repressed in Wood's scheme of things? The answer turns out to be that "our social structure demands the repression of the bisexuality that psychoanalysis shows to be the natural heritage of every human individual."[17]

At another point, Wood goes into greater detail:

> What then is repressed in our culture? First, sexual energy itself. . . . The "ideal" inhabitant of our culture will be the individual whose sexuality is sufficiently fulfilled by the monogamous heterosexual union necessary for the reproduction of future ideal inhabitants, and whose sublimated sexuality . . . is sufficiently fulfilled in the totally non-creative and non-fulfilling labor . . . to which our society dooms the overwhelming majority of its members. The "ideal," in other words, is as close as possible to an automaton in which both sexual and intellectual energy has been reduced to a minimum. . . . hence the necessary frustration, anxiety, and neuroticism of our culture.[18]

In Wood's scheme of things, in other words, sexual morality creates monsters by repressing our natural bisexuality: "In a society built on monogamy and family there will be an enormous surplus of repressed sexual energy, and what is repressed must always strive to return. . . . If we see the evolution of the horror film in terms of an inexorable return of the repressed, we will not be surprised by this final emergence of the genre's real significance. This is coupled with a sense that it becomes in the '70s the most important of all American genres and perhaps the most progressive, even in its overt nihilism—in a period of extreme cultural crisis and disintegration, which alone offers the possibility of radical change and rebuilding."[19]

In short, the horror film appeared during the 1970s because sexual repression was so great during that decade. Perhaps because Wood is a homosexual, he is more sensitive to repression. In his critique of *Alien*, the touchstone of 1970s horror, Wood makes clear that his assertion about the alleged sexual repression of the 1970s is in earnest. "The sexuality so rigorously repressed in the film," he writes giving his reading of *Alien*, "returns grotesquely and terrifyingly in its monster," leading him to conclude that "the more extreme the repression the more excessive the monster."[20]

In a sense it is true that "the more extreme the repression the more excessive the monster," but not in the sense that Wood intends. Wood clearly means repression of sexual desire in general and homosexual behavior in particular, an assertion that puts him in the bizzare position of seeing the 1970s as a sexually repressive decade. In order to make his theory of sexual liberation plausible, Wood needs to posit the 1960s and 1970s—precisely the time when Hollywood broke the Production Code and unleashed a flood of pornography onto the screen—as decades of reactionary Puritanism. Does the fact that *Deep Throat* was one of the ten top grossing films of 1973 indicate that American culture was in the grip of sexual repression? According to Wood's theory, it would have to mean just that. Wood's theory does, however, make sense if we specify that what was being repressed was not sexual desire—a patent absurdity—but rather sexual morality. Then the statement has about it the ring of truth, but that, of course, contradicts his ideology of sexual liberation.

Rather than adjust his theory, which seems determined more by homosexuality's effect on the human conscience than anything else, Wood places the horror movie he hopes to explain on the Procrustean bed of his Enlightenment ideology and then lashes out at the film's directors when it doesn't fit. Again and again, Wood summarizes the plots of horror movies he deplores as "reactionary" without the slightest hint that his homosexual hermeneutic may be blinding him to the essential message of the horror genre.

In an even more extreme example of the sort of thing we first saw with David Hogan's critique of *Blood Feast*, Wood denounces fellow Canadian and director David Cronenberg for making the wrong kind of horror movie. But as Wood's description makes clear, Cronenberg has made a classic version of the only kind of horror movie there is, the one in which the monster comes into existence because sexual norms have been violated. The plot by now is predictable enough— science has violated sexual norms, which protect the matrix of human life; horror is the result.

Cronenberg's film *Shivers* has all the components of the classic horror film. Dr. Hobbes, a mad scientist with a predilection for molesting twelve-year-old girls, invents an aphrodisiac that unfortunately also acts like a venereal disease. After introducing it into one of his teenage lovers (the film begins with him slicing her open in a futile attempt to destroy the disease), it spreads uncontrollably among the residents of Starliner Towers, a Gropius-inspired modern community on an island in the middle of the St. Lawrence River. Roger St. Luc, a medical doctor and former student of Hobbes, attempts to combat the parasite, but as the parasite-aphrodisiac spreads through the apartment complex, St. Luc finds the ensuing sexual frenzy overwhelming and eventually, at the end of the film, succumbs to it himself.

Cronenberg's film is overtly sexual and in the mode of classic horror. What continues to amaze is the critics' continuing inability to understand it. Wood's misreading of *Shivers* is exceptional in its wrong-headedness. He understands that *Shivers* is an explication of the trajectory of sexual liberation; what disturbs him is the suggestion that anyone could view the outcome of sexual liberation with, as he puts it, "unmitigated horror":

The entire film is premised on and motivated by sexual disgust. The release of sexuality is linked inseparably with the spreading of venereal disease, the scientist responsible for the experiments having seen fit (for reasons never made clear) to include a VD component in his aphrodisiac parasite. The parasites themselves are modelled very obviously on phalluses, but with strong excremental overtones (their color) and continual association with blood; the point is underlined when one enters the Barbara Steele character through her vagina. If the film presents sexuality in general as the object of loathing, it has a very special animus reserved for female sexuality (a theme repeated, if scarcely developed in Cronenberg's subsequent *Rabid*). . . . The parasites are spread initially by a young girl . . . the film's Pandora whose released eroticism precipitates general cataclysm; throughout, sexually aroused preying women are presented with a particular intensity of horror and disgust. *Shivers* systematically chronicles the breaking of every sexual-social taboo—promiscuity, lesbianism, homosexuality, age difference, finally incest—but each step is presented as merely one more addition to the accumulation of horrors."[21]

This is a fair description of the film; it is also a description of everything Wood does not like in the film. His quarrel is not so much with David Cronenberg, but with the very genre he seeks to explain. What Wood wants is a different film, one in which the release of sexuality is followed by universal peace and love; in other words, Wood wants a film that conforms to the Left's notion of sexual liberation. What he wants is a film that portrays sexual liberation as heaven on earth, not the genesis of horror.

As Wood recounted in an interview: "When I first saw *Shivers*, the unanimous reaction among people I talked to was disgust. . . . We were still in the aftermath of May '68 and its related events over the Western world. Even 'bourgeois humanists' like myself were beginning to become politicized and ideologically aware. We believed not only that a 'liberated society' was possible, but even that it might be within sight. Now, a decade later, a few of us are still trying to cling on to a radicalism the society around us (predominantly cynical and reactionary) appears to regard as increasingly ridiculous."[22]

The passage is instructive. Wood himself seems to indicate that the sexual revolution did not turn out as scripted by the savants of the Enlightenment, which makes him bridle all the more at Cronenberg's suggestion that its main consequence has been horror. How, Wood seems to be asking, can sexual liberation be associated with horror? Given his ideology, it cannot, but that also means that he cannot explain the horror films his book purports to explain, which, even he admits, inevitably have a sexual component. If, however, we substitute repression of the moral order for Wood's idea of monster as repression of sexual desire, all of the difficulties suddenly disappear. But since Wood's commitment to sexual liberation prevents him from making this point, he condemns himself to incoherence.

· · · · ·

Cronenberg, as artist, creates a horror film by adopting the tropes of the genre but cannot explain what he is doing any more than Wood can. It is clear from interviews that Cronenberg was drawn to the horror genre because he felt that it made some significant statements about the human condition, which lent themselves to visual representation. "When I looked at [Roger] Corman's and other people's films," Cronenberg said in one interview, "I thought, okay, these guys make mistakes. But *the genre* has enough power and clarity to help carry them through that. When the stuff they were doing suddenly did click it had enough momentum to make the film worth seeing. The field has a lot of flexibility to it. You can do some terrific stuff."[23]

But just because David Cronenberg makes films does not mean that he understands the films he makes, a point that Martin Scorsese has made. David Cronenberg was attracted to a genre, to characters and situations that articulated something that he didn't understand. Therein lay their attraction. When asked if his films *The Brood* and *Scanners* "deal with more defined moral absolutes than your previous films," Cronenberg gives an interesting reply: "I don't think, *consciously, anyway*, in terms of the struggle between good and evil. Martin Scorsese thinks I don't know what my movies are about. He said, 'I read your interviews, but it's obvious you don't know what they're about, but that's okay, they're still great.'"[24]

Cronenberg then goes on to define what he sees as the difference between himself and Scorsese in religious terms. Cronenberg is a nonobservant secularized Jew. Scorsese, on the other hand, is an ex-Catholic (in fact, a former seminarian) who "does deal with good and evil in very proto-Catholic terms, and I'm sure that what he meant was that when he saw my films he saw the struggle being played out. I don't see it quite that way, because I really don't see the lines drawn in those terms." Scorsese spends his time rebelling against a moral order he cannot ignore, primarily because of his Italian Catholic upbringing. Cronenberg, on the other hand, does horror because he cannot apprehend that moral causality in the first place:

> That's my curse, you see. I can't believe in the devil because I would have to believe in a purely evil being, and I don't feel that I've met anybody I could consider evil. I have difficulty thinking in terms of good and evil. I'm sure if I had been raised a Catholic I would have no trouble, because those issues are raised at a very early age. So I don't consciously think in those terms, and I certainly don't think in terms of moral absolutes, because I know what happens when you try to find a moral absolute. It's very difficult to come up with something that will hold for all men in all societies in all times. It's very hard whether it's murder or incest—whatever is taboo. It always varies—you can always come up with extenuating circumstances and my demon is that all sides appeal. . . . Is a person evil if you go back to his roots and see how he was made to be evil? Does his evil still feel the same? If we had seen Hitler as a little baby, he was probably a cute kid—who knows, maybe not. But if you saw him being battered and hammered psychologically you'd say ultimately he'd still have to be destroyed because he is still evil.[25]

The distinction is instructive for our purposes. Scorsese, the ex-seminarian, has not so much forgotten the moral order as he has declared war on it, but even in declaring war on the moral order, Scorsese retains its categories. His film *The Last Temptation of Christ* is in many ways the best example of a film where morality is very much on the mind of the director. The film is Scorsese's conscious attempt to get the upper hand on Jesus Christ, the Christ he repudiated when he ceased being a Catholic. *Last Temptation* is Scorsese's attempt to prove that he is right and that Christ was wrong. As a result, and as Cronenberg perceptively noted, the moral dimension of existence takes center stage, even if it is Scorsese's perversion and repudiation of the moral order.

Cronenberg, on the other hand, grew up in a milieu in which the moral had been subsumed into the therapeutic categories of late modernity. The *mise en scene* of his films is not Brooklyn with its *mafiosi* and misfits, but the clear geometric lines of Gropius-inspired *Wohnmaschinen*, buildings like Starliner Towers. And sexual license breaks out in Starliner Towers not because its inhabitants have chosen evil over good, not because they have given free rein to unruly passions that should have been held within the bounds of the moral order, but rather because a mad scientist has been experimenting with a leech-like parasite that is a combination aphrodisiac and venereal disease, and the experiment, intended for the good of mankind, got out of hand. Horror, in short, is the sign that the moral sources of human behavior have been either repressed or forgotten or never clearly acknowledged by the culture to begin with.

Scorsese is right in his judgment of Cronenberg. As anyone who has read one of his interviews could attest, David Cronenberg simply does not understand his own films or the forces that drive his characters. This is precisely why Cronenberg is so good at doing horror. He is himself so completely and successfully secularized, that he can only mirror the incomprehension of the society he was describing in his horror films. After citing Scorsese's penchant to see things in terms of right and wrong, all Cronenberg can say is that "I don't see it quite that way, because I really don't see the lines drawn in those terms." That is, Cronenberg is drawn to horror because he can't make sense out of contemporary events in light of the moral order.

In his interviews, Cronenberg tells us that the people who cause the calamities in his films are men of science who are really only trying to help humanity. But the films themselves tell a different story. Emil Hobbes, the doctor who creates the parasite that sends Starliner Towers into an advanced stage of Dionysian frenzy, first met the young woman he ends up killing at the beginning of the film, according to Hobbes's colleague, "when lecturing at a girls' school. They caught him examining her titties for breast cancer in the faculty lounge."

The moral, in other words, is not as remote at it would seem according to Cronenberg's explanation of his own beliefs. It is lurking right beneath the surface, repressed. Rather than being absent it is repressed in the notoriously ineffective way that most things get repressed. St. Luc is the man who finally tracks down the parasite; he is, if anyone meets the definition, the hero of the film. Cronenberg at one point even refers to him as a "saint." But Dr. St. Luc seems particularly obtuse. He examines a man who is manifesting symptoms of venereal disease but seems unable to make the necessary connection, even after the man admits to having had sexual intercourse with Hobbes's girlfriend. Before the examination, the man spends his time propositioning St. Luc's nurse who seems curiously unmoved by his advances. The nurse has a romantic interest in Dr. St. Luc, who is himself unmoved by her advances. And lest we think the nurse too subtle in this regard, she removes her clothes in front of St. Luc, who is preoccupied by a phone conversation.

Cronenberg seems to be determined simultaneously to reveal the sexual as the *radix malorum* at Skyliner Towers and deliberately to ignore the evidence he himself has brought up. This ambivalence characterizes Cronenberg's work. Cronenberg plants clues only to ignore them. *Shivers* is a film suffused with sexual disgust, yet also a film in which the moral roots of sexual behavior are simultaneously proposed and repressed. The horror stems from the repression. Things happen inexplicably because the director refuses to follow the chain of sexual causality to its root in the moral order.

Science, for example, in this universe, becomes simply a cover for sexual desire. "Hobbes," his colleague tells Dr. St. Luc by way of explanation, "believed that man is an animal that thinks too much. An over-rational animal that has lost touch with its body and its instincts. How do you like that? In other words, too much brains and not enough guts. So what he came up with was a parasite that is a combination of aphrodisiac and venereal disease that will hopefully help turn the world into one beautiful mindless orgy. He was using Annabelle as a guinea pig. He implanted her with the parasite and once it took over she went berserk. Hobbes wasn't ready for that. Then he had to kill her."

In describing the project of Dr. Hobbes, Cronenberg has given a fairly accurate description of the modern regime in general and the projects of "scientists" like Alfred Kinsey in particular. Modernity felt that sexuality could be liberated from the moral order for the benefit of mankind. The negative fallout—things like pregnancy and venereal disease—could be controlled by technology. What actually followed from the modern experiment was an unprecedented unleashing of sexual mayhem which smashed through the technological and bureaucratic tethers that were supposed to contain it like the monster it was often portrayed to be. But in *Shivers* Cronenberg, having indicted the modern regime, lets it off the hook by implying that Hobbes was after all a scientist who had the best interests of mankind in mind. In one interview, he not only denied the sexual disgust pervades his film, he went so far as to say that the orgy that destroyed the Starliner Towers was a good thing.

Why Cronenberg wishes to repress the moral is no mystery. If the source of the mayhem is sexual liberation, then the cure is the abandonment of sexual liberation and a return to the moral order, a prospect that few associated with Hollywood find palatable for personal and political reasons—including Wood and Cronenberg. Wood cannot see beyond his own sexual desires and the rationalized desires of those who provide him with his hermeneutic tools. David Cronenberg, on the other hand, intuits correctly that there is a connection between sex and horror by successfully appropriating the tropes of the horror genre in his films, but he cannot explain it any better than Wood because he is imprisoned in the same Enlightenment bind. And in this he is like the young Mary Shelley, also a captive of the Enlightenment, but one who saw that its application caused suffering and death.

. . . . .

In 1994, President Clinton attended a prayer breakfast in Washington, D.C. It is reported that he reached for a glass of water when the speaker started talking about abortion. The speaker that day was Mother Teresa, and her truth was this: "If we accept that a mother can kill even her own child, how can we tell other people not to kill one another? . . . Any country that accepts abortion is not teaching its people to love, but to use violence to get whatever they want."

As the chief representative of abortion culture, President Clinton was led back to the truth that our culture cannot face, which is also the truth that our culture cannot escape: By following our illicit desires to their logical endpoint in death, we have created a nightmare culture, a horror-movie culture, one in which we are led back again and again to the source of our mysterious fears by forces over which we have no control. It is a little like watching the *Texas Chainsaw Massacre* over and over again and watching the hippies drawn inexorably to their doom in the uncanny house (*das unheimliche Heim*) that has become not a place of refuge, but of slaughter instead. That house is our culture.

We are all being led into that house of horrors by a mysterious force over which we seem to have no control. That force is our conscience. The only way we can escape its clutches is by admitting that what it has to say about our guilt is true.

# *Notes*

## 1   *Why the French Revolution Failed*

1   Richard Holmes, *Shelley: The Pursuit* (New York: E.P. Dutton, 1975), 193.

2   William Godwin, *Enquiry Concerning Political Justice* (NewYork: Penguin, 1985), 7-8.

3   Ibid., 11.

4   Ibid., 8.

5   Erik von Kuehnelt-Leddihn, *Leftism Revisited: From de Sade and Marx to Hitler and Pol Pot* (Washington, D.C.: Regnery Gateway, 1990), 75.

6   William St. Clair, *The Godwins and the Shelleys: The Biography of a Family* (New York: W.W. Norton & Co., 1989), 45.

7   Lester G. Crocker, *Nature and Culture: Ethical Thought in the French Enlightenment* (Baltimore: The Johns Hopkins Press, 1963), 333.

8   Julian Offray de La Mettrie, *Man a Machine.* (LaSalle, Ill.: Open Court, 1953), 140-41.

9   A. Barruel, *Memoirs Illustrating the History of Jacobinism* (Fraser, Mich.: Real View Books, 1995), 133-4.

10   Ibid., 17.

11   Crocker, *Nature and Culture*, 332.

12   St. Clair, *The Godwins and the Shelleys*, 34.

13   Goethe, *Faust*, 1:2038-9.

14   Marquis de Sade, *Justine, Philosophy in the Bedroom & other writings*, ed. and trans. Richard Seaver & Austryn Wainhouse (New York: Grove Press, 1965), 605.

15   St. Clair, *The Godwins and the Shelleys*, 44.

16   Claire Tomalin, *The Life and Death of Mary Wollstonecraft* (New York: Harcourt Brace Jovanovich, 1974), 121.

17   Ibid., 123.

18   Simon Schama, *Citizens: A Chronicle of the French Revolution* (New York: Vintage Books, 1990), 210.

19   Ibid., 211.

20   Kuehnelt-Leddihn, *Leftism Revisited*, 66.

21   Schama, *Citizens*, 635.

22  Sade, *Justine*, 605.

23  Tomalin, *The Life and Death of Mary Wollstonecraft*, 120.

24  Ibid., 124.

25  Barruel, *History of Jacobinism*, xii.

26  Tomalin, *The Life and Death of Mary Wollstonecraft*, 147.

27  St. Clair, *The Godwins and the Shelleys*, 182.

28  Mary Wollstonecraft, *Collected Letters of Mary Wollstonecraft*, ed. Ralph M. Wardle (Ithaca, NY: Cornell Univ. Press 1979), 40.

29  Ibid.

30  Tomalin, *The Life and Death of Mary Wollstonecraft*, 171.

31  Wollenstonecraft, *Collected Letters*, 279.

32  Ibid., 236, 289, 291, 263.

33  Tomalin, *The Life and Death of Mary Wollstonecraft*, 189.

34  Wollenstonecraft, *Collected Letters*, 40.

35  Ibid., 321.

36  St. Clair, *The Godwins and the Shelleys*, 500.

37  Tomalin, *The Life and Death of Mary Wollstonecraft*, 172-3, 185.

38  Wollenstonecraft, *Collected Letters*, 321.

39  Ibid., 317.

40  Ibid., 46.

41  St. Clair, *The Godwins and the Shelleys*, 176.

## 2    *Passion and Electricity*

1  St. Clair, *The Godwins and the Shelleys*, 315.

2  Holmes, *Shelley: the Pursuit*, 17.

3  Percy Bysshe Shelley, *The Poems of Shelley*, ed. Geoffrey Matthews (London: Longman, 1989), 409.

4  Holmes, *Shelley: the Pursuit*, 209.

5  Ibid., 24-5.

6  Ibid., 37-8.

7  Ibid., 45.

8  Ibid., 47, 46.

9  Emily W. Sunstein, *Mary Shelley: Romance and Reality* (Boston: Little, Brown, & Co, 1989), 65.

10  Holmes, *Shelley: The Pursuit*, 103, 122.

11  Ibid., 168.

12  St. Clair, *The Godwins and the Shelleys*, 81.

13  Shelley, *The Poems of Shelley*, 296, lines 176-80.

14  Ibid., iii.

15  Ibid., 311, lines 18-21.

16  Ibid.

17  Ibid., 353, lines 40-51.

18  Ibid., 354, lines 76-86.

19  Ibid., 360, lines 1-5; 361, lines 6-12.

20  Ibid., 391, line 334.

21  Ibid., 368, lines 40-48.

22  Ibid., 371.

23  Ibid., 372-73.

24  Holmes, *Shelley: the Pursuit*, 230.

25  Sunstein, *Mary Shelley*, 76.

26  Ibid., 77.

27  Holmes, *Shelley: the Pursuit*, 273.

28  Ibid., 233.

29  Sunstein, *Mary Shelley*, 83, 84.

30  St. Clair, *The Godwins and the Shelleys*, 366.

31  Barruel, *History of Jacobinism*, 209.

32  Ibid.

33  Ibid., 74, 833-34.

34  Ibid., 56, 833-34, 820.

35  Crocker, *Nature and Culture*, 328.

36  Ibid., 352.

37  Ibid.

38  Ibid.

39  Sade, *Justine*, 300.

40  Ibid., 315.

41  Ibid., 316.

42  Ibid.

43  Ibid., 317.

44  Crocker, *Nature and Culture*, 356.

45  Sade, *Justine*, 119-20.

46  Ibid., 120.

47  Ibid., 329.

48  Crocker, *Nature and Culture*, 414.

49  Sade, *Justine*, 332.

50  Barruel, *History of Jacobinism*, 108, 403.

51  Ibid., 419, 115, 112.

52  Ibid., 454.

53  Ibid., 623.

54  Ibid.

55  Holmes, *Shelley: the Pursuit*, 126.

56  Barruel, *History of Jacobinism*, 401.

57  Ibid.

58  Friedrich Nietzsche, *Werke in Drei Baenden*, vol. 1 (Munich: Carl Hanser Verlag, 1955), 56-57 (my translation).

59  Holmes, *Shelley: the Pursuit*, 262.

60  Ibid., 257.

61  Ibid., 260.

62  Ibid.

63  Ibid., 261.

64  Ibid., 291.

## 3  *Frankenstein*

1   Holmes, *Shelley: the Pursuit*, 322.

2   Kenneth Neill Cameron, ed., *Shelley and His Circle*, vol. III (Cambridge, Mass.: Harvard University Press, 1961), 400-1.

3   Holmes, *Shelley: the Pursuit*, 322.

4   Ibid., 327.

5   Leonard Woolf, in Mary Shelly, *The Annotated Frankenstein* (New York: C.N. Potter, 1977), xii.

6   Barruel, *History of Jacobinism*, 13, 17.

7   Schama, *Citizens*, 44.
8   Holmes, *Shelley: The Pursuit*, 328.
9   Ibid., 329.
10  Ibid.
11  Sunstein, *Mary Shelley*, 117.
12  Holmes, *Shelley: the Pursuit*, 360.
13  Ibid., 375.
14  Woolf, in Shelly, *The Annotated Frankenstein*, 142.
15  Leslie Alexis Marchand, *Byron: a Biography*, vol. II (New York: Knopf, 1957), 559 n.1.
16  Sade, *Justine*, 519, 521.
17  Ibid., 605.
18  Ibid., 551, 555-56.
19  Ibid., 603.
20  Ibid., 606, 606-7, 607.
21  Ibid.
22  Ibid., 671, 608.
23  Holmes, *Shelley: the Pursuit*, 306.
24  Sade, *Justine*, 695-96.
25  Shelley, *The Annotated Frankenstein*, 67.
26  Ibid., 102-3.
27  Ibid., 128.
28  Ibid., 139.
29  Sunstein, *Mary Shelley*, 169.
30  Ibid., 216.
31  Shelley, *The Annotated Frankenstein*, 272, 282, 325.
32  Ibid., 331.
33  Sunstein, *Mary Shelley*, 297, 343.
34  Holmes, *Shelley: the Pursuit*, 20.
35  Sunstein, *Mary Shelley*, 343.
36  Ibid., 370, 374.
37  Ibid., 120.
38  Ibid., 119-20.
39  Sade, *Justine*, 634.
40  Shelley, *The Annotated Frankenstein*, 107.
41  Holmes, *Shelley: the Pursuit*, 214.
42  St. Clair, *The Godwins and the Shelleys*, 411.
43  Shelley, *The Annotated Frankenstein*, 139.
44  St. Clair, *The Godwins and the Shelleys*, 412.
45  Holmes, *Shelley: the Pursuit*, 279.
46  Ibid., 353.
47  Ibid., 415.
48  Sunstein, *Mary Shelley*, 320.
49  Kenneth Branagh, *Mary Shelley's* Frankenstein: *The Classic Tale of Terror Reborn on Film* (New York: Newmarket Press, 1994), 82.
50  Sunstein, *Mary Shelley*, 4.

## 4   Dracula and Sin

1   Stanley L. Jaki, *The Road of Science and the Ways to God* (Chicago: The University of Chicago Press, 1978), 286.
2   J.B.S. Haldane, *Daedalus or Science and the Future* (New York: E.P. Dutton, 1924), 44.

3   Jaki, *The Road of Science*, 286, 288.
4   Ibid., 283.
5   Andrew Carnegie, *Autobiography of Andrew Carnegie* (Garden City, NY: Doubleday Doran Company, 1933), 327.
6   Jaki, *The Road of Science*, 447.
7   Bram Stoker, *Dracula* (New York: Bantam, 1981), 338.
8   Ibid., 38, 39.
9   Ibid.
10  Ibid.
11  Ibid., 41, 42.
12  Ibid., 39, 110.
13  Ibid, 110.
14  Ibid., 110-1.
15  Ibid., 111.
16  Ibid., 118, 119, 131.
17  Ibid., 134.
18  Ibid., 169, 171, 172.
19  Ibid., 222, 223.
20  Bram Stoker, *The Lair of the White Worm* (London: W. Foulsham & Co, Ltd, 1911), 155.
21  Ibid., 61.
22  Ibid.
23  Ibid., 62.
24  Claude Quetel, *History of Syphilis* (Baltimore: John Hopkins University Press, 1990), 10.
25  Ibid., 20, 21.
26  Ibid., 16.
27  Ibid., 57.
28  Ibid., 123, 166-67.
29  Ibid., 146.
30  Ibid., 209.
31  Ibid., 240.
32  Ibid., 154-5.
33  Ibid., 220, 211.
34  Stoker, *Worm*, 178.
35  Ibid., 29, 60, 56.
36  Johannes Fabricius, *Syphilis in Shakespeare's England* (London, Bristol, PA: Jessica Kingsley, 1994), 233.
37  Quetel, *History of Syphilis*, 68.
38  Ibid., 196.
39  Ibid., 52.
40  Ibid., 257.
41  Stoker, *Dracula*, 226.
42  Ibid., 247.
43  Andrea Dworkin, *Intercourse* (New York: The Free Press, 1987), 118.
44  Ibid., 119.
45  Ibid., 158.
46  Jaki, *The Road of Science*, 301.
47  Stoker, *Worm*, 129.
48  Ibid., 58.
49  Stoker, *Dracula*, 252.
50  Stoker, *Worm*, 67, 179, 172.
51  Ibid., 173-4.
52  Ibid., 174.

53  Ibid., 176.
54  Ibid., 179.
55  Ibid., 181.
56  Ibid., 184, 185.


5   *Blood and Berlin*


1   Christopher Isherwood, *Christopher and His Kind 1929-1930* (New York: Farrar, Straus, Giroux, 1976), 128.

2   Paul Johnson, *Modern Times: The World from the Twenties to the Nineties* (San Francisco: Harper Collins Publishers 1983), 114.

3   Ibid., 115.

4   Siegfried Kracauer, *From Caligari to Hitler: A Psychological History of the German Film.* (Princeton, NJ: Princeton University Press, 1947), 76.

5   Erwin J. Haeberle, "Swastika, Pink Triangle and Yellow Star—the Destruction of Sexology and the Persecution of Homosexuals in Nazi Germany," *The Journal of Sex Research*, 17:3: 270-87.

6   Charlotte Wolff, *Magnus Hirschfeld: A Portrait of a Pioneer in Sexology* (London & New York: Quartet, 1986), 190-1.

7   Isherwood, *Christopher and His Kind*, 34.

8   Wolff, *Magnus Hirschfeld*, 193.

9   Magnus Hirschfeld, *Von Einst Bis Jetzt: Geschichte einer homosexuellen Bewegug 1897-1922* (Berlin: Verlag Rosa Winkel, 1986), 211.

10  Wolff, *Magnus Hirschfeld*, 234.

11  Adolf Hitler, *Mein Kampf* (Muenchen: Zentralverlag der NSDAP, F. Eher, Nachf., 1941), 751 (my translations).

12  Isherwood, *Christopher and His Kind*, 16.

13  Ibid., 17.

14  Scott Lively and Kevin Abrams, *The Pink Swastika: Homosexuality in the Nazi Party* (Keizer, OR: Founders Publ.Corp. 1995), 13.

15  Isherwood, *Christopher and His Kind*, 26-7.

16  Ibid.,. 432.

17  Hitler, *Mein Kampf*, 283, 384.

18  Ibid., 317.

19  Johnson, *Modern Times*, 116.

20  Hitler, *Mein Kampf*, 339-40.

21  Ibid., 340.

22  Ibid., 357, 358.

23  Joachim C. Fest, *Hitler: Eine Biographie* (Frankfurt: Propylaen, 1975), 87-8 (my translation).

24  Johnson, *Modern Times*, 342.

25  Hitler, *Mein Kampf*, 269.

26  Quetel, *History of Syphilis*, 183.

27  Fest, *Hitler*, 141.

28  Hitler, *Mein Kampf*, 270.

29  Ibid.

30  Ibid., 271.

31  Robert G. L. Waite, *Adolf Hitler: The Psychopathic God* (NewYork: Basic Books, 1977), 24.

32  Fest, *Hitler*, 144.

33  Samuel Igra, *Germany's National Vice* (London: Quality Press, Ltd, 1945), 67.

34  Quetel, *History of Syphilis*, 171.

35  Ibid., 193.

36  Ibid., 199.

37  Ibid., 206.

38  Ibid.

39  Ibid., 206-7.

40  Paul Weindling, "Sexually Transmitted Diseases between Imperial and Nazi Germany,"in *History of Medicine* (Oxford: *Genitourin Med,* 1994), 284.

41  Isherwood, *Christopher and His Kind*, 10

42  Ibid., 11.

43  Joseph Nicolosi, *Reparative Therapy of Male Homosexuality* (London, Northvale, NJ: Jason Aronson, 1991), 207, 164.

44  Ibid., 213, 103.

45  Isherwood, *Christopher and His Kind*, 12.

46  Ibid., 5.

47  Nicolosi, *Reparative Therapy*, 157.

48  Ibid., 24.

49  Ibid., 163.

50  Ibid., 116, 125.

51  Ibid., 126.

52  Isherwood, *Christopher and His Kind*, 128.

53  Haeberle, "Swastika, Pink Triangle and Yellow Star," 280.

54  Lively and Abrams, *The Pink Swastika*, 96.

55  Fest, *Hitler*, 131.

## 6  *The Difference Between Us and Them*

1  Donald J. Elia and Stephen M. Krason, eds., *We Hold these Truths and More: Further Catholic Reflections on the American Proposition, The Thought of Fr. John Courtney Murray, S.J. and its Relevance Today* (Steubenville, OH: Franciscan University Press, 1993), 87-88.

2  Alexis de Tocqueville, *Democracy in America*, 304.

3  Ibid.

4  Ibid, 304, 305.

5  John Courtney Murray, S.J., *We Hold These Truths, Catholic Reflections on the American Proposition* (New York: Sheed andWard, 1960), 29, 36.

6  Ibid., 36-7.

7  Edward L. Bernays, *Propaganda* (New York: Horace Liveright, 1928), 9.

8  Edward L. Bernays, *Public Relations* (Norman, OK: University of Oklahoma Press, 1952), 78.

9  Bernays, *Propaganda*, 12, 20, 24, 12.

10  Ibid., 20, 35.

11  Ibid., 46.

12  Ibid., 45.

13  Ibid., 66.

14  Ibid., 51, 52.

15  Ibid., 52-3, 114, 56.

16  Barruel, *History of Jacobinism*, 623.

17  Elia and Krason, *We Hold These Truths and More*, 112.

18  Bernays, *Propaganda*, 156.

19  Quetel, *History of Syphilis*, 250.

20  Stuart M. Kaminsky, *Don Siegel: Director* (New York: Curtis Books, 1974), 103, 104.

21  Ibid., 106.
22  Jack Finney, "The Body Snatchers," *Colliers*, December 10, 1954: 120.
23  Ibid., 124.
24  Ibid., 123.
25  Ibid., 65.
26  Ibid., 67.
27  Ibid., 72.
28  Paul Sammon, "Interview with David Cronenberg," *Cinefantastique* 10:1 (Spring 1981): 30.

## 7  *The Body Snatchers*

1  René Wormser, *Foundations: Their Power and Influence* (New York: The Devin-Adair Company, 1958), 3, xiii (my emphasis).
2  Ibid., xii.
3  Ibid., 4.
4  Ibid., 82 (his emphasis).
5  Ibid., 42.
6  Ibid., 21.
7  Ibid., 74, 180.
8  Ibid., 173, 174.
9  Ibid., 39.
10  Ibid., 229-30.
11  Ibid., 89, 93, 95.
12  Ibid., 32.
13  Ibid., 94.
14  Ibid., 100-1.
15  Ibid., 101.
16  Ibid., 102, 129-30.
17  Ibid., 104.
18  Ibid.
19  Ibid (his emphasis).
20  Ibid., 184-86 (his emphasis).
21  Ibid., 351 (his emphasis).
22  Ibid., 355.
23  Michel Schooyans, *Power over Life Leads to Domination of Mankind* (St. Louis, MO: Central Bureau, Catholic Central Verein of America, 1996), 36.
24  Ibid., 55-56.
25  Ibid., 59.

## 8  *Hollywood and Death*

1  Donald Spoto, *The Dark Side of Geniius: The Life of Alfred Hitchcock* (Boston: Little Brown, and Company, 1983), 15.
2  Ibid., 17.
3  Ibid., 269.
4  Linda Lovelace with Mike McGrady, *Ordeal* (New York: Berkeley Books, 1980), 115, 117.
5  Ralph Blumenthal, "Deep Throat," *New York Times Sunday Magazine*, January 21, 1973: 28, 30.
6  Ibid., 32.

7  Paul L. Montgomery, "Behavior in *Throat* Termed Normal," *New York Times*, December 30, 1972: A22.

8  Paul L. Montgomery, "Johns Hopkins Professor Lauds '*Throat*' as a 'cleansing film,'" *New York Times*, January 3, 1973: A34.

9  Paul T. Montgomery, "Professor says *Deep Throat* lacks redeeming social value," *New York Times*, December 22 1972: A22.

10  Paul T. Montgomery, "No-Jury, 20 Day *Throat* Trial; 'Obscene' Ruling by Judge Tyler Foreshadows fine of $2 million," *New York Times*, March 7, 1973: 6

11  Vincent Canby, "What Are We to Think of *Deep Throat*," *New York Times*, January 21, 1973: B1.

12  Ibid.

13  Nora Ephron, *Crazy Salad* (New York: Borzoi, 1975), 64.

14  Ibid., 67, 66.

15  William S. Pechter, "Deep Tango," *Commentary* 56 (1973): 65.

16  Blumenthal, "Deep Throat," 33.

17  Ellen Farley and William K. Knoedelseder, Jr., "*The Texas Chainsaw Massacre*: The film that made a name for Director Tobe Hooper was a legal nightmare of film business chicanery" (originally appeared in two installments as "The Real Texas Chainsaw Massacre"), *The Times* September 1982: 29.

18  Farley and Knoedelseder, 30.

19  Lovelace, 209.

20  Lovelace, 35, 50, 87.

21  Public Hearings on Ordinances to Add Pornography as Discrimination against Women: Minneapolis City Council Government Operations Committee, December 12 and 13, 1983: 16.

22  Ibid., 19.

23  Attorney General's Commission on Pornography Final Report, July 1986: 771.

24  Ibid., 67-8.

25  Ibid., 76, 86.

26  Public hearings, 86.

27  Arlene F. Carmen et al., *The Meese Commission Exposed: Proceedings of a National Coaliton Against Censorship*, public Information briefing on the Attorney General's Commission on Pornogrpahy, January 16, 1986: 42.

28  Ibid.

29  Attorney General's Commission, 110.

30  Michael Medved, *Hollywood vs. America: Popular Culture and the War on Traditional Values* (New York: Harper Collins, 1992), 14.

31  Ibid., 111.

32  Janet Smith, *Humanae Vitae: A Generation Later* (Washington, D.C.: Catholic University of America Press, 1991), 80.

33  Sigmund Freud, "Das Unheimliche," in *Gesammelte Werke*, vol. 12 (Frankfurt am Main: S. Fischer Verlag, 1947), 236, 250.

## 9  *Alien and Contraception*

1  Marc Mancini, "Thunder and Lightning: Dan O'Bannon interviewed by Marc Mancini," *Film Comment* (July/August 1983): 52.

2  Ibid., 53.

3  Ibid., 54.

4  Ibid.

5  H.R. Giger, *H.R. Giger's Necronomicon* (Beverly Hills: Morpheus International, 1991), 14.

6   Dan O'Bannon and Ronald Shusett, *Alien Movie Novel* (New York: Avon books, 1979).
7   Ibid.
8   Ibid.
9   Ibid.
10  Ibid.
11  Ibid.
12  Barbara Creed, *The Monstrous Feminine: Film, Feminism, Psychoanalysis* (London and New York: Routledge, 1993), 16, 18.
13  Ibid., 25.
14  Ibid., 5, 2.
15  Ibid., 16.
16  Ibid., 27.
17  Public Hearings, 17.
18  Dworkin, *Intercourse*, 119.

## Conclusion: Misreading Horror

1   Branagh, *Mary Shelley's* Frankenstein, 19.
2   David Hogan, *Dark Romance* (Jefferson, NC: McFarland, 1986), xii.
3   Ibid., 73.
4   Ibid., 236.
5   Ibid., 239.
6   Ibid., 259.
7   Sade, *Justine*, 217.
8   Ibid., 300.
9   Ibid., 249, 346.
10  Hogan, *Dark Romance*, 259.
11  Andrew Britton, Richard Liffe, Tony Williams, and Robin Wood, *American Nightmare: Essays on the Horror Film* (Toronto: Festival of Festivals, 1979), 10.
12  Ibid., 7.
13  Ibid., 10, 16.
14  Ibid., 14.
15  Ibid.
16  Ibid., 7.
17  Ibid., 8.
18  Ibid.
19  Ibid., 84.
20  Ibid., 27.
21  Ibid., 24.
22  Ibid., 127-8.
23  Paul Sammon, "Interview with David Cronenberg," 21 (my emphasis).
24  Piers Handling, ed., *The Shape of Rage: The Films of David Cronenberg* (New York: Zoetrope, 1983), 181.
25  Ibid., 181, 183.

# Index

## A Note on the Author

E. Michael Jones is the author of several best-selling critiques of contemporary culture, including his highly-praised trilogy on modernity, *Degenerate Moderns*, *Dionysos Rising*, and *Living Machines*. Dr. Jones earned his doctorate in American literature at Temple University and taught at the university level before founding *Fidelity* magazine, which in 1997 became *Culture Wars* magazine. He lives in South Bend, Indiana, with his wife and five children.

This book was designed and set into type
by Mitchell S. Muncy,
and printed and bound
by Edwards Brothers, Inc.
Ann Arbor, Michigan.

The text face is Caslon,
designed by Carol Twombly,
based on faces cut by William Caslon, London, in the 1730s,
and issued in digital form by Adobe Systems,
Mountain View, California, in 1989.

The cover illustration is *The Nightmare* (detail) by Henry Fuseli,
reproduced by permission of The Detroit Institute of Arts,
Detroit, Michigan,
on a cover designed by Stephen J. Ott.

The index is by IndExpert, Fort Worth, Texas.

The paper is acid-free and is of archival quality.

24